ENTERPRISE 2.0

ENTERPRISE 2.0

How Technology, eCommerce, and Web 2.0 Are Transforming Business Virtually

Volume 2: The Behavioral Enterprise

Tracy L. Tuten, Editor

PRAEGER

AN IMPRINT OF ABC-CLIO, LLC

Santa Barbara, California • Denver, Colorado • Oxford, England

Library of Congress Cataloging-in-Publication Data

Enterprise 2.0 : how technology, ecommerce, and web 2.0 are transforming business
   virtually / edited by Tracy L. Tuten.
     p. cm.
   Includes bibliographical references and index.
   ISBN 978–0–313–37239–1 (set : alk. paper) — ISBN 978–0–313–37241–4 (v. 1 : alk.
   paper) — ISBN 978–0–313–37243–8 (v. 2 : alk. paper) — ISBN 978–0–313–37240–7
   (set : ebook) — ISBN 978–0–313–37242–1 (v. 1 : ebook) — ISBN 978–0–313–37244–5
   (v. 2 : ebook)
1. Electronic commerce. 2. Web 2.0. 3. Information technology. I. Tuten, Tracy L., 1967– II.
Title: Enterprise two point oh.
HF5548.32.E567   2010
658'.054678—dc22   2010006057

ISBN: 978–0–313–37239–1 (set)
ISBN: 978–0–313–37241–4 (vol. 1)
ISBN: 978–0–313–37243–8 (vol. 2)
EISBN: 978–0–313–37240–7 (set)
EISBN: 978–0–313–37242–1 (vol. 1)
EISBN: 978–0–313–37244–5 (vol. 2)

14 13 12 11 10   1 2 3 4 5

This book is also available on the World Wide Web as an eBook.
Visit www.abc-clio.com for details.

Praeger
An Imprint of ABC-CLIO, LLC

ABC-CLIO, LLC
130 Cremona Drive, P.O. Box 1911
Santa Barbara, California 93116-1911

This book is printed on acid-free paper ∞

Manufactured in the United States of America

For Leia

Contents

Acknowledgments

Every accomplishment, every project, and every success are ultimately the result of a team of people working together, directly and indirectly, and in no situation is that truer than in the completion of *Enterprise 2.0*. *Enterprise 2.0* is ultimately the work of the authors who contributed to its development—I extend my most sincere gratitude to them for contributing their expertise, knowledge, and time to the development of this book. On their behalf, I also recognize the support and commitment they had from family, friends, and colleagues who listened, waited patiently while they wrote, cheered them on, and offered the intangible resources all authors require. Though these "silent contributors" are not recognized by name, I feel certain they will nod knowingly as they read this, recognizing the role they played. I thank Jeff Olson (and the rest of the Praeger family) for believing in this project and for his encouragement and advice as it developed. I also thank Brian Romer for seeing this project through to its completion. I expressly thank my new colleagues and the administration at East Carolina University's College of Business and Department of Marketing and Supply Chain Management for their support of this project. Finally, I am thankful for my "silent contributors," David, Dad, and Susan, who inspire me to be better in all that I do, whether it's making the evening's meal or editing a volume on technology in business.

1

THE BEHAVIORAL ENTERPRISE

Tracy L. Tuten

Sue Bushell, writing for *CIO* magazine on Enterprise 2.0, pointed out that a survey from Gartner found that only one in seven organizations has a Web 2.0 strategy and even fewer acknowledge the implications of social software in the organization.[1] Gartner (quoted in Bushell's article) stated, "Given the importance and the potential impact of Web 2.0, we can only conclude that the absence of strategy stems from an inability to determine the implications for the organization's business models, Web presence, customers and employees. Organizations must increase their Web 2.0 awareness and capabilities now to prepare for the storm of innovation to come."[2] Indeed, the impact of Web 2.0 technologies affects the enterprise at a strategic macro level related to business models and corporate processes, and it also affects the enterprise at a micro level—at the level of employees and customers.

For organizations to develop a competitive advantage using Web 2.0 tools, all levels must be considered. This is a point of contention for many Enterprise 2.0 experts, with disagreement on whether Enterprise 2.0 technologies are internally focused exclusively or also inclusive of external stakeholders. Addressing this very question of scope, Prem Kumar Aparanji writes, "there is a clear necessity for Enterprise 2.0 and Social CRM (customer relationship management) to coexist, since efficient employees lead to better customer experience."[3] Dion Hinchcliffe parrots this notion, writing for ZDNet, "The key point here is that where online tools let customers have a social relationship with a business—in other words, interaction that is visible to them and other customers whenever possible—then some Social CRM is taking place."[4]

In this volume, we follow Andrew McAfee's view when he defined Enterprise 2.0 as "the use of emergent social software platforms within companies or between companies, their partners, or customers."[5] With that in mind, our focus herein is the Behavioral Enterprise, beginning with managerial implications and applications of Enterprise 2.0 technologies for employees. From there, we explore several topics related to the consumer experience of Web 2.0.

ENTERPRISE 2.0 AND HUMAN RESOURCE MANAGEMENT

What human resource applications exist for social software in the Enterprise? There are several possibilities including enhanced colleague-to-colleague communication, remote employee/telecommuting applications, leader-employee communications, employee recruitment, employee onboarding, orientation and training activities, building peer relationships, project and team management (even at the global scale), and corporate human resource requirements such as providing regulatory information. For example, project management can be enhanced with the use of internal social networks, wikis, and advanced communication tools like instant messaging and online meetings. Corporate human resource information can be delivered via wiki on the corporate intranet to enable employees to ask questions and get answers all the while maintaining a trail for other employees to later access. Employee onboarding, the process of introducing a new employee to the organization and orienting and socializing the employee, can be conducted using virtual-world exercises and games. In fact, several employee recruitment and development activities can benefit from virtual interactions and games, including screening interviews for prospective employees in the pool, employee orientation sessions, and training seminars. Employees can be kept abreast of the goals and concerns of upper leadership with blogs, microblogs, and podcasts. And, all forms of internal communication—both peer to peer and leader to subordinate—can utilize instant messaging and texting as collaborative tools. It's not surprising, reviewing this list of applications, that 83 percent of respondents to a McKinsey survey who had adopted Web 2.0 technologies in the organization reported they did so to "manage knowledge."[6]

The McKinsey Global Survey, "Building the Web 2.0 Enterprise," reported that in 2008, 58 percent of participating organizations used Web services, 34 percent used blogs, 33 percent used RSS feeds, 32 percent used wikis, 29 percent used podcasts, and 28 percent used social networking.[7] In terms of the type of use of these technologies, 94 percent reported using Web 2.0 tools internally, 87 percent said they use these technologies to interface with customers, and 75 percent use them for interfacing with partners and suppliers.[8] Examples of collaborating internally included internal recruiting, product development activities, enhancing company culture, managing knowledge, training, and fostering collaboration. Examples of

interfacing with customers included activities like getting customer participation in product development, improving customer service, courting new
customers, and encouraging customer-to-customer interactions.

There are many benefits for Enterprise 2.0 applications. As the McKinsey
Quarterly report emphasizes, the latest wave of Web 2.0 technologies have
more intensive applications for organizations with implications for enterprise resource planning, customer relationship management, and supply
chain management.[9] Aside from the benefits to the ease and efficiency of
communication and collaboration, Enterprise 2.0 at the task level also helps
organizations to reduce its carbon emissions. Cisco's Jeff Sheard explains
that every Cisco employee has access to a Second Life account, a suite of
tools for online meetings and videoconferences, and a secure Facebook
group. These tools enable Cisco employees to collaborate and communicate
more effectively (as well as better enjoy their working environment), but
using such Web 2.0 tools reduces the need for employee travel. Cisco ends
each net meeting with an estimate on the carbon credits saved by using
the virtual meeting instead of a physical one.[10] Sabre Holdings, a company
with 9000 employees in 59 countries, has developed its own private social
network known as SabreTown. Employees maintain a personal profile.
About 60 percent of Sabre employees are active on the network.[11]

The report "Six Ways to Make Web 2.0 Work" from the McKinsey
Quarterly classifies these technologies into five categories: (1) broad collaboration, (2) broad communication, (3) collective estimation, (4) metadata
creation, and (5) social graphing. Broad collaboration (wikis and shared
workspaces) is described as the facilitation of co-created content and
applications across many dispersed participants. Broad communication
(blogs, casts, peer-to-peer communication) occurs when individuals share
information with a broad set of other individuals. Collective estimation
(polling, prediction markets) refers to harnessing the power of crowdsourc-
ing to solve problems. Metadata creation (tagging, social bookmarking,
RSS, ratings, filtering) explains the added value of supplementing primary
content with other forms of data. Social graphing (social networking,
network mapping) describes the connections between people and the value
of these connections.[12] A key point is that these categories are used by both
internal (employee) and external (customer) participants.

A Look at Internal and External Behavioral Aspects of the Enterprise

In this, our second volume exploring Enterprise 2.0, we begin with
employee implications for social software applications and then shift to
consumer innovations in the social sphere. Dr. Elizabeth C. Ravlin, a professor at the University of South Carolina and expert on virtual team collaboration, explains the shift for virtual teams to use mobile collaboration

tools. She identifies the positives and negatives of this type of teamwork and explains how managers can overcome barriers to effectiveness for truly mobile virtual teams. Next, Dr. Rudy Nydegger presents the special challenges of managing the group interactions among members of virtual teams. We continue the focus on virtual teamwork with a chapter on the coordination challenges facing teams using virtual-world project management. Virtual worlds can help minimize many coordination concerns but they present others. Employee recruitment is one of the corporate human resource management tasks that can benefit from Web 2.0 tools, and we are primed on such recruiting techniques. In chapter 6, Dr. Peter Otto proposes a framework derived from anthropology to help us understand online social networks. Josh Bernoff of Forrester Research and Charlene Li of Altimeter, authors of *Groundswell*, reveal how organizations can leverage and build on "groundswell," the power that comes from interpersonal connections made possible by social media. Dr. Cheryl L. Adkins and Dr. Sonya F. Premeaux speak to the frustrations of employees who are enabled by Web 2.0 tools. Indeed, such tools mean that employees can work every day, all day from anywhere in the world. They investigate the effects of Enterprise 2.0 on employee perceptions of work-life balance.

At this point, we shift from internal behavioral concerns to the external realm of customers. Earlier we noted that Enterprise 2.0 adoption has a green component, reducing companies' carbon emissions. Jason D. Oliver writes on a related topic, understanding the consumer adoption tendencies toward sustainable products. Emphasizing that companies can do good while doing well, Oliver presents do's and don'ts for companies offering sustainable products in the marketplace. In chapter 10, we hear from advertising expert and blogger Scott Sherman on the advent of conversational media. He explains the primary characteristics that must be present to encourage customers to communicate and collaborate with your brand. Brands must offer stories that are tellable, emotional, and tangible. Dr. Robert V. Kozinets, one of the authors of the book *Consumer Tribes*, introduces us to the fanaticism of brand fans—those customers who provide the passionate collaboration in social media. Then in chapter 12, Dr. Natalie T. Wood, an expert in virtual-world behavior, explains our future customers and employees in her chapter on growing up virtual. Indeed, Wood captures the core differences between virtual natives and virtual immigrants. Ellen Kolstö reveals her insights into how build an active and vibrant virtual community. Although this chapter is targeted to consumer worlds, organizations developing virtual-world resources for employee use should consider these tips to encourage adoption. Kolstö points out that virtual worlds can become "real" places where people come together as avatars or icons to have shared experiences whether it be as simple as having conversations or more involved such as playing games, taking classes, viewing art, or watching films.

The development of such communities must start with an understanding of the elements needed to attract and keep users in your space.

In chapter 14, Dr. Thomas R. Donohue presents examples of the evolution of viral marketing and the building of buzz so important to social-media communications with customers. Dr. Erika Pearson of the University of Otago in New Zealand exposes the reader to a relatively new phenomenon of the exchange of digital gifts. That social network participants are exchanging digital gifts provides evidence of the importance of these communities in the lives of their members. She explains that the exchange of gifts plays a key role in the upkeep of social life online just as it does in offline spaces. Our final chapter reviews the development of social commerce and social shopping behaviors. Just as organizations are incorporating Web 2.0 technologies for employees, and consumers are using the tools for their own entertainment, research purposes, and community building, customers are using social commerce tools to shop collaboratively online.

NOTES

1. Sue Bushell, "Enterprise 2.0—What Is It Good For? A 12-Step Guide to Getting the Most out of Web 2.0 Tools and Making It Safe-for-Purpose," *CIO*, May 6, 2008, http://www.cio.com.au/index.php/id;1127599955

2. Ibid.

3. Prem Kumar Aparanji, "Enterprise 2.0 vs Social CRM—Fight or Tango?" Customer Think, August 15, 2009, http://www.customerthink.com/blog/enterprise _2_0_vs_social_crm_fight_or_tango.

4. Dion Hinchcliffe, "Using Social Software to Reinvent the Customer Relationship," Enterprise Web 2.0, August 18, 2009, http://blogs.zdnet.com/Hinchcliffe/ ?p=699.

5. Andrew McAfee, "Enterprise 2.0: The Dawn of Emergent Collaboration," *MIT Sloan Management Review* 47, no. 3 (2006): 21–28.

6. C. G. Lynch, "Enterprise Web 2.0 Adoption Still Growing, McKinsey Report Says," *CIO*, July 30, 2008, http://www.cio.com/article/440165/Enterprise _Web_2.0_Adoption_Still_Growing_McKinsey_Report_Says

7. McKinsey Global Survey Results, "Building the Web 2.0 Enterprise," *The McKinsey Quarterly*, July 2008, http://www.mckinseyquarterly.com/Building _the_Web_20_Enterprise_McKinsey_Global_Survey_2174

8. Ibid.

9. Michael Chui, Andy Miller, and Roger Roberts, "Six Ways to Make Web 2.0 Work," *The McKinsey Quarterly*, February 2009, http://www.mckinsey quarterly.com/Six_ways_to_make_Web_20_work_2294

10. See Note 1.

11. "Interview with John Samuel, VP Of Sabre's Innovation Lab," *Social Networking Watch*, January 1, 2009, http://www.socialnetworkingwatch.com/2009/01/ john-samuel-vp-of-sabres-innovation-lab.html

12. See Note 9.

2

THE NEXT EVOLUTION: KNOWLEDGE SHARING AND INFLUENCE IN TEAM MOBILE COLLABORATION

Elizabeth C. Ravlin

Imagine yourself at a gathering of individuals, all of whom can, with the flip of a PDA, push of a button, or even a word, communicate with whomever they would like, anywhere in the world. What is going to determine who they choose to contact? Attraction? Ease of communication? Motivation regarding the topic to be discussed? Perhaps the most important question is when will these individuals go out of their way to communicate with others with whom they may have little or nothing in common, no joint history, limited ability to understand and be understood, and no motive to make the effort to develop a relationship? This description may sound extreme, but in fact, it is increasingly the situation in which we find ourselves at work and in our personal lives. The driving force behind these dramatic changes in the social landscape is the continued advancement of the ease, reliability, and mobility of technology-mediated communication. Organizational structures have been entirely revamped based on these new communication and knowledge sharing capabilities, and the changes are nowhere more apparent than in the implementation of virtual teams as vehicles for improving organizational effectiveness. The scenario described here, however, is not fully recognized as applying to the work world because the assumption tends to be made that the work of the organization will somehow effectively drive appropriate contacts.

Virtual teams are commonly considered to be task groups whose members are non-collocated but work interdependently, typically using computer-mediated interaction, on a common task.[1] Many variants of such teams exist, in that multiple communication technologies may be utilized to accomplish needed member interaction. As technology evolves, the structure and process of these teams evolve as well. Technological developments that are currently making themselves felt more broadly are focused in three areas: (1) they enhance mobility, (2) they impact the user's feelings of social presence, and (3) they provide added richness to the media of communication. Web 2.0 is a common phrase used to conceptually capture these phenomena. Here, I summarize the current development of virtual teams toward mobile collaborations, identify potential positives of and problems with this type of teaming, and examine how managers and leaders can overcome barriers to effectiveness in developing truly mobile virtual teams.

WHY MOBILE COLLABORATION?

Collaboration conducted via computer-mediated technologies has often been acclaimed for the potential it holds to provide avenues for participation on the part of all members of an aggregate, and knowledge held in teams utilizing such technologies is considered to be a distinctive competence.[2] As compared to face-to-face groups, theoretically, teams operating virtually should be better able to facilitate broad member input and open knowledge sharing. Cues regarding the relative status of contributors are muted or absent; turn-taking no longer dictates who will speak; normative pressure for conformity is reduced; and everyone involved should have access to the same information via the technological system used by the team. As we move into the next evolution of technology-facilitated collaboration, once again, barriers are falling with regard to influence and participation. As Personal Digital Assistants (PDAs) become the locus of technology-mediated communication, all who have such a device will have access, from virtually any location, to their coworkers, Internet-stored information, and software. Availability of information continues to increase, and presumably, access to individual members of a collaboration is nearing a 24-7 phenomenon.

These characteristics are of growing importance, as the value of virtual teams is generally considered to lie in the extreme ease with which people in different locations can work together using this structure. The globalization of business and the pace of change we now experience have altered the needs of the business community. The old expatriate model, in which an individual executive, often from the home-country headquarters operation, would be sent for a long period of time (3 to 5 years) to a subsidiary location to facilitate collaborative work, is declining in use. Today, business travelers range from technical professionals to top executives, the length of their stay in other locations more often is a few days as opposed to years, and they are sent to multiple locations and thus have reduced opportunity to build knowledge about the cultures in which they travel or the people with whom they interact. Further, projects change rapidly and continuously, and most individuals find themselves switching teams frequently, and/or working on multiple teams simultaneously. Virtual teams can be composed and reconfigured rapidly, given that the location of the redeployed human resources is irrelevant. The 50-foot collaboration rule (most collaboration in organizations takes place between colleagues who are located within 50 feet of one another) can, with the help of a strong mobile collaboration model, be safely abandoned. This also indicates that locating specialized competencies at each organizational location, as was common for divisionally organized firms, is no longer needed. Other advantages of virtual teaming include a reduction in travel, which not only helps hold down expenses, but also can be an integral part of a greening strategy. In sum, virtual teams may be the answer to increased globalization and change, the knowledge intensity of today's work, and the increased expense, difficulty, and undesirability of travel.

New technologies support these evolving needs on the part of business. Although PDAs have been available for some time, wireless access functionality continues to increase, and cost is diminishing. In the past, two major hindrances to using PDAs as significant work tools beyond their cell phone capacity were noted. First, there were severe constraints on storage of data, and, second, the ability to input information in the form of text was limited. Technological developments, however, are now on the way to making these constraints vanish. Most organizations are moving to a net storage model of data and software; therefore, the most important aspect of the PDA is its Internet access. In addition, the advent of virtual keyboard technology (in which the keyboard is typically projected onto a flat surface for the user), allows for greatly expanded use of convenient mobile devices such as PDAs and handheld PCs. Another issue that is being addressed is the ability of these devices to run multiple applications at once. Technology forecasts suggest the demise of the laptop as a primary component in the near future.[3] Even teleconferencing systems are moving toward at least a limited mobility in terms of the ability to set up in various locations on a temporary basis.

POTENTIAL PROBLEMS IN MOBILE COLLABORATION

These newer technologies promise not only to make distance between team members unimportant, but to make the current location of these individuals irrelevant as well. We can realize some immediate benefits (reductions in costs of travel and redundant personnel, increases in efficiency, for example), but how do these technologies fit with our knowledge of human behavior in our efforts to enhance team and organizational outcomes? More than 60 years ago, consultants and scholars identified a lack of fit between the technical system an organization uses

and the social system requirements as a key barrier to realizing the benefits of the new technology of the time. Interestingly, this socio-technical
systems view, the concept that the technical and social systems used in
the workplace must be integrated with each other for optimal performance, also was a fundamental contributor to growing interest in team
forms of organization.[4] In our current environment, we must have a clear
understanding of how people actually use the resources provided, as
opposed to how they could be used in a technologically Utopian world.

Organizing collaborative structures using technology as the basis for
communication differs from traditional collocated teaming in two fundamental ways. First, the media used to communicate may greatly reduce
the richness of the messages they are able to convey. Different types and
amounts of information are transmitted by different technologies,[5] ranging from pure data, which have no contextual or interpretive components,
to teleconferencing, which attempts to reintroduce the ability to observe
nonverbal contextual cues. Second, the psychological experience of social
presence (the presence of other humans) can be reduced or eliminated by
distance technologies. Differing socio-emotional and motivational effects
are produced by varying levels of social presence[6] based on technological
characteristics. Both media richness and social presence approaches
argue for changes in group processes based on the type of communication
media utilized.

Given these two broad differences, several issues drawn from group
dynamics can be identified as creating barriers to realizing some of the
highly touted benefits of virtual teams utilizing technologically-mediated
communication. I discuss these in the context of the performance of
essential team task and maintenance activities. Task activities encompass
behavior that directly addresses the team's work assignment, whereas
maintenance activities involve behavior aimed at forming and maintaining
relationships among the team members.

Team Task Activities: Participation in Team Decision-Making

Most virtual teams face the fundamental problem of sharing information in a variety of decision-making, judgment, or problem-solving contexts. Typically, a rational team decision protocol (a process designed to
be optimally effective) is composed of several steps. These steps most frequently include problem definition, goal setting, process planning, information gathering, alternative identification, evaluation, and selection.
Once an alternative is selected, implementation of the decision, adherence
to and evaluation of the decision, and solicitation of feedback from key
stakeholders should follow. Each of these steps is influenced by member
individual differences, including personality, experience, functional background, culture, and other demographic characteristics, as well as team
characteristics like the degree to which members are interdependent,

team norms and values, and leadership structure. As team members become more diverse, the amount of information the team has relevant to each decision step will grow, but agreement is very likely to diminish. Ideally, the effective team finds and uses the important information it holds, and gives it the most weight in the decision process.

The Role of Status

In traditional face-to-face teams, status characteristics provide a summary dimension that helps us to understand how team member characteristics typically affect each member's ability to influence team decisions.[7] All aggregates tend to form status hierarchies within their membership quickly based on perceptions of competence.[8] Perceived status is influenced by task-relevant qualities of members such as expertise (termed "specific characteristics"), but it also is a function of demographic or other salient attributes that are construed in some way (perhaps through stereotypical judgments) to be related to team goals (termed "diffuse characteristics"). If status is truly based on competence regarding the team task, the status hierarchy will confer more weight to the input of the appropriate individuals, and the team decision will be optimally effective. Typical arguments with regard to the role of technological mediation in virtual collaborations suggest a leveling of the playing field over time with regard to diffuse status characteristics, and a stronger emphasis on task-relevant contributions.[9] The thinking was, of course, that diffuse status characteristics such as gender, race, or ethnicity were either not known, or were not salient in the context of technologically mediated communication, and, therefore, that the focus would be on the work product alone. Early research comparing teams using technologically mediated communication with face-to-face groups indicated that some "status equalization" occurred, in that individuals who were of lower status in the team were able to contribute fully in the absence of status cues, conformity pressures, and the need for turn-taking.[10] However, more recent research indicates that although minority or lower status members may participate more in such settings than in face-to-face venues, they may actually have less influence.[11] This finding means that although these lower status individuals are more willing to speak up in computer-moderated forums, their contributions are not used by the team in formulating its decision.

The idea that virtual teams can potentially base their decisions on unbiased information exchange is drawn in part from the lack of contextual cues present in impoverished media such as e-mail. We don't have the usual information used to judge the importance and/or validity of the shared data, namely, information that is commonly thought to speak to the credibility of the source. Status cues and characteristics are not readily available,[12] beyond knowledge of the communicator's organizational position. However, the presumed equalization (or merit basis) of influence is unlikely to occur without intervention, despite these technological changes. In some cases, it appears that when other cues are missing, familiarity of the sender becomes an increasingly important cue in deciding whether and to what extent a message should be processed.

Although there may be situations in which less rich information is actually better, there are many in which a lack of status cues would not offset the loss of other useful content. It is certainly less likely to be interpreted in the way the sender intended. Cues regarding our confidence in our information, our actual expertise in the area under discussion, and the extent to which a full picture of the information held was shared may all be missing. Teams have a strong tendency to more fully discuss shared information (information team members have in common),[13] and ultimately, this tendency is unlikely to be reduced simply through the use of technology, although the initial mention of unique information may increase. Team members will still prefer to discuss shared information because it validates what they already know, does not generate conflict, and provides familiar solutions. In situations in which people have little else in common, and little knowledge of one another, we might even expect this phenomenon to increase, rather than decrease because of a greater need to find a common ground.

Both technological and human characteristics suggest that tendencies both to look for status cues (that indicate to whom one should attend) and to discuss shared information should continue as technology evolves to support fully mobile collaborative efforts. The amount of information available today at any location is virtually infinite via mobile connection to the Web, and this requires people, as limited information processors, to invoke heuristics to pick and choose what to incorporate in their thinking. Technological characteristics that improve our ability to screen this information rapidly continue to develop. From the days in which an individual had to pick up a phone to find out who was calling, we have now moved to an environment in which we have the ability to screen communications based on information about the sender without accessing these messages at all (e-mail, smart voicemail, incoming calls and texts). And, as noted in the introduction to this chapter, individuals may, in a veritable ocean of possibilities, make easier and more pleasant choices about with whom they will communicate.

These choices also can become habitual to the point where they occur without thought at some point. Psychologists believe that many routine behaviors are carried out at the unconscious level, and hitting the "delete" button while processing e-mail is one such habitual behavior. It is not a coincidence that e-mails from undesirable communication partners or about undesirable topics are often "lost." Although some portion of this phenomenon is surely deliberate, it is also influenced by habitual screening protocols that individuals use to quickly sort through what may be untenable amounts of information. Automatic cognitive process-ing[14] may enhance this effect with very little effort or input on the part of the screener, thus reducing the amount of information that must be examined.

The Role of Social Identity

What, then, determines who receives the attention of team members? The dominant paradigm in understanding group process today is the Social Identity Theory.[15] Individuals have a desire to create, maintain, or enhance the characteristics of fellow in-group members that distinguish them from opposing out-group members. In this way, positive identifica-tion with the in-group is maintained. The fundamental motives underly-ing in-group favoritism are the need for self-enhancement, or the quest for positive comparisons with others, and the need for uncertainty reduc-tion to maintain or increase one's understanding of the self in the context of interpersonal interactions.[16] Based on this thinking, similar others are likely to receive attention because they are most likely to validate our viewpoint, thus reducing our uncertainty about the information con-veyed and increasing self-enhancement by strengthening the position of the in-group.

Because of its lack of collocation and likely diversity of composition, identification with the virtual team or mobile collaboration as a unit is more difficult to develop than identification with a face-to-face group or similar others,[17] as the team is unlikely to have a clear or strong social identity that members can adopt as their own. Therefore, motives for self-enhancement and uncertainty reduction are less likely to be met by membership in a virtual team, and the processes of in-group favoritism and out-group distancing may well occur in reference to other social aggregations, or subgroups within the team, such as subgroups of mem-bers who are collocated, or who are from the same culture or functional area. This lessened degree of identification should reduce the extent to which favoritism based on virtual team membership should occur. That is, being a virtual teammate may confer no advantage in terms of whether one's input is seriously considered or not. If identification with the team does not develop, it is unlikely that the team will agree about the decision or weight the most germane input appropriately because the team goal is not the focus of attention.

The Role of Perceived Competence

In addition to identifying as a member of the in-group, another charac-teristic that provides for increased influence of a specific team member is the extent to which that individual appears to be particularly competent in the team's work. If team members judge competence based on specific work output, as opposed to qualities that may invoke stereotypical inferences regarding ability, then virtual teams can improve the quality of decisions made by weighting the input of more competent members more heavily. On the other hand, stereotypes regarding an individual's location or functional background may still play a role in providing an interpretive screen for work products. Unfortunately, communication technologies do not somehow erase the heuristics and biases that occur in everyday human information processing.

The status characteristics approach is based on the assumption that team members are strongly, if not entirely, task motivated. Thus, influence goes to the most competent of teammates once these individuals are identified. However, if the team itself is not the locus of social identity, the success of the team, as opposed to a subgroup of the team, may be unimportant to individual members, and they may be motivated not to identify input that is best for the team as a whole but for the subgroup with which they identify—for example, their functional group or those individuals with whom they are collocated. Beyond this motivational issue, we also know that performance is difficult to assess and presumably is more so at a distance. Members may also be distracted by technological expertise, in that those individuals who are good at using the communications media are considered to be more expert on the team task as well.[18] Therefore, virtual team members are disadvantaged in identifying their best contributors by biased information processing and the ambiguity of performance data.

The Role of Connections

One additional reason that individual input is given weight in collaborative decision-making is the extent to which the contributor is perceived to be connected to other people that we believe to be important (high in status). In the limited structure of a virtual aggregation, it is less likely that a different or distant other will be perceived as having influence with others outside the team who are of importance to us. For example, in cross-functional teams, each individual may be a well-regarded member of his/her functional area and have many connections throughout the organization and external professional community. These connections might in some contexts ensure that the individual is influential in his/her own right. However, within the cross-functional team, these contacts are not important to other members, who have their own functional constituents to consider. Again, influence may not be accorded to those people outside the immediate functional subgroup of the team.

Ultimately, in a world in which at any given moment we have the capacity to communicate with whomever we would like, whenever we would like, it would appear to be somewhat *less* likely that status barriers will fall. Research suggests that demographic group separation is in part self-chosen, and that people connect across these barriers when "forced" to do so in the context of work or school.[19] The ability to communicate with essentially infinite numbers of other partners at any moment in time should increase the likelihood that individuals continue to communicate with members of their in-group or with those of higher status in an effort at self-enhancement. In the meantime, those of higher status may be targeted by many communications from below,[20] and have the technological tools to screen these lesser members out. An example of this effect that clearly illustrates its necessity was the news that although President Barack Obama was allowed to keep his BlackBerry upon election, many of those considered to be in his inner circle prior to his election no longer have his number.

The Role of Accountability

As technology is adapted and developed to provide for greater richness in communication, we see the reintroduction of visual status cues into the process. While these systems have the advantage of providing an increased social presence, video conferencing, and in particular telepresence systems that provide life-sized images of team members, makes status cues such as demographic characteristics available and relatively salient. Research has shown that these images can be influential—in one case, camera angles were used to make individuals look taller or shorter. Not only did 'taller' individuals *think* they were more influential on the team's decision process, they actually *were* more influential.[21] Telepresence systems provide the strongest visual evidence of team members' activities during meetings, that is, their nonverbal behavior such as posture and facial expression that can indicate whether they are paying attention and their reaction to the discussion. This technology, although sometimes interpreted as having a component of surveillance, will engage members more fully through the mechanism of social presence, that is, the experience that one is in the presence of others. Of course, any device that provides mechanisms for accountability (for example, sign-in for availability to be called upon during a meeting) represents an alternative method of ensuring the active participation of virtual members. Other technologies beyond traditional video conferencing and telepresence systems also address this issue. Second Life approaches the problem by creating online venues for virtual encounters in which the team members are represented by avatars. Although this technological device for invoking social presence may seem too similar to gaming applications for serious use in business environments, digital natives find it to be an easy and natural way to interact. It moves team members far beyond a Web interface that provides pictures of the participants and their placement around a virtual table and into a type of alternative social interaction. All of these methods should enhance the accountability that members feel toward the other people with whom they are interacting.

Team Maintenance Activities: Forming, Maintaining, and Strengthening Interpersonal Bonds

From the organization's standpoint, the focal issue is the accomplishment of the work assignment of the team. However, in order for the team to function well, relationships must form between the members. Interdependence requires that individual members coordinate their activities with one another, and that they count on each member playing his or her part over the length of the project, and possibly longer if members may be reassigned to a new project together in the future. Such relationships must receive a certain amount of attention to be maintained. In face-to-face teams, it is often noted that one or more members will take on the role of relieving tension or conflict between members, using humor or soothing hurt feelings. How this happens in virtual teams with relatively impoverished communication mechanisms is a matter that should be given some attention. In particular, the role of trust in teammates one doesn't really know or see very often, if ever, is central to our understanding of how virtual teams can be effective. In addition, as noted earlier, the extent to which team members come to identify with the team will also have a significant impact on how effective the team can be.

The Role of Trust

Early views of team development suggested that it takes years for a team to reach a level of maturity that allows it to perform at an optimal level. Over time, however, the notion of "swift trust" gained acceptance. In swift trust, rather than waiting to gather evidence that work partners can be counted on to fulfill their part of the work agreement, individuals will simply assume that these partners will act appropriately. Supporting this notion of swift trust, some research has found that face-to-face and fully virtual teams are similar in their positive perceptions of teammates, whereas members of partially virtual teams, in which some members are collocated and others are not, exhibit a preference for those members with whom they are located.[22] Although there is evidence that suggests that virtual team members may start out with the assumption of trust, a number of psychological processes make it difficult to maintain in the abstract, or absent evidence of true performance. In conditions where we can't observe our work partners, our assumption tends to be that when performance falls short of expectations it is their fault, as opposed to having been caused by technological problems or other causes outside of their control.[23] Because people are not very good at accurately estimating how long a task will take to perform or the obstacles that will be encountered, it is likely that some goals for performance will be missed. In the absence of prior history that a partner is competent and motivated, the assumption may quickly become that the partner is not fully invested in the team's work. This type of trust has to do with the work or task, and is based on the extent to which we believe our teammates will fulfill their work commitments. In addition to work-based trust, relationship-based trust is also important. This type of trust is based on our knowing our interaction partners to the extent that we like them, and can formulate realistic expectations of them in the relationship context. If no social communication occurs between team members, the likelihood that relationship-based trust will form is low, and this problem can be exacerbated by technology aimed at social communication, in that those who extend social networking site privileges to some teammates, but not others, are likely to actively generate mistrust from the excluded subgroup of the team.

The Role of Commonalities

Because of the diversity among team members, obvious work- or social-oriented common ground may not exist. Opportunities for discovering this common ground may not be naturally forthcoming in the course of the work process. However, members need to find something on which to base a common identity. Technology experts are increasingly recommending that technology be used for some degree of socializing in virtual teams.[24] Because technology is increasingly integrating our personal and work lives, it has become natural to use equipment and applications in both venues,[25] and this may provide an avenue for workplace socializing. Whereas social networking sites such as LinkedIn provide opportunities for professional connections, other sites don't limit the application to one life domain. Evidence suggests that Twitter and other forms of blogging can enhance feelings of closeness and intimacy between people because of the nature of the communication. If team members have avenues for exchanging some of the minutiae of their lives, they can, over time, develop more substantive relational bonds. Even WILBing (workplace Internet leisure browsing) has some proponents who argue that what appears to be misuse of time and resources at work actually has benefits in terms of concentration and productivity.[26]

Not all evidence supports the formation of social connections as a positive outcome, however. Of course, clear limits must be placed on the use of organization resources, and employees may need guidance regarding what and how much to reveal in the realm of Internet communication, given its propensity to live on indefinitely. In addition, research has shown that, initially, the fact that technology-mediated communication may be less rich than face-to-face discussion actually can reduce conflict in heterogeneous groups because there is less opportunity for disagreements to be noticed.[27] This limited-communication approach may be more effective for less complex or less ambiguous tasks, but seems to potentially prevent the team from recognizing and dealing with important conflicts in the performance of the task and from making good use of the heterogeneity of team members' backgrounds in more complex environments.

We can identify a number of challenges to the effective management of virtual teams in the phenomena described above. In general, use of virtual as opposed to face-to-face collaboration changes the extent to which communication media provide for rich multifaceted information exchange and the degree to which members experience the social presence of other human beings. In summary, the challenges that arise from these changes in how people interact include finding ways of using communications technology to:

- Exchange and identify important task-related information fully despite distance and technological limitations.
- Reach agreement despite team heterogeneity and the increased ease with which manifest disagreement can be avoided.
- Fully implement agreed-upon decisions across locations.
- Ensure accountability among all members despite limited opportunity to observe others' work.
- Develop task-based trust in teammates.
- Develop relationship-based trust in teammates.

In the final section of this chapter, recommendations for meeting these challenges are described.

MEETING THE CHALLENGES: WORKING TOWARD MORE EFFECTIVE MOBILE COLLABORATIONS

It is clear that despite increasing access to the information and technology needed to participate in virtual collaborative aggregates, real and relevant psychological and sociological barriers still exist to limit the effectiveness of these forms of teaming. However, managers are not, of course, helpless in the face of these forces on behavior. The guidelines presented here provide steps toward more productive virtual teams.

Find the Common Ground

As with most aggregates, there is no reason to assume that the individual members share goals, processes, or normative behaviors when they first begin working together. Because virtual collaborations tend to be shorter-lived and provide less opportunity for social interaction, members have less opportunity to find out what they have in common, whether it is in the work or non-work domain. Providing some opportunities for face-to-face interaction for virtual teammates appears to be more successful in developing satisfaction and cohesion than purely virtual interaction,[28] and, if feasible, is a primary way to help the team overcome the barriers that distance imposes. When face-to-face interaction is not possible, managers should recognize that the use of richer media appears to increase cohesion,[29] and allowing for personal and socio-emotional communication of some kind is important to facilitating relationship building among members.[30] Some organizations use social networking sites to enhance ties between members, and allow time during work for employees to connect with distant team members in this way. Once we know something about the people with whom we are dealing, we have an increased feeling of social presence, and that feeling can be enhanced by some use of media that allow users to see and/or be aware of one another's presence.

Formulate Reasonable Expectations of One Another

Based on an improved understanding of other team members and the circumstances distant collaborators face, more accurate expectations should be formed regarding what resources and performance outcomes teammates can provide and when. It is common for individuals located in developed countries to assume that the resources and technology available to them are available throughout the team, whether or not the other members are working in a developed economy. For example, in many parts of the world, the local power supply routinely goes out several times a day, and the organization's own generators, which typically start when this happens, may or may not be reliable. These and other differences in working conditions, including other responsibilities team members may have, should be discussed. Once expectations are established, mechanisms for accountability should be utilized.

Establish a Social Identity

A social identity brings with it many important attributes for a virtual team, including commitment and a desire to see the collaborative effort succeed. Establishing a strong virtual team identity should aid in increasing communication among the team members as well. Procedural justice, or using processes and procedures that are perceived to be fair by all team member, appears to influence this formation of social identity positively in virtual teams.[31] Developing team norms that emphasize cooperation between members, inclusion of all, and recognition or understanding of member differences appear to be important, especially when less rich media, such as e-mail, are used.[32] Inculcating these practices should add to the perception of fairness across functions, locations, and cultures.

Work to Develop Task- and Relationship-based Trust

As a leader, you have the opportunity to demonstrate the trust you want members to model by transferring some leadership functions to the team. This shows your trust in them and suggests that they should trust each other. Increased leadership behaviors within the team may also facilitate performance.[33] Although it may be preferable to have all members of the collaboration be in communication with one another, this may not be possible, given language barriers or time zone constraints. In these situations, trust in the team can be developed by the presence of at least one trusted person who is able to communicate and connect with everyone, and convey needed task and context information to all.

Identify the Puzzle Pieces and Fit Them Together

As with any group, a primary task is to motivate the contribution of task-relevant information and appropriate weighting of all such contributions, regardless of the source. In some sense, this guideline is the opposite of the mandate to find common ground for the collaborators. Here, it is necessary to discover what is unique and different about potential contributions of the members, and to determine how these contributions can most effectively be integrated. It is a mistake simply to assume that technological communication tools will enhance access to the power structure on the part of lower status participants without active management of this process. Research points to several opportunities in this area. Although some early research indicated a reduction in the role of liking in the evaluation of virtual teammate contributions as opposed to face-to-face groups,[34] other findings indicate that such biases remain in computer-mediated domains. Although comments suggesting negative outcomes made by a majority member (high status) tend to be heard, such comments made by the minority are not given full attention. An understanding of the impact of the source of a comment (majority, minority) and the positivity or negativity of the message on the extent of influence will also be key to effecting change.[35] These findings can be utilized as levers in the continuing effort to provide avenues for input from all members as opposed to a select few.

Know and Use the Technology

One of the most common complaints about virtual communication or management systems is that they don't get used. Typically, for a technology to become a success, it must reach some level of usage at which it is going to provide utility to the majority of potential adopters to actually engage with it and learn to use it effectively. The average person is not likely to use new technology for "fun"; she must see a benefit to her work. The technology must help individuals do their work either more effectively or more efficiently. As more people start using the technology, it becomes more costly to avoid its use than to join in. The manager's role may well be to lead the way. By using the technology early, and using it consistently, you indicate the need for adoption to others who may wait to ensure that it will be worthwhile.

With few exceptions, the path to successful mobile collaborative efforts will be through technology, not through attempts to provide "enough" face-to-face contact. There are too many benefits to be realized with technologically mediated communication—with its increasing mobility and capacity for addressing the full complexity of the work environment—for a retreat on this front. As with most business problems, the solution lies in understanding the fundamental ways the environment changes through technologically mediated communication and proactively addressing these changes in ways that integrate with the social systems in which humans exist. As noted in the early days of the use of collaborative technologies for work groups,[36] the success we have in realizing the benefits of these technologies will rest on resolving the social issues that changes in human interaction raise.

NOTES

1. J. E. Driskell, P. H. Radtke, and E. Salas, "Virtual Teams: Effects of Technological Mediation on Team Performance," *Group Dynamics: Theory, Research, and Practice* 7 (2003): 297–323.

2. M. Harvey, M. M. Novicevic, and G. Garrison, "Challenges to Staffing Global Virtual Teams," *Human Resource Management Review* 14 (2004): 275–294.

3. C. C. Miller, "Sharing Consumers' Tastes in Cellphone Web Surfing," *New York Times*, February 23, 2009, http://www.nytimes.com/2009/02/23/technology/23buzz.html?th=&emc=th&pagewanted=print.

4. F. Emery, "Designing Socio-Technical Systems for 'Greenfield' Sites," *Journal of Occupational Behavior* 1 (1980): 19–27.

5. R. L. Daft and R. H. Lengel, "Organizational Information Requirements, Media Richness, and Structural Design," *Management Science* 32 (1986): 554–571.

6. J. Short, E. Williams, and B. Christie, *The Social Psychology of Telecommunications* (New York: Wiley, 1976).

7. J. Berger, B. P. Cohen, and M. Zelditch, "Status Characteristics and Social Interaction," *American Sociological Review* 37 (1972): 241–255.

8. M. H. Fisek, and R. Ofshe, "The Process of Status Evolution," *Sociometry* 33 (1970): 327–346.

9. S. Kiesler, J. Siegel, and T. W. McGuire, "Social Psychological Aspects of Computer Mediated Communication," *American Psychologist* 39 (1984): 1123–1134.

10. P. Wallace, *The Internet in the Workplace: How New Technology Is Transforming Work* (Cambridge, UK: Cambridge University Press: 2004).

11. P. L. McLeod, R. S. Baron, M. W. Marti, and K. Yoon, "The Eyes Have It: Minority Influence in Face-to-Face and Computer-mediated Group Discussion," *Journal of Applied Psychology* 82 (1997): 706–718.

12. See Note 1.

13. G. Stasser, "Pooling of Unshared Information during Group Discussions," in *Group process and productivity*, ed. S. Worchel, W. Wood, and J. A. Simpson (Newbery Park, CA: Sage, 1992).

14. J. A. Bargh and M. J. Ferguson, "Beyond Behaviorism: On the Automaticity of Higher Mental Processes," *Psychological Bulletin* 126 (2000): 925–945.

15. H. Tajfel, *Differentiation between Social Groups* (London: Academic Press, 1978).

16. S. A. Reid and M. A. Hogg, "Uncertainty Reduction, Self Enhancement, and Ingroup Identification," *Personality and Social Psychology Bulletin* 31 (2005): 804–817.

17. See Note 1.

18. A. H. Anderson, R. McEwan, J. Bal, and J. Carletta, "Virtual Team Meetings: An Analysis of Communication and Context,"*Computers in Human Behavior* 23 (2007): 2558–2580.

19. L. G. Martin and J. M. Ross-Gordon, "Cultural Diversity in the Workplace: Managing a Multicultural Workforce," *New Directions in Adult and Continuing Education* 48 (1990): 45–54.

20. P. M. Blau, *Inequality and heterogeneity* (New York: Free Press, 1977).

21. W. Huang, J. S. Olson, and G. M. Olson, "Camera Angle Affects Dominated in Video-Mediated Communication," in *Proceedings of CHI*, Short Papers (New York: ACM Press, 2002).

22. J. Webster and W. K. P. Wong, "Comparing Traditional and Virtual Group Forms: Identity, Communication and Trust in Naturally Occurring Project Teams," *The International Journal of Human Resource Management* 19 (2008): 41–62.

23. C. D. Cramton, "Attribution in Distributed Work Groups," in *Distributed Work*, ed. P. Hinds and S. Kiesler (Cambridge, MA: MIT Press, 2002).

24. M. Villano, "The Online Divide Between Work and Play," *New York Times*, April 26, 2009, http://www.nytimes.com/2009/04/26/jobs/26career.html?_r=1&th=&emc=th&pagewated.

25. T. Bisoux, "Making Connections," *BizEd* (January/February 2009), 16–22.

26. Larry Magid, "Study: Leisure Browsing Increases Productivity," Cnet News, April 3, 2009, .

27. D. S. Staples and L. Zhao, "The Effects of Cultural Diversity in Virtual Teams versus Face-to-Face Teams," *Group Decision and Negotiation* 15 (2006): 389–406.

28. R. S. Gajendran and D. A. Harrison, "The Good, the Bad, and the Unknown about Telecommuting: Meta-Analysis of Psychological Mediators and Individual Consequences," *Journal of Applied Psychology* 92 (2007): 1524–1541.

29. L. A. Hambley, T. A. O'Neill, and T. B. Kline, "Virtual Team Leadership: The Effects of Leadership Style and Communication Medium on Team Interaction Styles and Outcomes," *Organizational Behavior and Human Decision Processes* 103 (2007): 1–20.

30. R. K. Hart and P. L. McLeod, "Rethinking Team Building in Geographically Dispersed Teams: One Message at a Time," *Organizational Dynamics* 31 (2003): 352–361.

31. M. Hakonen and J. Lipponen, "Procedural Justice and Identification with Virtual Teams: The Moderating Role of Face-to-Face Meetings and Geographical Dispersion," *Social Justice Research* 21 (2008): 164–178.

32. B. Rosen, S. Furst, and R. Blackburn, "Overcoming Barriers to Knowledge Sharing in Virtual Teams," *Organizational Dynamics* 36 (2007): 259–273.

33. T. A. Carte, L. Chidambaram, and A. Becker, "Emergent Leadership in Self-managed Virtual Teams," *Group Decision and Negotiation* 15 (2006): 323–343.

34. S. Weisband and L. Atwater, "Evaluating Self and Others in Electronic and Face-to-Face Groups," *Journal of Applied Psychology* 84 (1999): 632–639.

35. R. Martin and M. Hewstone, "Majority versus Minority Influence: When, Not Whether, Source Status Instigates Heuristic or Systematic Processing," *European Journal of Social Psychology* 33 (2003): 313–330.

36. M. H. Olson (Ed.), *Technological Support for Work Group Collaboration* (Hillsdale, NJ: Lawrence Erlbaum Associates: 1989).

Suggested Reading

Anson, R., and B. E. Munkvold. "Beyond Face-to-Face: A Field Study of Electronic Meetings in Different Time and Place Modes," *Journal of Organizational Computing and Electronic Commerce* 14 (2004): 127–152.

Bowers, C., E. Salas, and F. Jentsch. *Creating High-Tech Teams: Practical Guidance on Work Performance and Technology.* Washington, DC: American Psychological Association, 2006.

Dekker, D. M., C. G. Rutte, and P. T. Van den Berg. "Cultural Differences in the Perception of Critical Interaction Behaviors in Global Virtual Teams," *International Journal of Intercultural Relations* 32 (2008): 441–452.

Driskell, J. E., P. H. Radtke, and E. Salas. "Virtual Teams: Effects of Technological Mediation on Team Performance," *Group Dynamics: Theory, Research, and Practice* 7 (2003): 297–323.

Duarte, D. L., and N. T. Snyder. *Mastering Virtual Teams.* San Francisco: Jossey-Bass, 1999.

Naquin, C. E., T. R. Kurtzburg, and L. Y. Belkin. "E-mail Communication and Group Cooperation in Mixed Motive Contexts," *Social Justice Research* 21 (2008): 470–489.

Rosen, B., S. Furst, and R. Blackburn. "Overcoming Barriers to Knowledge Sharing in Virtual Teams," *Organizational Dynamics* 36 (2007): 259–273.

Wallace, P. *The Internet in the Workplace: How New Technology Is Transforming Work.* Cambridge, UK: Cambridge University Press, 2004.

Weisband, S., Ed.. *Leadership at a Distance: Research in Technologically Support Work.* New York: Lawrence Erlbaum Associates, 2008.

3

BEHIND THE SCREEN: UNDERSTANDING VIRTUAL ORGANIZATIONAL BEHAVIOR

Rudy Nydegger

ORGANIZATIONS IN THE WORLD TODAY

That the world is changing is not a new phenomenon—it has been a fact since the beginning of time. However, today the world is changing faster than we can keep up with it, and the rate of change increases each year. This problem was recognized in 1970 with the publication of Alvin Toffler's book *Future Shock*[1] in which Toffler forecast that we are changing the world faster than we can adapt to the changes. This is an issue that confronts every organization in every country in the world today.

Today organizations deal with pressures, conflicts, and issues that could not have been imagined a few decades ago. For example, the Internet has changed the way business is conducted from the smallest organization to the largest. We have the luxury (and curse) of having more information available to us than we can ever access or use, as well as the challenge of procuring the most helpful information. The amazing advances in information technology have impacted all of us dramatically and have changed the ways organizations function and deal with their customers, suppliers, and competitors, as well as their own employees.

Organizations today face increased competition, new markets and labor pools, and new technologies, and must meet these challenges if they are to survive and thrive. The workforce is changing around the world as well: becoming more diverse, more educated, and more technologically savvy. This alone produces unique challenges for managers as they begin to reflect on the increased complexity of organizations, the workforce, and the world itself. New information and communication technologies are not only changing the way organizations operate, but also the way work is performed and how people relate to and communicate with one another.

Leaders in organizations today are looking for innovative ways to organize employees and how they do their jobs. For example, organizations use modern communication technology to distribute work to people who physically may not be in the same location as their coworkers or supervisor, or who may not even be working at the same time. Permitting people to telecommute (work from home or another location with a computer that links to the workplace) is only one example of how technology is impacting the workplace. These advances are also supporting an increased interest in the use of "virtual teams"—teams whose members are not at the same location and may not be working at the same time. In fact, some feel that because work team boundaries are expanding and shrinking in response to changing project necessities, virtual teams are going to become vitally important to organizations and many different types of groups.

As important as changing technology is for organizations to relate to and meet the needs of their customers, it is also a necessary and important way for people in the organization to stay in touch with one other. It used to be that work teams had fixed and stable membership that changed very little over time, but today it is not unusual for team membership to be dynamic and to shift as needs dictate. It is also common for teams to include people from outside the organization who can offer special skills or knowledge that is important for the team to complete its work. Similarly, it is common for workers to be members of several teams working on different projects simultaneously. Often, teams of workers are not collocated (in the same place) and may be distributed (in different places). Traditionally, work teams had specific projects that had specific beginnings and end points, but today projects are often large, dynamic, and may continually change as needs and constraints dictate. Finally, many employees who work on different teams will have to relate to different managers, and in matrix organizations there will frequently be multiple reporting relationships that employees will also need to navigate.[2]

This chapter will address some of the implications of change in the workplace today and how these changes will affect workers, teams, organizations, and society as a whole. The use of information and communication technologies has dramatically changed how work is performed, how people interact with one another at work, and how organizations function.

ORGANIZATIONAL BEHAVIOR IN VIRTUAL TEAMS AND GROUPS

Organizational behavior (OB) deals with the behavior of people and groups in organizations and with the functioning of the organization as a whole. It examines the effects of various psychological, social, organizational, and environmental factors on the thoughts, feelings, and behaviors of people in organizations as well as on group dynamics and team performance. It also looks more broadly at organization-wide factors like organizational culture, climate, and performance. OB is a multidisciplinary field drawing from the social sciences psychology, sociology, anthropology, and political science, as well as from fields such as management and engineering.

Because of dramatic changes in the workplace and advances in information and communication technology, many organizations are beginning to use "virtual teams" much more widely and in many contexts. According to D. L. Duarte & N. T. Snyder,[3] virtual teams operate "without the physical limitations of distance, time, and organizational boundaries. They use electronic collaboration technologies and other techniques to lower travel and facility costs, reduce project schedules, and improve decision-making time and communication." More simply, D. Gould says that virtual teams = teams + electronic links + groupware.[4]

Additionally, many organizations are geographically dispersed and require employees to work on projects or initiatives with people from different sites and time zones. As many organizations merge, acquire other organizations, or are acquired themselves, the need for distributed work increases along with the need to contain costs. Through telecommuting and virtual work, teams can dramatically save money, time, and commuting expenses allowing for travel to be more strategically focused. Finally, virtual groups and distributed work can reduce the time-to-market cycle, an advantage for companies and a distinct benefit for customers.

Many organizations use more modern forms of self-managed teams, including virtual teams, to improve efficiency. L. G. Boiney[5] found that 68 percent of *Fortune* 1000 companies are using self-managed and virtual teams, and, according to W. R. Cascio,[6] there are numerous business reasons companies should consider using a virtual workplace:

- Reduced real estate expense
- Increased productivity
- Higher profits
- Improved customer service
- Access to global markets
- Environmental benefits

As attractive as the opportunity for virtual teams and the virtual workplace may seem, it is not always easy to make the switch to this form of organizational design and management. The virtual team "can offer flexibility, responsiveness, and diversity of perspectives in ways that differ from traditional groups."[7] However, virtual groups differ from more traditional ones in other important ways. For example, because they are often geographically distributed, the communication among members may be the only visible artifact of the group's existence. Virtual groups also tend to work within a less formal structure and are often more self-managed than traditional teams. There are, therefore, new secondary roles and differing status for members of the group, and roles and status in the virtual group may be totally independent of their roles and status in the home organization. More so than in traditional groups, the roles and status of members in the virtual group depend on the resources they bring to the group and the extent to which they offer something of value to the group.

Virtual teams can take a number of different forms. For example, virtual groups can be normal work teams, or they can involve executive teams that are relatively permanent groups of managers who may work at different sites but who need to continually coordinate their efforts. Project teams that only exist only for the life of the project can also find virtuality useful, and the members of these teams are usually selected because they can offer to the home organization a specific expertise. An interesting variant of virtual organizational teams is called the *community of practice team* that involves people from different organizations working on similar projects who get together to support the ongoing work of all of the members in the different organizations.[8]

Many things set virtual groups apart from traditional groups, including the effects of anonymity and the lack of physicality,[9] and this implies that maintaining a clear group identity could be a problem.[10] Interestingly, individual performance is at least as vital in virtual groups as in collocated groups because of the importance of drawing on the expertise of those involved in the success of the group venture. In fact, group performance within any team depends on individual performance, which in turn depends on the structural position (individual centrality) of the person as well as their individual role characteristics (e.g., functional role, status, communication role).[11] To help us understand group functioning in the virtual team, we must also consider social needs versus task needs within the group, as well as the social identity and self-concept of the members. As with any group, virtual groups must function under a stable set of group norms as well as develop leadership patterns and functions within the group.[12]

VIRTUALITY AND INDIVIDUAL/TEAM PERFORMANCE

OB strives to understand how people, teams, and organizations function, as well as the factors that impact them. Although it is tempting to treat virtual groups as if they are a completely different animal, we must remember that virtual groups are, nonetheless, still groups with many of the same issues, constraints, and strengths that other groups experience. If we define a group as two or more people who interact, are interdependent, and who share a common purpose, then virtual groups clearly meet these conditions. When we look at the factors that determine the effectiveness of an individual's performance in a distributed group, we find that their functional role, status, and communication role are as important as their centrality within the group, similar to what is found in traditional groups. A team member's functional role reflects that individual's attributes, such as the activities a person performs that require special skills, although it is not necessarily associated with a formal role. Status is based on how long a person has been a group member and their rank within the group—this usually has a direct impact on performance. The communication role is defined by the actions a person takes to directly interact, share, and receive information from others. One study shows that individuals who contribute more information to the group than they seek will be perceived as performing better.[13] Another factor, centrality, is the number of connections a person has with group members and how closely she or he is attached to the group. It was found that centrality is a stronger predictor of performance than individual characteristics, but a clear functional role seems to enable a person to achieve better centrality.[14]

While communication is an important factor in determining the performance of individuals and teams, numerous studies have also demonstrated the importance of communication to group and organizational functioning. Much of the prior work on computer-mediated groups suggests that they are unable to support the fuller range of communicative acts that are typically employed by face-to-face (FtF) teams. As people and groups gain more experience, however, they usually adapt to the medium's restrictions by imbuing their text-based messages with both task and social information.[15] Thus, the use of pictures, symbols, shortcut jargon, and other ways of communicating nonverbal and other social information soon becomes part of our interaction patterns. Of course, this does not replace the richness of FtF communication, but it does indicate how important these subtler elements of communication have become, and the efforts that are people willing to employ in order to enrich a leaner communication medium.

Communication is the fuel that keeps any group moving forward, and it also impacts the nature of the relationships among the members as well as the dynamics of the group or team. Interestingly, in normal FtF groups, individual liking among members is largely based on nonrational or nontask bases of attraction, whereas in virtual groups people seem to like those who contribute most to the group's performance.[16] Therefore, as group work in organizations becomes increasingly virtual, communication becomes even more important as a determinant of group functioning, both task-based and interpersonal.

Another important aspect of group functioning and effectiveness is trust. Trust becomes extremely important in virtual groups because many of the social and nonverbal cues that are so important in establishing trust between people are lacking. Box et al.[17] point out that, as with other relational dynamics, trust tends to diminish when there are fewer visual and vocal cues as found with computer-mediated communication (CMC). Certainly, trust is based in large part on social information exchange,[18] and therefore having virtual groups develop ways to improve the richness of their social communication is very important. Trust is important among group members so that they will enjoy their job and feel a part of the group. While trust was found to be positively related to performance in groups,[19] the conditions that lead to trust are unquestionably more difficult to establish among members of virtual groups and teams. Feeling connected to and part of a group is what is referred to as "cohesiveness," and this is based on all of the factors that make a person feel (and want to continue to be) part of a group. It has been clearly demonstrated that cohesiveness exerts considerable influence over work group performance,[20] and yet work on virtual groups has consistently found that group members in CMC groups experience lower cohesiveness and feel more loosely connected to their groups.[21] In order for cohesiveness to improve, trusting and liking one another are the main factors when working with virtual groups.

When CMC or virtual groups run effectively, the resulting outcomes can be extremely positive:

- Greater liking for and acceptance by other group members
- Negating the effects of social anxiety
- Decreased feelings of isolation and loneliness
- Increasing one's social network
- Coming together and feeling part of a group[22]

While teams, including virtual teams, perform well under most circumstances, a lack of trust and openness can interfere with important communications or with coordinating efforts among team members. Effective leadership is vitally important in any group, and although it is sometimes difficult within virtual groups, it is no less important. However, mistaken and misleading beliefs about virtual team leadership in virtual groups can affect group functioning. Myths include:

- Virtual teams don't need supervision—members are usually working alone and don't need leadership.
- Virtual team members can't be trusted to work alone—they must be monitored to make sure members aren't avoiding their work.
- You can't manage what you can't see—leaders can't do much in virtual groups because they can't relate directly to the members at other locations.
- Virtual groups are less complex and easier to manage—they don't use as many social cues and interactions.

- Because people aren't working as closely together, trust isn't as big an issue in virtual teams.
- It is not important for members to have FtF contact—most of the work is done individually and through a computer.

It turns out that the style and quality of leadership may be more important in virtual groups than "normal" groups because virtual groups use fewer social cues. In traditional groups it is easier to adjust or adapt to the style of the leader and to fulfill leadership functions. With limited cues in the virtual group there are fewer options and opportunities to make adjustments, making leadership more difficult and fragile.

An effective leader in virtual groups must be able to facilitate various types of meetings in a way that establishes a positive tone and atmosphere. Coaching, mentoring, and timely feedback become critically important to a leader in order to have a positive impact. From a motivational standpoint, a good leader will establish clear and meaningful goals that are consistent with the needs of the organization. Demonstrating proficiency with virtual communication tools and relevant technology and being able to analyze the group's data is vitally important to foster the trust and respect of the group's members.

One of the challenges for leaders of virtual teams is that they cannot see their employees working and often do not know what or how much they are doing; this exemplifies the importance of the leader's role and the importance of trust and meaningful communication. A leader should also be prepared to transition team members onto or off a team in ways that are advantageous to them and to their careers. Leaders should focus on results, schedules, and budgets rather than on less tangible outcomes, and they should plan to spend around 75 percent of their time with team members who are not collocated with them; contact is vitally important in order for team members to remain involved and committed to the team. Leading a virtual team can be a challenge and requires that a leader understand virtual team development and dynamics and model the behavior that is expected of all members. Dealing with different types of employees across cultural lines is especially important as most organizations are becoming increasingly diverse and work is done with members in different locations.

Continuous improvement is expected of all teams and members, and leaders should consistently strive for improving their leadership knowledge and skills. Being able to recognize problems and to take action requires constant involvement, monitoring, and possessing up-to-date knowledge and information. Other hints for leaders of virtual teams include:

- Members who are not collocated with the leader should feel a part of the team.
- All members need to receive timely and specific feedback.

- Team processes must not unfairly favor those collocated with the leader.
- Reward and recognition must be fair and consistent for all members of the team.
- The leader should participate in most if not all team meetings.
- The leader must have some direct contact with all members of the team before actual work begins—face to face if possible.
- The leader needs to be aware of progress (of lack of same) and meet frequently to discuss progress and processes.

Team diversity is another important group variable, as it is associated with increases in communication problems, conflict, and turnover. One interesting finding is that in diverse teams, members often develop a negative view of the team experience regardless of how well the team performs or is recognized for its performance.[23] One diversity factor that is more obvious in most workplaces is gender. In the United States, women comprise approximately 46 percent of the workforce and by 2020 they will number about half, which means that over the next decade, most new employees will be female, making work teams increasingly diverse with respect to gender. This means that we are dealing with two different "cultures" with respect to work norms and expectations. Of course, not all men or all women have similar approaches to work, but it is clear that very often they approach work and their jobs differently. These types of differences will also affect the virtual workplace and how male and female workers utilize computer-mediated communication.[24] For example, women tend to be more comfortable with team-based evaluations and rewards and overall report higher levels of perceived team performance than do men. Women also express higher levels of satisfaction with being members of a virtual team and perceive fewer severe team problems than do men, with the exception of sharing information among members. After having served on a virtual team, 66 percent of the women interviewed said they would have liked more face-to-face contact, while only 37 percent of men said that more face-to-face contact would have been helpful.[25] One study found that women in virtual groups perceived the group as more cohesive and able to help each other more than did men. They were also more satisfied with the virtual group than were men and felt that conflict was more readily resolved. However, in face-to-face groups women were less satisfied than those in virtual groups and felt that conflict was only smoothed over rather than being resolved. Perhaps the most important finding is that there are no differences in general between the genders with respect to the quality of work in groups, teams, or individually,[26] and in general, men and women tend to report good experiences in virtual teams.[27]

Other aspects of OB affect performance of virtual groups, and sometimes differently from traditional groups. For example, personality and perception will have different impacts on the virtual group because team members will have different types of information and perhaps less information than they might have in the traditional FtF group. Perceptions would be different because the information base would be different, and, whether considering social perception or perception of other group factors, the different information would yield different perceptions. Both the leader and team members should be cognizant of the fact that the information that is relevant in a virtual group is likely to be different from that found in the traditional group.

While the members in a group learn differently from individuals alone, learning in a virtual group is even more different. When designing the training programs for people in virtual groups leaders must consider the nature of the work, the tasks and knowledge involved, the individuals and their learning styles, plus the nature of information exchange and technology.

In recent years, motivating employees has also become much more complicated. First, with a more diverse workforce, motivation becomes a more complex issue, and with more work being done in teams, this adds another dimension as well. For example, when people are working in teams should the manager focus on motivating the group or individuals? The answer, of course, is "Yes." That is, we must consider motivation, incentives, and rewards from both the group's and the individual's perspective. When we add the dimension of virtuality, motivation becomes even more complex and complicated. The manager must remember that people work for different reasons and with different expectations, and in the new dynamic and complex environment this fact is even more relevant.

Finally, issues of power and politics do not disappear because an organization is utilizing more distributed work strategies including the use of virtual teams. Power is simply about influencing people to act in ways that are preferred by the person in power, and politics are simply the ways in which people use their power to influence outcomes in their own interest. In the virtual or distributed work situation, power and politics are still issues to be managed, but they will certainly look different from a more traditional setting. Although a virtual team manager or member does not have to be an organizational politician to work effectively in virtual teams, he does have to be aware of the political climate and work accordingly. The best remedy for dealing with a highly politicized situation is to insist on open and honest communication, and while this can be a challenge, it is not impossible.

ADVANTAGES AND DISADVANTAGES OF THE VIRTUAL TEAM

Differences between virtual groups and FtF groups are due to relational dynamics, discretionary and asynchronous participation, free-riding, difficulty integrating information, and other information-processing aspects of virtual work that make virtual groups particularly challenging to manage.[28] However, virtual groups allow for very efficient communication with people all over the world, and some find the virtual group even more intimate (possibly because they can work and interact in more comfortable conditions). These attributes seem to make virtual groups very powerful and appropriate,[29] and many are reporting significant advantages of virtual teams. A more efficient exchange of information leads to an easier and faster spread of "best practices" among employees, and it is simpler to connect "islands of knowledge" into self-organizing, knowledge-sharing networks of professional communities that foster cross-functional and cross-divisional collaboration. It also becomes easier to initiate and contribute to projects across organizational boundaries.[30] As we gain more exposure to and experience with virtual teams, we notice that very few teams are 100 percent virtual, and they tend to take on the same structure as "real" teams. We are also finding that people can be trusted to work remotely and that virtual teams tend to get the job done.[31] Other advantages of a virtual team include that they:

- Save time and money providing easier access to experts
- Can be organized regardless of the location of its members
- Allow organizations to expand their potential labor markets, enabling them to hire the best employees regardless of their physical location
- Make it easier to hire and utilize effective workers who are disabled
- Make it easier for employees to accommodate their personal and professional lives
- Enable dynamic team membership, which in turn allows people to move from one project to another as needed
- Allow employees to be members of multiple teams and projects
- Permit team communications and reports to be available online and accessible from any place at any time, which makes for more effective and efficient use of team resources[32]
- Allow people to work from any place at any time
- Eliminate commute time
- Minimize or eliminate travel, lodging, parking, and leasing/owning building space expenses[33]

The cost savings alone for distributed and virtual work is potentially significant. One U.S. government study showed that if 20,000 federal workers could telecommute one day per week, they would save over two million commuting miles, 102,000 gallons of gasoline, and 81,600 pounds of carbon dioxide emissions each week.[34]

In addition to the advantages of virtual groups, there are disadvantages as well. When using groupware and other technologies, it is often the technology that is blamed first when problems arise, although it is more often the individuals or social factors that really are responsible for subpar performance in virtual teams.[35] For example, both men and women report that the main problem areas in virtual teams are poor sharing of information, unclear or inappropriate expectations, and unclear lines of accountability or control.[36] Obviously, these issues all depend on the people or social aspects of the group rather than the technology. However, the technology aspects of virtual teams can provide some concerns as well and should also be considered when relevant.

Other disadvantages of virtual groups include the setup and maintenance costs associated with the installation and upkeep of the sophisticated communication and information technology infrastructure. By distributing the work there is the possibility of losing some of the cost efficiencies that can be gained if the work is concentrated in one location, and as mentioned above, personal or social issues can potentially exist in the virtual workplace as well. Cultural issues, feelings of isolation, and a lack of trust related to a more limited interaction with managers and supervisors must also be considered in the virtual workplace.[37]

The evidence, however, suggests that the most significant issue within virtual teams has to do with the fact that dispersion may lead to outcome problems such as difficulties with relational communication and trust, as well as productivity and the group's work quality. Relational communication is the reciprocal process of how members regard one another and how they express their regard. Because relational cues are often nonverbal their absence does put virtual and distributed groups at somewhat of a disadvantage,[38] leading some to assert that trust cannot be maintained in virtual teams.[39]

It must be asserted that geographic dispersion of work teams can have several disruptive effects. There are incongruities in the work environments and social structures, dissimilar organizational cultures and subcultures, and different time zones in which the work occurs.[40] Clearly, the main disadvantage of the virtual team is the lack of physical interaction and the limited nonverbal cues, as well as the synergies that often are part of FtF communication. This is particularly important in high context cultures like China, Japan, and many of the Middle-Eastern and South American countries where many aspects of the setting and nonverbal and social cues are very important.

One interesting problem area regarding distributed work teams has to do with managers' resistance to virtual work. It has been found that many managers of virtual teams feel a threat to their identity because they feel that their role, authority, and responsibilities are unclear. Further, there may be an issue with respect to status and esteem, and many think that they may have less control over the work for which they are responsible.[41] While these concerns are understandable, care must be taken to provide managers with the training and information necessary to understand, appreciate, and respect the reasons for using a virtual work environment. The managers' responsibilities may change, but their role is no less important in the new environment. If the virtual workplace is to be effective, the managers and leaders must be a positive contributing force that strengthens and facilitates the work and the processes related to it.

There are some distinct advantages in the virtual workplace, but there are some concerns and problems as well. As technology continues to advance, the use of CMC and virtual work will not totally replace the FtF workplace or the use of traditional groups, but it will also continue to be part of the new and emerging work environment. Looking at a meta-analytic study of CMC and FtF work teams, the results are inconclusive as to which is superior.[42] However, one conclusion to be drawn is that there is clearly a need for both types of groups. Research and training are now needed to help us to understand when and how best to employ the different work strategies that meet the needs of the organizations as effectively as possible.

TIPS FOR MANAGING IN A VIRTUAL WORLD

Organizations now and in the future will need to access and enhance their employees' commitment and their capacity to learn and work at all levels. Rather than managing learning and change, new managers will need to facilitate them.[43] The use of technology and distributed work will increase the number of dimensions and opportunities that people can access to improve the quality and amount of their work. Designing and improving communication environments are means of providing employees with databases as well as enabling and improving the dialogue between them.

Designing work around virtual teams takes advantage of technology, but it is equally important to remember that teamwork is fundamentally a social system, and when new information is introduced to a team it is best to use the social networks within the groups. Managers and team members need to facilitate all members experiencing the reality of being a team member. They must also engage in the practices of the group, both observation and participation in order to enhance their knowledge and expertise. Engagement is inseparable from empowerment, and "failure" to perform often results from exclusion from the process.[44] In the early stages of any group's or team's formation, proximity and FtF interactions are important for establishing a basis for trust and the empowerment of collaborative relationships. In the latter stages of a group's evolution richer social cues are necessary for accurate communication. While both of these conditions are more difficult in virtual groups, they are nonetheless important and must be considered a part of the healthy functioning of the group.[45]

According to L. Kimball,[46] when designing a virtual team a few factors can be critical to the group's success:

- **Purpose**. Schedule more frequent and explicit check-ins, because there is a lack of FtF meetings, in order to achieve a unified sense of purpose.
- **Roles**. Give each virtual team member a clearly defined role to fulfill that is understood by all the group members. Role ambiguity and confusion are recipes for poor performance.

- **Culture**. Use technology to support a virtual team based on the prevailing culture of the whole organization; that is, how it will affect and be affected by that culture.
- **Conversation**. Use technology to support conversation among the members, not just to store and exchange data.
- **Feedback**. Spend more time on the use of technology to improve the quality of communication among team members (especially the older ones) as it is the primary means of producing frequent, timely, and helpful feedback.
- **Pace**. Facilitate the pace at which work is performed, because some members will access the shared environment more or less frequently than others. In an asynchronous environment it is a challenge to ensure that employees do not feel as though they are being left behind or excluded.
- **Entry and reentry**. Introduce new members to the often fast-paced virtual team process as quickly and comfortably as possible. It is vitally important for managers and leaders to bring them on board and integrate them efficiently.
- **Weaving**. Tell employees where they have been, where they are, and where they might want to go next through "weaving," a networking term that refers to the process of summarizing and synthesizing multiple responses in virtual groups.
- **Participation**. Pay attention to the cues that are unique to virtual teams and which indicate when people are engaging and actively participating in the group. In the absence of nonverbal cues that are more readily available in FtF groups, it is important to notice other sources of information like emoticons (a textual representation of a writer's mood or emotional state) and other "paramessages" that will give some richness to a fairly "lean" type of communication.
- **Flow**. Be sure to know what is transpiring and how the group is functioning. There will be times when the group in general or its members are more or less active.

As managers start to structure organizations with the intent of increasing the use of virtual teams several steps need to occur. First, the process for managing and developing the teams needs to be designed, defined, piloted, tested, and refined *before* the teams are fully brought online. Second, managers and team members must be trained to work in the new virtual team environment. Third, the culture and structure of the organization must be reshaped in order to support the use of a different type of team model. Fourth, the reward system must be modified to reflect the changes in how work is performed and evaluated. Finally, new management, measurement, and control systems must be designed and integrated into the processes as they relate to the new types of groups and incorporate into the organization as a whole.[47] Specifically, suggestions for managers include:

- Start by changing the culture, and then use the new technology to support the change.
- Change the reward system to evaluate the employees' teamwork and their ability to share information.
- Encourage bottom-up, grassroots efforts.
- Be sure the new software fits the new processes, is properly installed, and that people are adequately trained in its use.
- Start collaboration with FtF meetings, when possible, within the virtual teams.
- Use role modeling for spreading the effective use of groupware.
- Use training programs for teaching and collaboration of skills and software.[48]

Gould[49] points out that the most frequent complaint by virtual teams is communication, and he suggests that leaders schedule FtF meetings when possible, particularly for the initial meeting of the group. Another strategy that will help to avoid delays and to reduce the amount of dysfunctional conflict is to establish a code of conduct that all members are expected to follow. It is important for members to augment their text-only messages with FtF information that will enrich communication and help nurture a sense of trust that is essential for teams are to be successful.

When organizations begin to use virtual teams, leaders should follow some basic rules that can lead to success:

Rule 1: Start right away—don't drag your feet.
Rule 2: Communicate frequently to all members of the team.
Rule 3: Multi-task the organizing and performance of substantive work simultaneously.
Rule 4: Overtly acknowledge that you have read one another's messages.
Rule 5: Be explicit about what you are thinking and doing.
Rule 6: Set deadlines and stick to them.[50]

When these rules are followed, it is found, both in research and in practice, that virtual teams were more effective, and the members reported more satisfaction with being on the team and with the other team members.

Engaging the team to set their own goals and expectations for both behavior and performance is helpful to clearly define each member's responsibilities and obligations. To ensure that they fully understand, rigorous project management disciplines are vitally important. Establishing the tone of the team as well as setting positive and proactive standards can make a big difference in how the team functions. An atmosphere of openness and honesty among team members will be one of the most important aspects of a successful team. To manage occasional conflicts, leaders must encourage individuals to voice their differences of opinions or ideas, and instruct them as to how issues will be addressed and managed. Managers must ensure that communication is open, frequent, and accurate, and is as rich as the medium and circumstances permit. It is important that leaders encourage and support frequent feedback and regular formal and informal communication sessions to ensure that all members are engaged and productive and that no issues lurk below the surface. By clearly communicating expectations and ensuring that the rewards system is consistent with those expectations, managers can have a significant impact on the amount and quality of work their team produces.

Being effective in the virtual workplace will require a new mind-set for managers. Rather than assuming that traditional FtF meetings are always the best choice, managers will now need to access different environments that can effectively support high quality work. Collaboration will no longer be achieved by sitting in a room together, but rather through ongoing activity that has fewer time constraints and with boundaries that are fluid and permeable.

Managing virtual teams *is* about being people-oriented, but using newer technologies to make that happen. Managers must develop trust in their team members to do their jobs without direct supervision, a leap of faith for some, but nevertheless essential. It is important for managers to have an open, positive attitude that focuses on opportunities and solutions rather than on finding blame and making excuses, or on finding reasons to discontinue the virtual aspects of the work. Effective leaders who employ a management style that emphasizes results rather than processes and who are skilled communicators, both formally and informally, are successful with teams in traditional workplaces as well as those at different sites and times zones. Finally, the manager of any team must be able to delegate and follow up with support and feedback in order to be assured that work is being performed as it should.[51]

In summary, virtual teams can succeed if commitment to virtual work starts at the top and passes through to all members. Employees must feel connected to the team through frequent communication to track progress and problems. The team must share a view of the goals, which includes recognizing that diversity is a positive element of teams. Because diversity can pose communication issues and the potential for conflict, team members must get to know one another on a personal, human level and not just as technology-driven robots. The most important element of an effective virtual team is the fundamental notion that trust and respect are assumed, not earned.[52] Team members and managers must foster a culture that encourages openness, trust, and respect upon which all elements of team effectiveness can be built and supported.

To be successful, virtual teams must have appropriate:

- Technology
- HR policies
- Training and development for team leaders and members
- Standard organizational and team processes

- Appropriate organizational culture
- Effective leadership
- Leader/member competency[53]

The virtual world is here—there is no turning back.

NOTES

1. Alvin Toffler, *Future Shock* (New York: Random House, 1970).

2. L. Kimball, "Managing Virtual Teams," Speech given at the Teams Strategies Conference, Toronto, Canada: 1997.

3. D. L. Duarte and N. T. Snyder, *Mastering Virtual Teams* (San Francisco: Jossey-Bass, 1999), 4.

4. D. Gould, "Fifth Generation Work—Virtual Organization," 2006, http://www.seanet.com/~daveg/vrteams.htm (November 20, 2008).

5. L. G. Boiney, "Gender Impacts Virtual Work Teams," *Graziadio Business Report* 4, no. 4 (2001): 1–5.

6. W. R. Cascio, "Managing a Virtual Workplace," *The Academy of Management Executive* 14, no. 3 (2000): 81–90.

7. J. B. Walther, U. Bunz, and N. N. Bazarova, "The Rules of Virtual Group," *Proceedings of the 38th Hawaii International Conference on System Science*, 2005.

8. See Note 2.

9. K. Y. A. McKenna and A. Green, "Virtual Group Dynamics," *Group Dynamics: Theory, Research, and Practice* 6, no. 1 (2002): 116–127.

10. T. Finholt and L. S. Sproull, "Electronic Groups at Work," *Organization Science* 1, no. 1(1990), 41–64.

11. M. K. Ahuja, D. F. Galletta, and K. M. Carley, "Individual Centrality and Performance in Virtual R&D Groups: An Empirical Study," 2002. Unpublished manuscript.

12. See Note 9.

13. See Note 11.

14. See Note 11.

15. J. B. Walther, "Interpersonal Effects in Computer-Mediated Interaction: A Relational Perspective," *Communication Research* 19, (1992): 51–90.

16. S. Weisband and L. Atwater, "Evaluating Self and Others in Electronic and Face-to-Face Groups," *Journal of Applied Psychology* 84 (1999): 632–639.

17. N. Box, J. Olson, D. Gergle, G. Olson, and Z. Wright, "Effects of Four Computer-Mediated Communications Channels on Trust Development," *Proceedings of the Special Interest Group on Computer Human Interaction* (2002): 135–140.

18. S. I. Jarvenpaa and D. E. Leidner, "Communication and Trust in Global Virtual Teams," *Journal of Computer-Mediated Communication* 3 (1998): 4.

19. See Note 6.

20. P. S. Goodman, E. Ravlin, and M. Schminke, "Understanding Groups in Organizations," *Research in Organizational Behavior* 9 (1987): 121–173.

21. M. Lea and R. Spears, "Computer-Mediated Communication, De-individuation, and Group Decision-making," *International Journal of Man-Machine Studies* 34, (1991): 312–321.

22. K. Y. A. McKenna, "Influences on the Nature and Functioning of Online Groups," In *Psychological Aspects of Cyberspace: Theory, Research, Applications*, ed. A. Barak (Cambridge, UK: Cambridge University Press, 2008): 228–242.

23. See Note 5.

24. M. R. Lind, "The Gender Impact of Temporary Virtual Work Groups," *IEEE. Transactions on Professional Communication* 42, no. 4 (1999): 276–285.

25. See Note 5.

26. See Note 24.

27. See Note 5.

28. J. Y. Smith and M. T. Vanacek, , "Dispersed Group Decision Making Using Non-simultaneous Computer Conferencing: A Report of Research," *Journal of Management Information Systems* 7(1990): 71–92.

29. B. Dean, , "The Psychologist as Virtual Coach," *The Independent Practitioner* 18, no. 4 (1998): 188–189.

30. See Note 2.

31. D. Gould, 1997, "Leading Virtual Teams," *Virtual Organization*, http://www.seanet.com/~daveg/ltv.htm (November 27, 2008).

32. See Note 6.

33. See Note 4.

34. See Note 6.

35. See Note 2.

36. See Note 5.

37. See Note 6.

38. See Note 7.

39. C. Handy, "Trust and the Virtual Organization," *Harvard Business Review*, no. 73 (1995): 40–50.

40. See Note 7.

41. B. M. Wiesenfeld, S. Raghuram, and R. Garud, "Managers in a Virtual Context: The Experience of Self-Threat and Its Effects on Virtual Work Organizations," in *Trends in Organizational Behavior, vol. 6: The Virtual Organization*, ed. C. L. Cooper and D. M. Roussear (Chichester, UK: John Wiley & Sons, Ltd., 1999).

42. P. L. McLeod, "An Assessment of the Experimental Literature on Electronic Support of Group Work: Results of a Meta-Analysis." *Human-Computer Interaction* 7 (1992): 257–280.

43. See Note 2.

44. See Note 2.

45. B. Nardi, and S. Whittiker, "The Place of Face to Face Communication in Distributed Work," in *Distributed Work: New Research on Working Across Distance Using Technology*, ed. P. Hinds and S. Kiesler (Cambridge, MA: MIT Press, 2002), 83–110.

46. See Note 2.

47. See Note 2.

48. See Note 2.

49. See Note 31.

50. See Note 7.

51. W. F. Cascio, "Virtual Workplaces: Implications for Organizational Behavior," in *Trends in Organizational Behavior, vol. 6: The Virtual Organization*, ed. C. L. Cooper and D. M. Rousseau (Chichester, UK: John Wiley & Sons, Ltd., 1999).

52. "Seven Habits of Successful Virtual Teams," Web Worker Daily, 2006, http://webworkerdaily.com/2006/12/17/seven-habits-of-successful-virtual-teams/ (November 24, 2008).

53. See Note 3.

Suggested Reading

Cascio, W. R. "Managing a Virtual Workplace." *The Academy of Management Executive* 14, no. 3 (2000): 81–90.

Cooper, C. L., and D. M. Roussear, Eds. *Trends in Organizational Behavior, vol. 6: The Virtual Organization*. Chichester, UK: John Wiley & Sons, Ltd, 1999.

Duarte, D. L., and N. T. Snyder. *Mastering Virtual Teams*. San Francisco: Jossey-Bass, 1999.

Finholt, T., and L. S. Sproull. "Electronic Groups at Work." *Organizational Science* 1, no. 1 (1990): 41–64.

Goodman, P. S., E. Ravlin, and M. Schminke. "Understanding Groups in Organizations." *Research in Organizational Behavior* 9 (1987): 121–173.

Gould, D. "Leading Virtual Teams." *Virtual Organization*. 1997. http://www.seanet.com/~daveg/ltv.htm.

Handy, C. "Trust and the Virtual Organization." *Harvard Business Review* 73 (1995): 40–50.

Jarvenpaa S. I., and D. E. Leidner. "Communication and Trust in Global Virtual Teams." *Journal of Computer-Mediated Communication* 3 (1998): 4.

McKenna K. Y. A., and A. Green. "Virtual Group Dynamics." *Group Dynamics: Theory, Research, and Practice* 6, no. 1 (2002): 116–127.

McKenna, K. Y. A. " Influences on the Nature and Functioning of Online Groups." In *Psychological Aspects of Cyberspace: Theory, Research, Applications*. Ed. A. Barak, Cambridge, UK: Cambridge University Press, 2008, 228–242.

Walther, J. B. "Interpersonal Effects in Computer-Mediated Interaction: A Relational Perspective." *Communication Research* 19 (1992):55–90.

Walther, J. B., U. Bunz, and N. N. Bazarova. "The Rules of Virtual Groups." *Proceedings of the 38th Hawaii International Conference on System Science*, 2005.

4

Real-World Opportunities for Virtual-World Project Management*

Dawn Owens, Alanah Mitchell (née Davis), John D. Murphy, Deepak Khazanchi, and Ilze Zigurs

Virtual worlds such as Linden Lab's Second Life are pervading our everyday world and already impacting organizational practices involving virtual teams and virtual-world project management. Consider a world in which you can conduct training sessions and bring together experts from around the globe in a single, common environment; hold effective meetings in a shared space where distant resources and people can come together to communicate, laugh, and create artifacts quickly and easily; and coordinate a project with ease, overcoming cultural barriers to team effectiveness. Virtual-world technology can help realize these goals.

A virtual world (VW) is an instantiation of a metaverse—a fully immersive 3D virtual space in which people interact with one another through avatars and software agents. This virtual space resembles the real world, or "first life," but without its physical limitations.[1] Until recently, most people thought of VWs as social or gaming environments. However, VWs are garnering attention because they provide technology capabilities that can transform education, learning, organizational communication, and even virtual project management.

Virtual-world projects are those conducted partially or wholly in a VW through a collaborative team of avatars and people. In VWPs, activities can occur in-world, out of world, or a combination of the two. *Virtual-world project management* is the process of managing a project through coordination, communication, and control within the bounds of a VW environment and a traditional environment. VWs can enhance collaboration and VWPM through the unique technology capabilities these worlds provide. Using VW technology capabilities, VWP teams can gain access to richer, more engaging environments to help overcome collaboration barriers. Our goal is to highlight the unique technology capabilities in these new environments. We provide an example of these capabilities by describing a VW project that we conducted in Linden Lab's Second Life (SL). We also discuss opportunities and challenges for businesses interested in taking advantage of VWs.

GROWING INTEREST IN VIRTUAL WORLDS

A report from Forrester Research speculates that VWs such as Second Life (www.secondlife.com), There (www.there.com), and other more business-focused VWs are on the brink of becoming valuable work tools.[2] SL is one of the most popular examples of a VW. In fact, according to a Gartner report, 80 percent of active Internet users (around 2.4 billion people) will have a "second life" by the end of 2011.[3]

Today, SL has more than 15 million residents, up from just 3 million in early 2007 (http://secondlife.com/whatis/faq.php). Residents come to this world from more than 100 different countries, with approximately 60 percent of them being men and 40 percent women. User ages range from 18 to 85 years, with an average age of 33. SL distributes space by partitioning the environment into virtual islands. As of October 2008, there were more than 26,000 islands, with 689 new islands added that month alone.

VWs such as SL are not only for individuals. Organizations such as IBM, STA Travel, Sears, and BP are exploring potential uses of VWs in business contexts through SL.[4] Such entities can own an entire island or inhabit portions of one; for example, SciLands is a community of islands in SL devoted to science and technology, where more than 20 science and technology organizations have facilities.[5] These organizations include government agencies, universities, and museums, and occupants of the island include the U.S. National Space Society, the U.S. National Library of Medicine, and the Tech Museum of Space Innovation. The collaboration between IBM and China's Palace Museum is an example of recent efforts to build a major historical and cultural attraction within a VW. The two worked together to build a virtual version of the famous Forbidden City.[6] The virtual Forbidden City (www.beyondspaceandtime .org) is a fully immersive, 3D online world intended to recreate the sense of space and time of this Chinese cultural treasure. The project took three years, involved 12 project team members, and cost U.S. $3 million to build. The final product is available in the form of a download.[7] Following are further examples of how organizations (and exemplar organizations) are using SL in a business context:

- Meet and greet customers, host employee meetings, and conduct global interaction and collaboration (IBM, BP)
- Conduct marketing and e-commerce in a virtual showroom (Sears, BP)
- Provide product information and updates (STA Travel)
- Provide a virtual campus and online collaborative learning (Harvard Law School)
- Communicate vision and build relationships with the public and customers (NASA, IBM)
- Host a virtual museum for brand recognition and e-commerce (International Spaceflight Museum)
- Provide a 3D hospital with free online consultation on resources for medical conditions or issues (Health Info Island)
- Conduct market research and test hotel designs (Starwood Hotels)
- Interview, recruit, and hire employees (Ogilvy Interactive, TMP Worldwide Advertising & Communications)
- Provide training simulators and learning programs (MIT, IBM, Nike, EMC, Discovery Education, BP)

These examples show that a growing number of successful organizations and entities are taking VWs seriously. Innovative companies and educational institutions are finding ways to use VW technology to enhance business processes and to experiment with novel ideas in new contexts. Yet many companies are still asking why they should spend time and resources exploring these worlds. We examine this question on the basis of our own research and provide insight into how companies can use VWs and their inherent technology capabilities for virtual-team interaction and VWPM.

VIRTUAL-WORLD TECHNOLOGY CAPABILITIES

What is so unique about VWs? For one thing, they let you create a world of your choice, complete with access to brainstorming tools as well as buildings and artifacts that perform specific tasks, such as playback of recordings, slide show displays, simulations and models. Avatars in VWs can also walk, fly, and even teleport to other areas. They can interact with other avatars or explore the world independently.

The ability to interact with objects and people through another medium is not unique. What is unusual about VWs is the environment's vividness and the technology capabilities that provide opportunities to enhance interaction and collaboration. These environments can support virtual-team collaboration in ways that are not possible with other technologies.[8]

Current collaboration technologies such as Web conferencing, video conferencing, and video walls strive to emulate face-to-face communication, but they have not yet done so. For example, video conferencing provides communication through what is referred to negatively as "talking heads." Video walls such as HP's Halo provide more life-size images and depth perception, but even these technologies present a physical boundary such as a wall or a computer that separates individuals. VWs are unique because physical boundaries no longer exist. The distinctive features of VW technology include:

- 3D lifelike conversation and an immersed environment for interaction
- Purposeful nonverbal communication, including the ability to touch
- The ability to control avatar appearance, avatar behavior, and the environment

Because avatars can touch things in the environment, move objects, import objects from real life, and create their own in-world objects, these capabilities provide an opportunity for immediate feedback regarding communication and project deliverables. VWs bring people together in real time to enable collaboration, while their avatars explore simulated worlds.[9]

People can control the appearance of their avatars, including hair color, clothing style, and body type. They can also control their avatar's behavior through verbal and nonverbal communication cues. The technology provides purposeful nonverbal communication with deliberate body language, gestures, and nonverbal expressions, including touch. In real-world communication, some nonverbal communication cues occur unconsciously, such as changes in facial expression, which could provide more information than intended. In VWs, the ability to deliberately control cues that are near-automatic reactions in the physical world is a new concept in virtual-team collaboration and interaction. For example, avatars can perform deliberate actions such as smiling, clapping hands, and jumping up and down. These capabilities provide the opportunity for people to express themselves (and their feelings) in a controlled way.

Besides their own appearance and behavior, people can control their environment's appearance and functions. They can also implement additional tools such as those for voting and brainstorming. These features can enhance the collaboration process or help manage specific tasks on a project. Finally, individuals can choose their preferred method of communication—whether text in the form of individual or group notes, audio, video, facial expressions, body language and gestures, or Internet lingo (LOL, BRB, PLZ, and so on) in text chat. Thus, a person has the freedom to express and interact with others using one or more technological forms. This ability enhances the communication process and makes the interaction between people more interesting.

These and other technology capabilities are available in VWs through advanced scripting and graphics not found in previous forms of collaboration technologies. These capabilities result in features that present a flexible, tailored environment in which meaningful, contextual, and rich communication between parties is possible. The list below shows the unique technology capabilities of VWs and their support for virtual-team interaction and VWPM, based on our research.[10]

- Various communication channels enable communication in team meetings, where team members can express themselves freely. They can eliminate geographic and cultural boundaries. They provide the ability to communicate using nonverbal expression.
- Rendering of people and the real world allow team members to express themselves through their appearance and to control their own behavior.
- Real-time interaction provides an environment for real-time problem-solving and discussion. It provides improved coordination and control by facilitating interaction between team members in the VW environment. It fosters mobility and the ability to change locations quickly and easily. It supports real-time immediacy of artifacts through creation and building of figures (3D models or images that can be left behind for others to interact with).
- Team process tools and artifacts foster team interaction and leadership. They allow for recording of meetings for subsequent viewing. They provide 3D brainstorming tools, voting tools, or visual problem-solving, in which avatars "stand" on their vote (that is, move here for yes, and move there for no). Team process tools and artifacts also support avatar training using software agents.

MOVING FROM FIRST LIFE TO SECOND LIFE

Project managers have many opportunities for moving into a VW environment such as SL. To illustrate the possibilities, we used VW technology capabilities in a series of experiments conducted in SL with project teams recruited from SL residents. We placed each participant into a VWP team consisting of four or five individuals with varying skills and backgrounds. Team members had no prior history together, so the members had to learn one another's backgrounds and skill sets. We provided each team the same set of task instructions. The project task was to construct a Rube Goldberg machine that resided on an island within SL. Each team was allowed one hour to complete the task.

We created an island that contained a meeting place for project members. The island had a sandbox area, which allowed project teams to develop their machines. We also developed and made available additional team process tools for brainstorming, voting, and recording of meetings.

We recorded the activities of the project teams as they used the technology capabilities available within SL. Our goal was to examine how these teams interacted and collaborated to complete the project task. Interestingly, those teams that used the technology completed the task in the time given. The teams that struggled and did not complete the task were those that also did not take full advantage of the VW's capabilities to collaborate and interact. Our research suggests various opportunities for members of VWP teams.

Opportunities for VWP Teams

VWs can affect team dynamics in virtual projects by removing interaction boundaries. Virtual teams tend to behave differently from traditional face-to-face teams.[11] These behavioral differences are the result of geographic distance, temporal distance, and limited face-to-face interactions. VWs can overcome these obstacles by breaking boundaries in terms of geographic and cultural differences. Geographic distance is no longer an impediment, because avatars come together in a shared space to interact with one another. Cultural differences between individuals can be minimized because participants can create a generic appearance independent of racial or cultural variations. In addition, avatars can use Internet lingo, including acronyms and emoticons, to express various sentiments.[12]

By removing these boundaries, VWP teams can develop trust, which is typically difficult in traditional virtual teams because team members cannot interact directly with one another. VWs can enhance the development of trust through:

- The use and control of verbal and nonverbal communication cues
- Simultaneous use of multiple communication channels and the combination of verbal and nonverbal cues
- A playful environment that lets users socialize and develop member and group well-being

In our research, teams in which participants used VW technology capabilities to interact with one another established trust and had successful project outcomes. We also found that appearance was important in the process. Participants could control their avatars' appearance, and some outfitted theirs in professional attire to participate in the project. In fact, participants often commented on the appearance of one another's avatars.

Understanding individual roles and authority on a team is important. Roles often emerge through interaction of team members; leadership roles are easily expressed when team members can interact and provide immediate feedback on behavior. Leaders typically emerge through verbal and nonverbal cues, which are lost in a typical computer-mediated environment. However, VW technology allows expression of these cues and more. Because people can control their avatars, they can control their placement in meetings—whether they sit or stand, where they sit, and whom they sit next to. They can also control their body language, in addition to their style of dress. VWs provide an environment in which leaders can emerge on the basis of their behavior and actions.

Many of the challenges related to virtual teams lie in the inability to mimic face-to-face interaction. In our research, project team members carried traditional face-to-face behaviors into the VW, including nonverbal communication, eye contact, and team positioning. Team members used instant messages and notes with Internet lingo to represent emotions as well as nonverbal cues such as laughing or frowning. In terms of eye contact, project team members would physically turn their avatar toward the avatar or group of avatars they were talking to, so as to make eye contact. Finally, the position of an avatar in relation to the rest of the team indicated the avatar's level of interaction on the project. Although VWs are not intended to replace face-to-face communication, they can incorporate face-to-face behaviors to enhance interaction and the overall experience, thus potentially improving team performance.

Opportunities for VWPM

The unique technology capabilities of VWs lead to increased flexibility regarding how a team behaves, which provides opportunities for VWPM. Project coordination is a major element of project management, and it presents an enormous challenge in virtual projects. VWs can help minimize coordination challenges by

- Enabling immediate feedback during team member communication
- Establishing trust through multiple channels of communication
- Removing geographic boundaries
- Viewing one another's artifacts as team members work on them—that is, immediacy of artifacts

In our research, the VW technology capability that had the greatest impact on projects was immediacy of artifacts because of the potential for instant feedback among team members. Immediacy of artifacts is the ability of users to collaborate jointly in the real-time creation and use of artifacts such as text, images, and 3D models. The ability to immediately touch and interact with artifacts can improve team performance. The SL project teams in our research used this capability to facilitate coordination and communication and to increase shared understanding of a task. The teams were immediately able to share their contributions; for example, they created a list of tasks needed to implement their solution, and they divided those tasks among themselves. When a team member completed a task, the outputs of that task were immediately visible to the rest of the team. Team members could interact with the artifact—they could see it, move it, and touch it. This interaction allowed for real-time adjustments or changes on the basis of feedback. Anything within SL can become an artifact—an idea, a preference, or a decision—and it becomes visual through instantiation in 3D space.

VWs also facilitate informal communication that can lead to great discussions about the project at hand. In a traditional environment, these discussions might occur in the hallway, after a meeting, or even around the water cooler. VWs support informal communication, as avatars linger in the VW after a project meeting or before teleporting to another meeting.

Not surprisingly, our experiments showed that traditional project management practices are still important. For example, in addition to having the available resources, employing the right skill set for a project is critical to success. The SL project team members in our research who lacked the necessary skills to execute the project tasks were not able to actively participate in the project. Leadership was also essential. Like traditional virtual teams, VWP teams require a clear definition of roles and an effective team leader. In our study, VWP teams without a clear project leader struggled with understanding the task and with effectively assigning individual responsibilities. In contrast, VWP teams that had a leader were able to more effectively work on the project. Those teams with leadership discussed and understood the overall goals of the project and were able to distribute tasks to members on the basis of individual skills and experience while synergistically working on the overall project goals.

CHALLENGES

VW environments are not without their challenges. There is a steep learning curve related to the technology. In our experiments within SL, participants did not use as many VW capabilities as we expected; for example, many people used text chat as the primary method of communication, ignoring other available communication channels such as voice chat and gestures.

Temporal dispersion, or time zone coordination, also remains a challenge that project teams using metaverse technologies cannot easily overcome. VWs support synchronous communication, but project tasks that require individuals to meet at the same time will still find it difficult to schedule team meetings.

Security is a major concern for many organizations interested in VW technology capabilities provided by environments such as SL. Organizations can limit access on their particular island or space, but there is still a risk in sharing proprietary information on a server that the organization itself does not own and maintain. Aside from the security risks, organizations might find it difficult to motivate employees to accept the technology because of its reputation as a gaming environment. (Clearly, though, organizations are moving past this bias by demonstrating the capabilities available in these VWs.) Finally, as more organizations accept this technology, the risk of unpredictable behavior will grow. As in the real world, there are no constraints in VWs regarding how people behave. In fact, because people are operating in a virtual space, they might show less respect or restraint when using technology to convey their thoughts. The following list explains these and additional challenges to consider when moving from first life to second:

- **Client software and hardware**. Each user must download client software that requires memory and graphics. VW audio capabilities are not robust, and desktops must be high end.
- **Learning curve**. Learning to operate within the environment to take full advantage of its capabilities can require considerable effort.
- **Balancing worlds**. Project managers must recognize that a VW is not a complete substitute for first life; there could still be a need to meet in traditional surroundings at the same physical location.
- **Acceptance**. Securing buy-in and support from managers and other employees for use of the technology is essential.
- **Distractions**. People's avatars might be tempted to explore and drift away.
- **Norms of behavior**. Some people might show less respect or restraint when using technology to convey their thoughts.
- **Uncertainty of behavior**. The behavior of other people's avatars cannot be controlled.
- **Representation**. Users might have to adjust to the idea of working as their virtual personas.
- **Security**. Second Life is a public space with limited security features.

Virtual worlds and their technology capabilities can help virtual teams find new ways to face the challenges of managing a global IT workforce. To appreciate the impact of VW capabilities on organizations of the future, consider a thought experiment: imagine you're part of a highly distributed project with globally dispersed team members who have come together to work within a VW such as SL. Using the VW's technology capabilities, you could immediately contribute to the project by meeting people "face to face" through your avatar in a synchronous shared virtual space. You could customize avatars to engender immediate trust. You could jointly and instantaneously design, build, and review richly textured artifacts—actually show people what you think rather than just state it. You could use 3D brainstorming tools to generate new ideas and rank them, and you could share virtual objects and documents seamlessly between the VW and other software tools. This is all possible using today's VW technology, and the potential for the future seems endless. There is much to be explored with this engaging and vivid environment for VWP teams.

Notes

1. W. S. Bainbridge, "The Scientific 1. Research Potential of Virtual Worlds," *Science*, July 27, 2007: 472–476.

2. E. Driver et al., "Getting Real Work Done in Virtual Worlds," *Forrester Research*, January 7, 2008, www.forrester.com/Research/Document/Excerpt/0,7211,43450,00.html.

3. "Gartner Says 80 percent of Active Internet Users Will Have a 'Second Life' In the Virtual World by the End of 2011," Gartner, April 24, 2007; www.gartner.com/it/page.jsp?id=503861.

4. B. Ives and G. Piccoli. "STA Travel Island: Marketing First Life Travel Services in Second Life," *Communications of the Association for Information Systems* 20, no. 1, 2007: 429–441.

5. "The U.S. Space Agency Orbits a Virtual World: NASA's Virtual Spaceflight in Second Life," *Space Today Online*, 2008, www.spacetoday.org/NASA/SecondLife/NASA_SecondLife.html.

6. "IBM and Palace Museum Announce Opening of the Forbidden City Virtual World Celebrating 600 Years of Chinese Culture," IBM press release, October 10, 2008; www-03.ibm.com/press/us/en/pressrelease/25379.wss.

7. C. Megerian, "A Virtual Path into a Once-Forbidden City," LinuxInsider.com, October 2008.

8. S. S. Kahai, E. Carroll, and R. Jestice, "Team Collaboration in Virtual Worlds," *ACM SIGMIS Database* 38, no. 4, 2007: 61–68.

9. J. Leigh and M. Brown, "9. Cyber-Commons: Merging Real and Virtual Worlds," *Communications of the ACM* 51, no. 1, 2008: 82–85.

10. A. Davis et al., "Avatars, People, and Virtual Worlds: Foundations for Research in Metaverses," *Journal of the Association for Information Systems* 10, no. 2, March 2009: 90–117.

11. I. Zigurs, "Leadership in Virtual Teams: Oxymoron or Opportunity?" *Organizational Dynamics* 31, no. 4, 2003: 339–351.

12. M. Zitzen and D. Stein, "Chat and Conversation: A Case of Transmedial Stability?" *Linguistics* 42, no. 5, 2004: 983–1021.

5

LEVERAGING 2.0 FOR INTERNET RECRUITING

Run Ren and Barry Brewton

The dramatic advance in technology and the remarkable growth of the Internet are probably the most important changes affecting organizations' business practices as well as their human resource management practices. For instance, electronic bill presentation and payment has eliminated paper checks and sped up payments to employees and suppliers.[1] Online training and learning programs have become more popular, taking over the place of traditional in-house training programs.[2] Employee databases have allowed employees to access or make changes to their personal data and benefit information without a visit to the HR office. Such practices have not only facilitated information flow and shortened the process and time but also significantly reduced company cost, which is a major concern for most organizations, especially in today's gloomy economic situation.

With this trend is the increasing use of the Internet in organizations' recruiting and selection process. It has long been realized that human resources are critical assets to create sustainable competitive advantages for firm success.[3,4] Many businesses are facing the challenging task of finding individuals with the right qualifications to meet their organizational needs. A potential solution is to take advantage of Internet recruiting, which utilizes the Internet to fulfill different tasks during the recruiting process, including posting the position advertisement, searching and identifying qualified applicants, collecting resumes and applications of job seekers, and even interviewing candidates through the Internet. Internet recruiting has existed for less than 20 years. It started with Bill Warren, who founded Online Career Center (OCC, now

Monster.com), the first employment site on the Internet in 1992. More than ever before, the Internet is providing a global platform where information about prospective employees and companies can be obtained quickly and inexpensively.[5,6] For instance, 178 million hours were spent on Monster sites worldwide, and 40,000 new resumes were posted to Monster.com every day in 2005.[7]

The benefits of Internet recruitment are quite obvious. Many organizations have found that Internet recruiting has yielded a high return on investment and given them the ability to gain a diverse applicant pool. It is fast, convenient, and cost efficient for both employers and job seekers. These factors are a key attribute because organizations are able to allocate unused funds toward other organizational goals and give them the ability to be competitive in an ever-changing economical environment. Although Internet recruiting provides a wide variety of benefits, it also has some limitations and disadvantages that companies need to be aware of. Unqualified and unserious applicants, increased amount of applications, and recruiters' lack of knowledge and experience on Internet recruiting will all decrease its efficiency. Nonetheless, the Internet is a valuable and inexpensive resource for even the smallest company, and it is the future of recruiting.

The last decade has witnessed a second generation of Web development and Web design, referred to as "Web 2.0." It aims to facilitate communication, information sharing, and collaboration on the Internet.[8] It has also led to the development and evolution of Web-based communities, hosted services, and Web applications. Examples of Web 2.0 applications include social-networking sites, video-sharing sites, wikis, and blogs. The advancement of Web 2.0 is forcing employers to adapt their recruiting strategies to be compatible with these new technologies. The purpose of this chapter is to discuss different ways companies can conduct recruiting via the Internet, including more traditional job posting or applicant searches, or "Web 1.0" applications, and more recent developments of recruiting through "Web 2.0" application. Some critical challenges of Internet recruiting are also discussed to help companies understand it correctly and choose the right method for their different objectives.

INTERNET RECRUITING METHODS

Though Internet recruiting has only been popular in recent years, there have been many different ways organizations can utilize the Internet for recruiting purposes. In general, four categories can be listed. First, and the easiest way, is to post position announcements on job search Web sites and company career sites, and/or to screen online databases for potential applicants. Second, many social networking Web sites have also served as a key component in Internet recruiting. Third, online videos have been used as an effective promotion tool by employers. Finally, more advanced technology has brought in video interviews and virtual worlds for Internet recruiting, thanks to Web 2.0 advancement.

Job Sites and Company Career Sites

Currently, there are over 40,000 different job search Web sites around the world.[9] The most popular among them include Monster.com, Yahoo! Hot Jobs, CareerBuilder, AOL Career.[10] These job search engines not only gather resumes but also allow users to view job trends, salaries, and relevant research conducted by professional recruiting companies. They are noted for their user-friendly features and the huge amount of traffic. Monster.com has about 150 million resumes stored in its database from past and current job seekers by 2008 and has over 1 million job postings at any time.[11] These search engines not only provide job listings for applicants; they also work as a versatile career tool, providing applicants various resources on career development, resume writing, job seeking advice, and information on salaries of different professions and locations. For recruiters, these search engines provide a large applicant pool without much effort. Recruiters can post a position advertisement that can reach millions of job seekers and/or access millions of applicant resumes in their database, which is more efficient than traditional newspaper/magazine recruiting and is available at a similar or even lower fee. Most of these search engines provide job opportunities both within the United States and abroad and attract applicants worldwide too. The success of these search engines has won them a notable reputation. For instance, SimplyHired has gained awards from *Time* Magazine, *Forbes*, *PC Magazine*, and CNet for outstanding results.[12]

Lou Adler, President of the Adler Group—a training and consulting firm—suggested that the main tools for online recruiting advertising are narrowcasting, search engine optimization, organic search, micro-sites, pay-per-click, and talent hubs.[13] These tools have been used for Internet marketing and have been proven to be efficient. Companies using the Internet for recruiting purposes can use all of these elements to help find the best candidates for their open positions. A key factor to all recruiters is to make sure that their advertisements should be easily found by the right applicant.

Narrowcasting is the process of setting up what one is looking for into narrow sets of choices and then using different techniques to reach members of those targeting groups. An example would be when a company plans to advertise their position only to professionals with a CPA (Certified Public Accountant) certificates. After narrowing down their target applicants, the company can post their positions on the Web site for the American Institute of Certified Public Accountants, for instance, instead of posting the position blindly on any job sites.

Search engine optimization is a process that improves the volume and quality of the traffic to a Web site from search engines. A company will bid on words or phrases that are related to their company or ones that people may use to search for a job in that company's area of business. If used successfully, the company will get the most qualified applicants. One of the main parts of search engine optimization is organic search, which is a search style with results listed by the degree of relevance.

Micro-sites and talent hubs are two similar online tools companies can borrow for Internet recruitment. "Micro-sites," or "mini-sites," are interchangeable Internet Web design terms that direct a user to a Web page or cluster of pages that are meant to function as a supplement to a primary Web site. Talent hubs are a form of micro-site but are more career-oriented. They are used to attract individuals who are looking for a certain type of career instead of a specific job, such as retailing. But once the individual has visited the talent hub Web site, he or she may be directed to specific jobs within this particular career. For instance, Microsoft has built talent hubs for all its major positions, such as finance, sales, marketing, and human resources, to name only a few. If designed successfully, these talent hub Web sites should directly drive job seekers to all position postings in the particular field. Unfortunately, Microsoft has not linked its talent hub Web sites to its job application pages.

Companies can also advertise on the Internet with banner advertisements that require them to pay a fee depending on the number of times their advertisement is clicked. This is also called Pay-Per-Click. Search engines, and content Web sites such as blogs, are where these types of advertisements are placed. In using pay-per-click, companies bid on keywords and phrases as well.

Another useful tool is cross-posting. Several services are available to recruiters that allow them to cross-post the same position between several different job boards, again saving their time. Instead of having to submit the position announcement to each different job site, recruiters can enter the job posting into a centralized system and choose all or several job boards where they want their posting to appear. CareerBuilder.com provides cross-posting services to employers, besides their regular job posting services. For less than $200 a month, employers receive a standard cross-posting subscription that allows automatic distribution of their job listings to over 90 diversity partner sites and reaches far beyond the 25 million unique visitors that CareerBuilder.com receives.[14]

When companies select to use job search engines for recruitment purposes they need to be aware of some factors that may affect their recruitment effectiveness and efficiency. One concern for many organizations is job posting visibility and the ability to reach a large number of qualified job seekers. Recruiters need to be careful when writing a job posting. Using the right keywords can increase the chance of being viewed by the right candidates. Using multiple search engines could also be helpful, but at the same time, this means increased workload for recruiters, with applications flooding in.

Besides utilizing the various job sites, many companies today also set up their own career sites on company Web sites. This facilitates the job search process for those job seekers who know exactly which companies they want to work for, and they can directly upload their resumes and fill out an application. Companies can also share information about the organization, working environment, employee values, what to expect on the job, and much more on their own Web sites than on outside job sites, which may have a limit regarding how much they can put on a job posting. It also reduces the dependence on outside job sites, and does not require a subscription fee. However, there are a few basic requirements for employers who prefer to create their own career sites. First, companies must establish the capabilities of their IT department. Necessary software and hardware associated with their recruitment plan should be in place in order to effectively handle the traffic generated by job hunters. This will allow for fewer technical problems and the ability to process all the applications without missing anyone with a good potential. Companies will also need a good Web designer to make sure that job seekers browsing the company Web site can easily find the position posting. A survey found that U.S. firms could be losing $30 million every day because their recruiting sites are too difficult to use.[15] The survey looked at the problems job applicants experienced while applying for jobs on six companies' Web sites (including Cisco, Procter & Gamble, and Citibank). Over 70 percent of job seekers reported experiencing some degree of problem while applying for the job online.[16] Such problems can easily drive away a potential good employee.

Second, the human resource department of the company should keep an up-to-date and accurate job posting. It may bring some negative impact to the company when applicants see that the posting was a year ago. Applicants may feel that the company is not at all serious about recruiting and thus may not want to apply for its positions any more. All other rules of a good posting on professional job sites apply here, including concise description of the position, motivating and attractive language, and contact information.

Third, with the help of their own search engines or other recruiting software, the recruiter should establish a well-sorted applicant database and keep track of each applicant's progress during the recruiting and selection process. A systematic process will help recruiters to provide feedback to the applicant in a timely manner. This company-specific database will also facilitate future recruiting. Recruiters can first try their own database for possible candidates when a position comes up. There is a variety of well-established recruiting software available on the market. Each has its own strengths and weaknesses, but they all share several similar features. The purposes of such software are to make the recruitment procedure less manual (such as eliminating manual data entry), to reduce the expenditure in the process, and to increase the productivity. Most of such software creates an applicant database, provides applicant tracking systems, and is compatible with other computer programs such as Microsoft Word, Excel, and Outlook. Some software can also integrate candidate online testing ability and score the results automatically. A few popular examples of efficient recruiting software include Bullhorn, RecruitNEXT, Arithon, cBizOne, RecruitTrak, Taleo, and Gopher.[17] With so many choices, it is all about finding the one that fits a particular company the best. A few tips to effectively use the recruiting software include test driving free demos, receiving training from recruiting software providers, and referring to handbooks, manuals, and user guide before implementing the software in the company.[18]

Networking Web Sites

The Internet development in recent years has witnessed the introduction of many social networking Web sites, such as Facebook, MySpace, Twitter, and LinkedIn, just to name a few. Utilizing such social networks for company recruiting has been a hot topic recently and it will continue to increase its popularity among both employers and job seekers. The reason is simple. Recruiting is to find the right employee for the company and these social networks provide a good way to connect people with each other and to find out more about potential applicants. Different from online job posting, which is merely a one-way broadcasting; social networks provide a two-way communication between the two parties by allowing viewers to add their own comments freely.

Among most popular social networks nowadays, Facebook and MySpace are more general and have the most visitors compared with other networks. Many companies have realized the benefits of having a corporate presence on such social networks. KPMG created its own alumni network on Facebook—"KPMG Connect" to stay in touch with people who have worked at KPMG. But that is not all it provides. In addition, people can find out new career opportunities at KPMG Connect and may decide to go back. Hiring a former employee who knows about the company's culture and work ethic could save a lot of effort for both parties in the adjustment process. Burger King Corp is also trying out social networks. "We want to be ahead of the competition," said a senior corporate recruiter. "We're quietly using Twitter. We're using LinkedIn." Such effort has brought in good results. Burger King was included in a recent list of top Twittering recruiters.[19] Besides business organizations, one can also find various Facebook and MySpace pages for the U.S. Army to help with recruiting. On these pages, real people talked about the reasons they joined the Army and shared their experiences.[20] Such informal communication channels make recruiting more fun and less of a burden.

Another kind of network has a more professional focus, such as LinkedIn and Xing. The latter primarily focuses on Europe and China. LinkedIn strengthens and extends one's existing network of trusted contacts by helping them discover inside connections. As the premier provider of professional networking site, LinkedIn also allows users to find jobs or potential employees and business partners. A special feature of LinkedIn is its job site. It is different from other job sites in that both job seekers and recruiters can use the power of their network. In other words, LinkedIn Jobs incorporates the traditional referral program into the Internet recruiting. After finding a dream position on LinkedIn Jobs, applicants can click on the "Request Referral" button to see whom in his/her network connects to the job poster and contact that person. If the person linked to the job poster is two or three degrees away from the applicant, he/she can request an introduction through one of their connections. Such referrals can help applicants to put their feet in the door. For recruiters, LinkedIn offers a unique combination of job listings, candidate search, and trusted referrals. Through LinkedIn Jobs, recruiters can reach over 20 million candidates at a minimum cost. Some of these candidates may come referred to them by their trusted contacts on LinkedIn. So, it is no longer whom a person knows, but whom that person's contacts know. By leveraging the power of recruiters' network to announce position vacancies, the chance of a successful hire is greatly increased. By 2004, LinkedIn had facilitated over 15,000 successful referrals.[21]

Twitter is a most recent networking tool. Similar to LinkedIn, it is relationship-based. It is a text-based microblogging tool that allows one to write up to 140 characters at a time and send the message (called "tweets") to other people who have subscribed to them—known as followers. The tweets can also be sent to followers' mobile phone or Web sites. People communicating on Twitter post a tweet which answers the question, "What are you doing?" Founded in March 2006, Twitter has exploded to about 25 million users and has seen some weeks with a 40 percent increase in new users.[22] A February 2009 Compete.com blog entry ranked Twitter as the third most used social network, just following Facebook and MySpace.[23] The vital nature of Twitter is that one tweet can be re-tweeted and seen by thousands of people. In less than 3 months after using it, Oprah had gained nearly 1.8 million followers on Twitter as of July 1, 2009, which means such a big population will follow Oprah's tweets. Imagine a recruiter is trying to find some good candidates for a job position. How many people can he/she send out the word to? All the followers. Though recruiters may certainly not have so many followers as Oprah, it would still produce a good amount of response, with followers forwarding the news to others they know. More important, it is free and almost effortless. Because of its efficiency, Twitter was even used as a publicity mechanism in several 2008 U.S. presidential campaigns.[24]

The use of Twitter for recruiting is just at the beginning compared with other social networks, but it will probably pick up as the economy improves and Twitter becomes more popular. Currently, only a small number of companies worldwide have tried out recruiting on Twitter, including ones who are also active in Facebook and LinkedIn, such as Ernst & Young, KPMG, and Burger King.[25] These pioneer companies have benefited from Twitter. According to Divesh Sisodraker, founder of TheJobMagnet, after posting a job listing on Twitter, "within 15 hours, this tweet went from a few thousand to 15,000 people."[26] At the same time, though Twitter is not specifically designed as a job site, recruiters can nonetheless effectively search the bio section of Twitters profile by choosing the right key words. In addition, similar to LinkedIn, people can get connected through their followers who may refer them to job opportunities, and for recruiters, referrals are always the most successful recruiting source.

Social networks will definitely become an important part of every company's recruiting practice in the near future. There are both general networks like Facebook and MySpace, and more professional networks like LinkedIn and Xing. They also differ in their focused users and there are networks for China, Japan, and other places. Depending on its targeted applicant population, the company can choose a few most popular networks they want to present themselves. However, it is not recommended that the company create a profile on every different network site. Simply creating a profile will not help much unless the company spends time to keep updating their information and communicate with visitors who view their profiles. Recruiters will also need to be familiar with various features of these social networks and actively participate in online communication to utilize them best. Some training maybe needed for recruiters who are new to these networks.

Online Videos as a Promotion Tool

With so many companies recruiting online it can be hard for job seekers to determine which company is right for them and why. One way companies are getting the edge on their competitors is by allowing job seekers to view online employee testimonial videos. These videos allow job seekers to get a firsthand account from real employees about what a typical day at the office is like or why they enjoy working for this company. This strategy is helpful because "Human nature makes us all attracted to anything visual. It gives you a sense of what the people look like (who) work there, how they dress and how they sound," according to Jeff Wittenburg, Chief Leadership Officer with Kaye Bassman International.[27]

Meanwhile, such videos give job seekers insight into company culture and what to expect if they choose to accept a position with the company, which helps them to decide whether or not this company is truly right for them and if they should apply. This, in turn, could decrease the amount of unserious and unfit job applicants, and help recruiters to work more efficiently.

An advantage of online videos over other Internet recruiting methods such as job posting and applicant search is that it gives applicants a touch of realism that otherwise is not present in the online application process. This is very critical and beneficial for employers in the competitive labor market. Ernst & Young generally hire 5,500 college graduates a year from the United States and Canada. A recruiting, branding, and communication leader for the company stated, "Top talent is very much in demand. We need to be on top of our game, speaking and interacting in a way that is compelling and in touch with what students want."[28] To achieve this objective, Ernst & Young has set up a well-developed and sophisticated career Web site. EY Insight provides an exciting Web site experience with real insight into what they are all about—who they are, what they do, and how one can join them. There are three categories under it. *EY 360* shows their employees' in-and-out-of-the-office lives, at different offices within the country. *Picture Yourself* facilitates job applicants' exploration of their real career possibilities at Ernst & Young in a fun and informative way. Based on their major and interests, applicants can view a range of practices related to those choices and also compare different practices. As a result, applicants can apply for a position that better fits them and that they are interested in, and they can expect how their career will progress. *Interview Insider* provides a series of short videos with real advice and valuable information to job applicants on how to prepare for and behave in an interview. Not many companies tell job seekers what to do. This distinguishes Ernst & Young from its competitors and explains for its success in recruiting the top talent.

Besides putting employee testimonials on their Web sites, companies can take advantage of videos by putting them on popular social sites such as YouTube. Every day, many people around the world check out videos on YouTube. KPMG has interns and new hires who have been putting up videos on YouTube to show what it is like to work at the company through their own eyes. The company even holds a best-video contest for interns. Such videos give potential job applicants a more vivid image about the job and the company and is also a great way to promote the company worldwide without paying a penny. As a result, it brings in about 2,100 full-time college hires and 1,700 interns each year.[29]

Recently, a number of companies also started to try out using YouTube videos for recruiting announcement. It is similar to a traditional job posting on job sites, but instead of putting it into words, these recruiting videos give viewers a rich visual experience and more information through the speaker's tone, body language, facial expression, and the background. For instance, FusionStaffing, an employment agency, uploads video job announcements to YouTube regularly. Though some videos made still need improvement, it is a good start of a new Internet recruiting method in the age of Web 2.0. Not many companies are doing this. A thought for future development is that YouTube can develop a new category under videos as "job announcement." The advancement of Web 2.0 provides a great opportunity for companies to stand out from their competitors in the labor market to recruit the best employees.

Video Interviews and the Virtual World

The most epoch-making innovation of Web 2.0 on Internet recruiting is the use of video interviews and the virtual world. This idea is so new that not many companies are actually using these resources. Video conferencing has been more widely used among many companies to communicate with employees in different geographical locations worldwide. The advantages of video conference on saving traveling time and expenses, and being more flexible and convenient, have been acknowledged. But the use of video interview in the recruiting process has just begun. For the same reason, video interviews can dramatically reduce cost-per-hire under such tough economic situations. All one needs is a Webcam and high-speed Internet. Yet, it still guarantees the features of two-way face-to-face communication. Both recruiters and applicants can see each other's facial expression and body language and convey immediate feedback, without flying the candidate from thousands of miles away. This benefits companies especially when they are doing global recruiting. However, video interview cannot absolutely substitute traditional on-site interviews in all perspectives. For example, one of the purposes of on-site interviews is to give applicants a chance to experience workdays in the company, interact with other employees, and observe its organizational culture and operation. On-site interviews also give applicants a sense of the local atmosphere, where they will live if taking the position. What we suggest is to conduct video interviews with a few top candidates to make the decision of whom the company should invite to on-site interviews; or to have video interviews replace previous phone interviews. By doing this, the company can further reduce the possibility of flying in a wrong candidate and have the most suitable short list.

More recently, recruiting professionals have turned their eyes to the virtual world. Launched in 2003, Second Life (SL) is a free 3D virtual world that allows its residents to create avatars and interact with other real people from around the world. Residents can walk and fly to other 3D locations and can voice and text chat with others in the virtual world after downloading and installing the free Second Life viewer.[30] SL is similar to other popular multi-player online role playing games regarding its interface and display. However, it has two quite unique features—creativity and ownership. The SL virtual world provides almost unlimited freedom to its residents. This world really is whatever residents make it.

Residents also own anything they create and can get a land to live by paying a monthly lease fee, just like in the real world.[31]

SL also has its own economy and currency. Some real-world companies have established their presence in SL, including Reuters, IBM, and General Motors.[32] If residents can explore, meet other residents, socialize, participate in individual and group activities, and create and trade virtual property and services with one another, or travel throughout the world, there is no reason recruiting cannot be done in SL. Some recruiting professionals have pioneered this new opportunity. TMP Worldwide, an interactive advertising agency specializing in recruitment, is the first company to set up a *real-world* recruiting service on SL.[33] TMP's "island" in SL allows different clients to host recruiting events and build virtual replicas of their real-world offices. Through this recruiting service in the virtual world, a company still gets real-world resumes, along with a chance to promote its brand to a digitally sophisticated audience.[34] In May 2007, TMP hosted a virtual job fair with employers such as Hewlett-Packard, Microsoft, and Verizon.[35] "TMP Island represents the future of employment recruiting," said Russell Miyaki, VP, national interactive creative director, TMP Worldwide. "To reach a new generation of employees, successful recruiters will need to employ sophisticated, innovative technologies that extend their reach and demonstrate that they are smart and tech-savvy."[36]

The State of Missouri's Information Technology Services Division started using SL in November 2007 and set up an information kiosk for information technology career recruitment. A few job fairs were held. People from as far as Spain, England, and Scotland have attended the fairs, just like real-world career fairs. The division made its first hire from SL in September 2008.[37]

Such virtual job fairs provide impressing advantages. It saves companies travel cost for recruiters and it allows recruiters who otherwise cannot attend a chance to show up. However, a few things should be noted about virtual-world recruiting. Most of the same rules in the real world apply in the virtual world too. The job is a real job, and the interview should be therefore be professional in all regards. Some creativity is allowed, but don't go too far. Recruiters are still looking for the same qualities in a candidate. It is questionable if a SL interview should replace a real-world interview. It is more like a personal way to contact other people as other social networks. It may provide a good chance to recruit tech-savvy applicants if the position requires. On the other hand, it limits the chances for people who are not up-to-date with new technologies. In addition, some recruiting professionals are not used to interviewing in the virtual world either, which sometimes may send a wrong signal to the candidate. For example, at a SL recruiting event, a company executive's avatar accidentally slumped over and looked as if it were asleep.[38] Therefore, we suggest using SL virtual world as an additional step to narrow the applicant pool at the current stage, rather than to replace traditional on-site interviews completely.

The above methods, if used appropriately, will greatly save recruiters' time and effort and result in a pool of highly qualified applicants for the position. However, there is no one tool that is the best. The company should consider their resource and objectives before choosing the right Internet recruiting method(s). In addition, the Internet recruiting methods discussed in this chapter are by no means inclusive. Other Web 2.0 applications may bring recruiting opportunities as well, such as recruiters' blogs.

FUTURE CHALLENGES OF INTERNET RECRUITMENT

Though Internet recruiting is relatively new, it has greatly changed the way businesses look for and hire applicants, mostly because of the Web 2.0 applications. The cost-effectiveness and increased diversity in applicant pool of Internet recruiting greatly improve human resources management efficiency and allow companies to focus on other important organizational tasks. In addition, because of the availability of Internet recruiting, both large and small companies can benefit from it. In fact, more than 75 percent of HR professionals are using Internet job boards in recruiting,[39] and the Recruiters Network reports that 45 percent of companies surveyed had filled more than 20 percent of their positions through Internet recruiting.[40] Meanwhile, companies should be aware of some trends affecting the future of recruiting.

First, as more and more companies switch from traditional recruiting to Internet recruiting, the job of Internet search engines becomes greatly important. In the near future job search engines will face an increasing demand to narrow down their results based on more specific requirements. Though using the Internet to search for applicants is cheap and fast, that does not offset the cost and time of interviewing unqualified applicants. Job search engines allow people all over the world to look at and apply to positions companies post with just a few clicks, but this could have unintended consequences of extremely large amount of both qualified and unqualified applications. One of the biggest challenges for search engines is to come up with new and innovative ways to weed out the unqualified employees. For instance, the search engines need to be able to sort the applications based on multiple key words at the same time and with different ranking, in order to yield optimal results. In addition, it should be able to search not only the exact key word but also blurred key words to avoid missing any qualified candidates. The large number of applications generated from Internet recruiting also requires recruiters to be able to track and follow up with applicants. There must be good recruiting software to help recruiters with the overwhelming applications they have to deal with every day. Recruiters should also realize that even though Internet recruiting saves their time and effort to reach a larger applicant pool, they may need to spend more on sorting, tracking , and responding to these applications.

Second, search engines and recruiting software should be able to correctly classify applicants not only by their qualifications, but also their personalities. Recruiting and selection is a process where both parties (i.e., the employer and job applicants) need to find a fit between each other. Not only should applicants have the right KSAO (i.e., knowledge, skills, abilities, and other qualifications) to fit with the job requirement, they should also have the right personality traits to fit with the culture of the organization. If job applicants get into the organization despite a misfit, sooner or later they will either find themselves having trouble meeting the performance standards or having lowered job satisfaction. Some job search engines and recruiting software have provided personality tests to assess job applicants' personality. By doing so, part of the recruiters' job responsibility is fulfilled automatically in the initial screening process. But recruiters should have a good knowledge regarding what personality traits each job should look for and be well prepared to understand and interpret the test results properly, in order to have such tests aid the recruiting and selection process.

Third, the popularity of the Internet also poses the issue of authenticity and legitimacy of information on the Internet.[41] The level of spam and deceptive e-mail on the Internet has exploded dramatically in recent years. The spam to non-spam ratio was estimated to be 63 percent by March 2004.[42] Some of the spam is infected with viruses or worms that represent a serious threat to Internet privacy. To protect Internet users from such spam, many e-mail programs have developed built-in spam filter resulting in automatic deletion from the incoming mailbox. When job applicants register with the job boards, and select to be notified with new posts matching their qualification, such e-mails sometimes are filtered out before job applicants have a chance to view them. This may reduce applicants' chance to apply for potentially qualified positions and therefore decrease the effectiveness of Internet recruiting.

Fourth, the popularity of Internet recruiting requires certain ethical standards from both applicants and recruiters. Compared with traditional recruiting methods, Internet recruiting provides more convenience for applicants to fake the information on their profile, in order to be singled out into the next stage of the selection process. For instance, a motivated job applicant could tailor his/her response to match a company's culture and other requirements with minimum effort. Therefore, despite that Internet recruiting is an easy, convenient, and low-cost recruiting tool that generates a big applicant pool, it cannot absolutely replace the need for other recruiting and selection methods. Reference check and referrals will still be the primary source for successful recruiting and selection. A recent Execunet survey found that among more than

6,000 executives and executive recruiters surveyed, 70 percent indicated that networking and referral would be the key to either finding a job or finding candidates, compared to only 16 percent through online advertising.[43] Another survey of 800 corporate recruiters filling staff and mid-level manager positions also suggested that about 35–40 percent of their hires were through networking and employee referrals.[44] From employers' and recruiters' perspective, they should be careful too. Easy access to millions of job seekers' information from online job banks may create potential threat of identity theft. Online job banks must limit access to such information only to qualified recruiters. At the same time, the recruiters should have some proper ethics training on how to properly use and protect such abundant information. Recruiters should also be cautious with what they look for from the Internet. For instance, when using social networks for recruiting purpose, employers can easily find out a person's religion, politics, appearance, and sex orientation through their personal profiles on Facebook, MySpace, and blogs. Such information usually is not available through traditional recruiting methods and should not be used as a selection criterion. The popularity of social networks helps recruiters to know more about the potential candidate, but learning such information may also create a perception in the recruiter's mind unconsciously, and the recruiter may reject the candidate because of that additional information, leading to potential discrimination.

Fifth, companies using Internet recruiting should be aware that they are still constrained by Equal Employment Opportunity guidelines. The survey conducted by the U.S. Department of Commerce found that access to computers and Internet differs greatly depending on age, education, household income, race, and other demographic characteristics. For instance, people with a college degree are 8 times more likely to have a home computer and 16 times more likely to have Internet access at home than those with only an elementary school education. A low-income white family with a child is 3 times more likely to have Internet access than a comparable black family, and 4 times more likely than a comparable Hispanic family.[45] Even if people all go online, they will visit different Web sites and will differ on how well they know various Web 2.0 applications. Thus, companies should not depend on the Internet as their only recruiting tool. At the current stage, it would not be wise to give up traditional recruiting tools. Moreover, companies should investigate the target group of each recruiting tool and of each Internet recruiting method to make sure that they provide an equal chance for all kinds of job seekers. On the other hand, a company is not expected to use every recruiting tool at the same time. They need to compare carefully and choose the right tool for their own purposes.

Sixth, organizations using their own career sites should provide a user-friendly interface. With the technology development, many organizations that put position announcements on their own Web sites are trying to make it more interesting and attractive, with such features as animation, sound, and flash effects. However, when doing so, the organizations need to keep in mind whether applicants who view their postings have correct software to open the Web page smoothly. If they fail, it is quite easy for job seekers to give up and look for other available positions elsewhere. Organizations can provide necessary software downloads so job seekers can easily and quickly install the software and continue to view the posting, before their interest fades away. Alternatively, organizations can provide different formats of the posting and applicants can choose how they want to view it, either plain text or more interactive format. Some organizations may require the application material in special formats other than Word or PDF documents. For instance, when Tourism Queensland in Australia was recruiting an island caretaker for the Great Barrier Reef in 2009, they asked each applicant to make and upload a 60-second or less application video in English, explaining why they were the best person for the job in an entertaining way, in addition to an online application form. The innovative recruiting advertisement attracted over 34,000 applicants from more than 200 countries around the world.[46] But this required their Internet server to have a large storage for all the application videos and a large traffic volume so applicants can easily upload their application videos successfully without having to try multiple times.

Last, but not the least, managing different online recruiting techniques could be a challenge for recruiters. Some recruiters are not tech-savvy, and find these new ways of Internet recruiting sometimes confusing. Basic training and introduction of these new Web 2.0 applications could be helpful. But whose responsibility is it? Should the HR department take care of it or should the technical support be in charge? Another important issue is which job sites and/or social networks a company should choose to present itself on. With so many options available, it could be a hard decision. In addition, many of the Web 2.0 applications have blurred the boundary between work and non-work activities, which could lead to employee work-family conflict. With Internet access through cell phone, PDA, and iPhone, people are checking their e-mail and online profiles a million times a day. For instance, a recruiter from California Pizza Kitchen said, "I try to go in [Twitter] a couple of times a day and read Tweets, and try some re-Tweeting of my own. It's adding on to my normal, typically busy day. Some days I just don't find the time." There are no absolutely correct answers to the above questions. Each company needs to make their own decision based on their own objectives and resources.

CONCLUSION

More than ever before, companies are using the Internet to recruit, either by developing their own career sites, or by linking up with other job board services. Applicants have also changed the way they look up and apply for positions by electronically submitting their resumes and application without leaving their homes. According to the Society for Human Resources Management, more than 90 percent of HR people are now using the Internet to recruit.[47] CareerXRoads claims that Internet postings now result in 10 times as many hires as newspaper advertisements. Internet job posting revenue has grown 242 percent in the past five years according to Forrester Research.[48] In a recent survey of a smaller group, 75 percent of respondents claimed that they had landed at least one job in their career using the Internet. Internet recruiting is now a multi-billion dollar industry, and one that every firm is obviously using today! Despite its advantages, Internet recruiting can also bring some risks to organizations. To take full advantage of Internet recruiting, companies need to clearly understand and properly respond to these issues.

Internet recruiting is not merely a recruiting method. It also reflects the company's attempt to sell its employer brand. So, companies should have a detailed and clear objective regarding what message they want to convey to the potential applicants and the public and which methods of Internet recruiting will serve their purpose the best. More important, companies should work harder to find out what information and experience job applicants want, rather than what companies want to tell or deliver.

NOTES

1. Lisbeth Claus, "The Future of HR," *Workplace Visions* 6 (2001): 3–4.

2. W. C. Symonds, "Log on for Company Training," *Business Week*, January 10, 2000, 138–139.

3. David J. Teece, "Explicating Dynamic Capabilities: The Nature and Microfoundation of (Sustainable) Enterprise Performance," *Strategic Management Journal* 28, no. 13 (2007): 1319–1350.

4. Patrick M. Wright and Gary C. McMahan, "Theoretical Perspectives for Strategic Human Resource Management," *Journal of Management* 18 (1992): 295–320.

5. Joann S. Lublin, "To Find CEOs, Web Firms Rev-up Search Engines," *Wall Street Journal*, October 26, 1999, B-1.

6. Joann S. Lublin, "An e-Company CEO Is Also the Recruitment Chief," *Wall Street Journal*, November 9, 1999, B-7.

7. Telco 2.0, "Building a Monster 2-Sided Business," January 31, 2008, Http:// www.telco2.net.

8. Prashant Sharma, "Core Characteristics of Web 2.0 Services," November 28, 2008, http://www.techpluto.com.

9. The International Association of Employment Web Sites, 2009, http:// www.employmentwebsites.org.

10. HRFocus, "Hot Internet Recruiting Sites," *HRFocus* 8, no. 2 (August 2004): 8.

11. Monster.com, 2009, http://www.monster.com.

12. SimplyHired.com, 2009, http://www.simplyhired.com.

13. Lou Adler, "Four Trends Affecting the Future of Recruiting," June 6, 2008, http://www.ere.net.

14. CareerBuilder.com, 2009, http://www.careerbuilder.com.

15. Michael Pastore, "Corporate Recruiting Sites Need Help," ClickZ, September 9, 1999, http://www.clickz.com/197811.

16. Ibid.

17. SimpleThoughts, "Top 10 Recruiting Software," February 25, 2009, http://blog.taragana.com.

18. Stephanie Feaman, "Guide to Recruiting Software Education and Training," February 6, 2009, http://www.work.com.

19. Todd Raphael, "Recruiting's Smart Experiment with Social Media," June 15, 2009, http://www.ere.net/2009/06/15/recruitings-smart-experiment-with-social-media/.

20. Kevin Wheeler, "Four Required Recruiting Tools," September 4. 2008. http://www.ere.net.

21. Konstantin Guericke, and Laurie Thornton, "LinkedIn 'Links Up' with DirectEmployers to Transform Online Recruiting for Fortune 500 Employers," *JobCentral National Labor Exchange*, 2004, http://www.jobcentral.com/LinkedIn3_04.asp.

22. Michael Arrington, "Twitter Mania: Google Got Shut Down. Apple Rumors Heat Up," May 5. 2009, http://techcrunch.com/2009/05/05/twitter-mania-google-got-shut-down-apple-rumors-heat-up/.

23. Andy Kazeniac, "Social Networks: Facebook Takes Over Top Spot, Twitter Climbs," February 9, 2009, http://blog.compete.com/2009/02/09/facebook-myspace-twitter-social-network/.

24. Barack Obama, "Twitter / BarackObama," Twitter, 2008, http://twitter.com/BarackObama (May 7, 2008).

25. Susan, P. Joyce, "Top 50+ Employers Recruiting on Twitter," June 9, 2009, http://www.Job-Hunt.org.

26. Rachael King, "Is Twitter the Next Monster?" March 12, 2009, *Technology at Work*. http://www.businessweek.com/technology/technology_at_work/archives/2009/03/hunting_for_job.html.

27. Eve Tahmincioglu, "Firms Putting Best Foot Forward in Cyberspace," MSNBC, June 14, 2008.

28. Ibid.

29. See Note 19.

30. SecondLife.com, 2009, http://www.secondlife.com.

31. Ibid.

32. FOXNews, Recruiting Agency Plans Job Fairs, Interviews in 'Second Life'." February 14, 2007, http://www.Foxnews.com.

33. Ibid.

34. Ibid.

35. Anjali Athavaley, "A Job Interview You Don't Have to Show Up For," *The Wall Street Journal*, June 20, 2007.

36. BusinessWire, "TMP Worldwide Brings Recruitment to Second Life," February 12, 2007, http://www.businesswire.com.

37. Jena Thompson, "Second Life Meets Real Life Recruitment," *Columbia Missourian*, January 25, 2009.

38. See Note 35.

39. HR Focus. "Online Recruiting: What Works, What Doesn't," *HR Focus* 3, no. 1 (March. 2000): 11–13.

40. Joanne Charles, "Finding a Job on the Web," *Black Enterprise* 30, no. 8 (2000): 90–95.

41. C. Biever, "Spam-buster Sport out the Fakes," *New Scientist*, February 7, 2004, 26.

42. Robyn Greenspan, "The Deadly Duo: Spam and Viruses," June 7. 2004. http://www.internetnews.com.

43. See Note 13.

44. Ibid.

45. James C. Sharf, "As If g-loaded Adverse Impact Isn't Bad Enough, Internet Recruiters Can Expect to Be Accused of e-loaded Impact," *The Industrial-Organizational Psychologist* 38, no. 2 (2000): 156. http://www.siop.org/tip/tip.aspx.

46. Islands of the Great Barrier Reef, Queensland, Australia, http://www.islandreefjob.com.

47. Allan Schweyer, "Does Internet Recruiting Work?" March 2005, http://www.inc.com.

48. Ibid.

Suggested Reading

Arthur, Diane. *Recruiting, Interviewing, Selecting & Orienting New Employees*, 4th ed. New York: AMACOM Books, 2006.

Foster, Michael. *Recruiting on the Web: Smart Strategies for Finding the Perfect Candidate*. McGraw-Hill, 2002.

Pritchard, Christopher W. *101 Strategies for Recruiting Success: Where, When, and How to Find the Right People Every Time*. AMACOM, 2006.

Steckerl, Shally. *Electronic Recruiting 101*, 2007 ed. Arbita Consulting and Education Services, 2007.

Weddle, Peter. D. *WEDDLE's Directory of Employment-related Internet Sites: For Recruiters and Job Seekers 2005/6*. Weddle's Publisher, 2005.

Weddle, Peter. D. *Weddle's Guide to Employment Sites on the Internet: For Corporate and Third Party Recruiters, Job Seekers and Career Activists*. Weddle's Publisher, 2007.

6

HARNESSING COLLECTIVE KNOWLEDGE: GROUP COHESION IN ONLINE NETWORKS

Peter Otto

Given the growing complexity and dynamic nature of today's global markets, firms need to innovate continuously. To do this they need to learn faster than ever, certainly faster than their competitors. In order to facilitate this need for rapid learning, firms must find ways to help their knowledge-based workforce discover and share knowledge. While practices designed to encourage learning within and across organizations have been in place for some time now, only recently have organizations become aware of the potential benefits that can accrue to the firm from practices designed to facilitate learning from entities outside the organization including even nominal competitors. Knowledge sharing within an organization is highly structured and well defined in terms of corporate policies that establish rules for sharing and retrieving knowledge from organizational stakeholders. Effectively sharing knowledge within an organization, however, may be restrained by a lack of resources in terms of technology or human capital. Thus another critical challenge facing all managers relates to the allocation of firm resources.

Management typically has more opportunities than it has resources to commit. Deciding which direction to go and the best way to utilize these resources to compete, prosper, and survive is what strategy is all about. Ongoing changes in the competitive business environment mean that old strategies will undoubtedly become ineffective. As a result managers are constantly looking for new approaches to business strategy.

Two mainstreams have recently received considerable attention—the Industrial Organization (I/O) model and the Resource-Based View (RBV).

The Industrial Organization view contends that competitive advantage is achieved when firms implement the strategy dictated by the characteristics of the external environment, that is, economic and technical dimensions of the industry (number and size of buyers, extent of vertical integration, elasticity of demand, etc.). This approach assumes that most firms have strategically relevant resources and posits that competitive advantage can only be increased when a firm finds the industry with the most profit potential and learns how to use its current resources to execute the strategy required by the structural attributes of that industry. Typical strategies that have resulted from this view include cost leadership, differentiation, and focus.

Peter Otto and Salvatore Belardo in "Managing in the New Economy: New Strategies, New Structures" describe thoroughly the differences between the I/O and Resource-Based Views.[1] The I/O view suggests that the conditions and characteristics of the external environment are the primary inputs to and determinants of strategies firms should formulate in order to gain competitive advantage. Implicit in this model are three main assumptions: (1) The external environment with particular emphasis on the industry's structural environment is assumed to impose restrictions and tensions that determine strategies that would result in superior performance. (2) Most firms that compete within a particular industry or industry segment are assumed to control similar strategically relevant resources. (3) The resources used to execute strategies are largely mobile across firms, suggesting that firms that do not possess them, and that for this reason any resource difference that might develop between firms will be transitory.

The Resource-Based View, on the other hand, assumes that the critical factors for success lie within the firm itself in terms of its resources and capabilities. Accordingly, the firm is viewed as a bundle of resources. The firm's choices are not dictated by environmental constraints but by evaluating how the firm can exploit its resources relative to opportunities and threats in the environment. The strategy then is discussed in terms of balancing existing resources in order to utilize them toward advantage creation. The RBV of the firm is rooted in the traditional economic theory of the firm that holds that a firm is an administrative organism with a collection of resources—productive, physical and intangible and that these resources are the source of "economic rents."

The RBV research has focused on examining the link between a firm's internal characteristics and performance and subsequently builds on two alternative assumptions in analyzing sources of competitive advantage: (1) Over time, firms acquire different resources and develop different capabilities. As a result, firms competing in the same industry sector may be diverse with regard to the strategic resources they control.

(2) The resources those firms control may not be perfectly accessible across the entity and thus heterogeneity may be long lasting.

Unfortunately neither approach to strategy is adequate by itself to address the demands of today's complex ever-changing global economy. Limitations of the I/O view include: (1) Research suggests that structure only accounts for between 8 and 15 percent of the variance in profit rates across companies. (2) Little attention is given to discovering, innovating, and commercializing new sources of value. Because innovation has been shown to be the number one creator of organizational wealth, this is a major flaw. (3) The I/O view relies on a static picture of competition. It uses a snapshot approach to industry analysis and does not consider the fact that strategy can dramatically change industry structural characteristics. It focuses too much on what makes an industry attractive rather than on why some industries are attractive. (4) Traditional industry structural analysis, typical of what is found in most textbooks; focus on how to position products and businesses within the existing industry structure rather than how to transform industries to create new advantages.

The RBV is also lacking. It is too static and limiting. Subsequently, this may lead to a mind-set in which management is focused on the degree of fit between available resources and the current environmental opportunities, with the trade-off that the firm does not enough building of new resources and capabilities to create and exploit future opportunities. As proponents of the RBV have sought to distance it from the I/O approach, there is a danger of overemphasizing internal analysis thereby neglecting problems that stem from a rapidly changing environment.

Michael Porter, a major proponent of the I/O school, contends that the RBV runs the risk of being tautological. He argues that the logic of this theory is circular in that "successful firms are successful because they have unique resources."[2] They should, he argues, mature these resources to be successful. In response to the limitations of these two approaches to strategy, G. Hamel and C. K.Prahalad have proposed an approach that combines the best of each and addresses the deficiencies identified above.[3] It is called the Core Competency approach. This approach is a view of strategy that recognizes the need for more than an incremental improvement. It argues that what is needed is a strategic architecture that provides a plan for building the competencies needed to carve out a distinct position to serve future markets. It is fundamentally about improving the organization's capacity to absorb new ideas and new technologies from outside as well as from across the firm. It is about the ability of the firm to continuously and effectively manage external and internal sources of knowledge.

The Core Competency approach suggests that in order for a competency to be core, it must meet three criteria. First the competency must provide customer benefits. A good example of this is Sony; its core competence in miniaturization of electronic components provides benefits of pocket-ability to customers. Second, the competency must be extendable. In other words it must have intrinsic value that enables the firm to extend it to other products and markets. Honda is a good example of this feature. It has used its expertise in superior motorcycle engine design to move into the automotive, lawnmower, and even recreation vehicle (Jet Ski) markets. Third, in order for a competence to be core, it must also be inimitable; that is to say, it must be extremely difficult to duplicate.

An example of this competency can be found in IKEA, the unique furniture store from Sweden. Their philosophy is to build furniture that lasts a lifetime yet is rather inexpensive. IKEA is not only unique in the way it sells furniture—customers have to pick up and assemble what they buy in the store by themselves—but it is also unique in the way that it develops products. At IKEA, product development involves collaboration among designers, product developers, purchasers, and suppliers. Such cooperation encourages multidisciplinary thinking. While some of the previously mentioned companies have policies in place to encourage collaboration, they are more focused, however, on strategic needs and are bounded by hierarchical structures.

In response to these limitations, firms should establish linkages with outside organizations or individuals for the acquisition and sharing of knowledge that takes place free from the constraints of hierarchy and local rules. Professional associations often employ electronic networks as part of their membership benefits. Examples of successful networks include those engaged in open-source software development where programmers voluntarily code software for the benefit of a broader community. Examples of open-source initiatives range from building operating systems such as Linux or office applications to the Firefox Web-browser.

The practice of establishing linkages with entities outside the organization recently gained attention when the CEO of Pfizer, Jeffrey B. Kindler, announced that he wants his secretive researchers to open up and work more closely with outsiders. To encourage such collaboration Pfizer has decided to put the company's drugs pipeline on the Internet for all to see.[4] Its intention in doing this is to establish linkages to individuals and organizations outside Pfizer in order to leverage knowledge in hopes of improving the efficiency of Pfizer's research and development (R&D) efforts.

Managing these loosely structured electronic networks, without formal boundaries, is a challenging task for an organization, echoing Andrew McAfee,[5] who stated, "leaders have to play a delicate role [to ensure the success of Online Communities], and one that changes over time, if they want to succeed. They have to at first encourage and stimulate use of the new tools, and then refrain from intervening too often or with too heavy a hand." The main goal of an electronic network is to develop linkages with practitioners outside the boundary of the firm, while at the same time providing some structure so as to help ease access, facilitate collaboration, and ensure the quality of the knowledge being transferred. Networks of practice also have the characteristics to facilitate knowledge exchange in situations where an organization establishes an alliance with one or more partners to complement its knowledge repository.

An alliance can be broadly defined as a situation where two or more organizations come together because of their mutual interest in interorganizational learning and collaboration to leverage existing knowledge levels. The number of U.S. corporate alliances has grown by more than 25 percent annually for the past five years. P. E. Drucker[6] suggested that the greatest change in the way business is being conducted is the accelerating growth of relationships based not on ownership but on partnership. An important explanatory factor in the growth of alliances is that these forms of cooperation provide a platform for organizational learning and access to new knowledge gained during the alliance.[7]

The motivations for an organization to enter an alliance include, for example, attempts to achieve competitive advantages by gaining market access, improving scale economies, and developing competence through collaboration. While the number of alliances has grown over the last few years, the actual performance of strategic alliances seems to be disappointing.[8] Some suggest that a key to better understand the pitfalls of strategic alliances can be found in the benefits and difficulties of organizational learning among the cooperating firms. Other researchers have identified particular learning problems, such as the risk of uncontrolled information disclosure and asymmetric diffusion of core competencies to partner firms as constraints for a successful alliance.[9] While alliances have a defined beginning and end, networks of practice are established to achieve a long-term and sustainable online environment where members seek and contribute collective knowledge.

However, leadership must bring out the best in people and make those changes that will improve organizational performance. To do this, managers need to develop a better understanding of their organization's culture and its systems and values.

Besides the requisite ability to manage people, managers in today's chaotic business environment need other skills as well, skills that are essential to ensuring core competencies. When most people think of core competence they tend to think in terms of those abilities and skills that can be classified according to the various functional areas such as marketing, production, or R&D.

Another dimension of competence, one that has gained considerable interest in recent years, focuses specifically on the integrative characteristics of competencies within organizations. It is necessary to note that while previous resource-based work implicitly acknowledged the importance of an integrative view, it typically treats the evaluation of resources from a static perspective and ignores the nature of relationships between them how they interact to build synergy.[10]

We contend, however, that it is these integrative competencies, which emphasize the integration and combination of functional, technical, and organizational knowledge, that really provide firms with unique inimitable capabilities. Because the integrative dimension of competence emphasizes the critical importance of identification of new technologies and skills as well as the integration and combination of functional, technical, and organizational knowledge, learning, skills, and routines, it is essential that we examine the role of knowledge management in creating and enhancing these integrative competencies.

Ongoing research[11] suggests several ways that knowledge management can improve integrative competencies. First, knowledge management can help firms identify market trends as well as new and emerging technologies that can help firms with their innovation processes. To do this a firm must look outside its boundaries for new technologies and changes in environmental forces that might help identify threats as well as opportunities. Second, knowledge management can be employed to help leverage the knowledge that exists within and across departments in a firm. Information and knowledge sharing are essential in helping firms synthesize knowledge so that new knowledge can be created. Sharing helps departments learn from one another and permits firms to reapply competencies in different ways. Finally, firms need to ensure that people within the organization develop common codes of communication and common problem-solving skills that can help them anticipate what others need as well and also help them benefit from the knowledge that others have.

Once external information or knowledge about changes and trends in the environment has been identified, processed, and absorbed, internal integrative competencies determine how it will be used.[12] Such competencies are linked to the different functions and disciplines within an organization that interact. One important means by which these different groups coalesce and effectively pool resources to achieve the organizational goals is largely a function of how they communicate and disseminate information and knowledge. The ability to integrate knowledge flexibly across boundaries within the organization may be a fundamental source of competitive advantage.[13] G. P. Huber[14] suggests that combining information from different organizational subunits leads not only to new information but also to new understanding.

One aspect of information distribution is concerned primarily with a firm's ability to integrate knowledge effectively across the different functional domains within a firm. In turbulent environments, organizations that invest in cross-functional knowledge-sharing devices that explicitly focus on the systematic nature of complex products and on increasing the flow of information across functional boundaries significantly outperform those organizations that do not. Results from a study of the pharmaceutical industry[15] suggest that the ability to integrate knowledge within the boundaries of the firm is important determinants of heterogeneous competence. Information or knowledge dissemination across an organization can be greatly facilitated by infomediaries. One such infomediary, TACIT Knowledge Systems (http://www.tacitknowledge .com/) provides software that automatically produces user profiles and automatically and continuously inventories the skills and knowledge of the entire organization. To do this, the software analyzes the content of e-mails, Web pages, document repositories, and other sources of knowledge.

A second aspect of information and knowledge distribution is a firm's ability to effectively integrate knowledge across the different fields of discipline within a firm, or to reconvert discoveries in one applied field to another. The ability to integrate multiple disciplines into a technology, product or process within the organization may be a fundamental source of competitive advantage. However, to leverage the availability of integrated knowledge, firms should seek to extend the corporate boundaries by using new forms of collaboration.

Network of Practice

The concept of networks of practice (NoP) has lately achieved recognition within both academic and practitioner literature as a useful way not only to help facilitate learning but also to help create identity and even motivation within working groups. NoPs have been characterized as fluid social arrangements or relations enacted among a self-selected group of participants.[16] In contrast to communities of practice, where people may meet face-to-face to coordinate activities and communicate with each other, networks of practice consist of a larger, loosely knit, geographically distributed group of individuals engaged in a shared practice without the need to meet face to face.[17] With recent advances in computer-mediated communication NoPs can extend the reach and social interactions needed to sustain the community.

M. M. Wasko and S. Faraj[18] define an electronic network of practice as a self-organizing, open activity system focused on a shared practice that exists primarily through computer-mediated communication. Members of the network are willing to engage with one another to help solve problems or make contributions common to the practice. An important aspect of networks of practice is that members create, seek, and share knowledge and thus establish a community where new knowledge is acquired from the network and transferred among network members. But what motivates people to share knowledge and use their valuable time to build these online networks?

In an analysis of data from a study of members of a national legal professional association in the United States, Wasko and Faraj[19] found that network centrality is an important indicator of whether individuals choose to contribute knowledge; an actor with a high degree of centrality maintains contacts with numerous other network actors. A. C. Inkpen and E. K. Tsang,[20] though, argue that the concept of networks is one that suffers from being overstretched. They have shown that the extent and value of the knowledge transferred varies across network types and contend that all networks are, at their core, about social relationships, and, therefore, social dimensions have applicability, regardless of the network type.

While the literature is replete with contributions on knowledge transfer both within traditional and online communities, little is known about an organization's ability to intervene actively to encourage the growth of electronic networks of practice. For example, ease of access or openness helps to grow the network at the beginning, while there is little control over who gets into the network. As the network begins to grow, there is a need to have some rules and policies to maintain the quality of the content; this subsequently can affect the attractiveness of the network. To successfully establish an online network, organizations need to understand the social factors governing the network, for example, group cohesion and the policies to make structural interventions. A policy is an intervention to help sustain or grow the network such as imposing rules and regulations for people who participate in an online network or share resources. For example, if a member from the community is uploading information to the network, s/he must adhere to rules determined by the organization operating the network. Imposing rules and policies, in turn, might reduce the egalitarian nature of the network and subsequently the attractiveness for members to participate. Another policy, which may affect the growth of an online network, is group commitment. We can refer to group commitment as activities and incentives aimed at strengthening the cohesion of individuals in an online network. Group commitment can be strengthened, for example, by acknowledging those who contribute regularly, which may reinforce the motivation to increase the involvement in the online network. The result from this policy intervention may lead to stronger ties among individuals who are part of the online community.

HARNESSING COLLECTIVE KNOWLEDGE

One of the best-known examples for an online community that facilitates the creation of collective knowledge is Wikipedia, a popular online encyclopedia, written by volunteer contributors. Wikipedia is an international online project that attempts to create a free encyclopedia in multiple languages. Using Wiki software, thousands of volunteers have collaboratively and successfully edited articles. Within three years, the world's largest Open Content project has accumulated more than 1,500,000 articles in the English-language version and more than half a million in the German-language version. There are 250 language editions of Wikipedia, and 18 of them have more than 50,000 articles each.

The content of the Wikipedia encyclopedia is written collaboratively by volunteers, allowing most articles to be changed by almost anyone with access to the Web site. Wikipedia is an open-source project with a dynamic environment where people join and leave the network and collaborate on making knowledge available to a larger audience. The online encyclopedia consists of a number of administrators, a small number of experts who oversee the content quality, and editors, people who contribute by editing existing articles or uploading new knowledge. Wikipedia staidly grew from its launch in early 2003. By end of October 2006, 14,600 Wikipedians (or active contributors) participated in building collective knowledge for the English version of Wikipedia, guided by 250 Administrators. Wikipedia's reach per million hit 56,000 in October 2006, which means that about 5.6 percent of Internet users were visiting Wikipedia each day.

Like many other open-source projects relying on collective knowledge creation or sharing by volunteers, Wikipedia faces a number of challenges. For example, Wikipedia needs a lot of people to keep a project alive. Poor involvement of editors or even inactivity also challenges the sustainability of the project. Credibility of content is another issue; inexperienced editors need to build a certain level of credibility. If they fail to establish their credibility or take too long a time, the project might falter.

Another example of open-source collaboration, where knowledge is created collectively, is open-source software development. For example, the operating system Linux, a software program, is written by a larger community of individuals without any financial incentives to work on building software open accessible to the public.

The main problem in building and sustaining electronic networks of practice, however, is to balance a loosely structured environment with some control levers. Without any control over the network in terms of rules and procedures, the content quality may suffer, which will affect the sustainability of the network in the long run. To manage a loosely structure network effectively, we need a framework to better understand the social dimension or group cohesion in online networks. One way to look at network cohesion is to use the grid-group analysis, first proposed by social anthropologist Mary Douglas[21] and later developed for application to political cultures by M. Thompson, R. Ellis, and A. Wildavsky.[22]

The Grid/Group Typology

The Douglas typology suggests, "a person's behavior, perception, attitudes, beliefs and values are shaped, regulated and controlled by constraints that can be segmented into group commitment and grid control."[23] Applying the segmentation of extreme low and high for each variable results in four

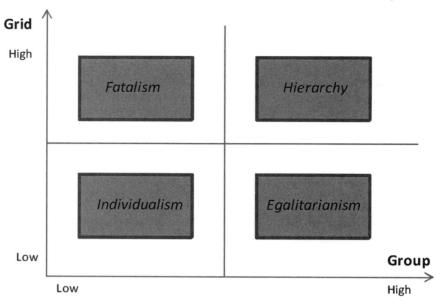

Figure 6.1 The Douglas Grid/Group Framework

possible social characteristics depicted by the Douglas grid/group typology: "fatalism (high grid, low group), egalitarianism (low grid, high group), individualism (low grid, low group), and hierarchy (high grid, high group)." The two-dimensional characterization derived from the grid/group framework has been empirically validated over the last years.[24]

Douglas[25] and J. L. Gross and S. Rayner[26] suggest that the strength in group ties (high or low) depicts the degree to which individuals are motivated or restricted in thinking and action by their commitment and involvement to a social group. In following the grid/group framework, high group strength is a result of considerable devotion of time and resources to interacting with other members in their unit. As group strength increases, the more activities members of the same unit do together and the longer they spend doing it. In turn, group strength may be low when members of the same unit are neither controlled nor constrained by other members in the same segment and activities in the network are centered on creating individual benefits.

The complementary bundle of constraints on social interaction is, according to the Douglas framework, "grid." This segment depicts a composite index of the extent to which the behavior of individuals will be constrained by normative roles. For example, grid strength is high in situations where activities of individuals are based on common social classification such as gender, race, or hierarchical position. The other end of the spectrum is a low-grid position, where access and activities are determined on personal abilities and skills, for example, in an online network to foster open-source software development. The four characteristic clusters of the Douglas grid/group model as shown in Figure 6.1 are:

Egalitarianism (low grid, high group) is a social context in which the external group boundary is typically the consideration and the social experience of the individual and is shaped by the "we" versus "them" ethos. All other aspects of interpersonal relationships are ambiguous and open to negotiation, with emphasis on egalitarianism and active participation.

Individualism (low grid, low group) represents a social context dominated by strongly competitive conditions, volatile circumstances, and a prescription for individual autonomy. This context allows the individual maximum options for negotiating contracts or choosing allies.

Fatalism (high grid, low group) is a social context dominated by insulation. In its extremity, the sphere of individual autonomy is minimal with little scope for personal transactions. The organizational correlate is a hierarchical environment with well-established and formalized individual roles.

Hierarchy (high grid, high group) is a social context with individual behavior and group boundary controls. Here everyone knows one's place, though that place might vary with time. Personal security is obtained at the expense of overt competition and social mobility.

Looking at group cohesion and possible effects from policy interventions in an online network, the Douglas grid/group framework can provide a number of advantages over traditional approaches to help understand cause and effect in managing online networks. The grid/group framework helps to capture accurately the social relationships and characteristics (social actions taken in hope or expectation of future positive responses) of individuals within an online network. Another advantage applying this framework is that at the core of a network are people. As such, the Douglas grid/group framework depicts the important social characteristics determining the behavior of groups. Finally, the Douglas grid/group framework provides a different approach to previous studies, where the focus was, for example, individual incentives,[27] impact of firms' participation on individual motives,[28] impact of community participation on individual motives[29] and relationships between incentives and technical design.[30]

BUILDING AND SUSTAINING AN ONLINE NETWORK

There are many challenges to successfully establish and sustain an online network of practice. Wikipedia, for example, deployed a robust, clever, and easy-to-use Web-based technology called "Wiki" to post and edit articles on its Web site. (Wikipedia defines a wiki as a "page or collection of Web pages designed to enable anyone who accesses it to contribute or modify content, using a simplified markup language.") Wikipedia's early success was the result of a certain seeding structure that motivated individuals in creating a vibrant online community. The element that helped to scale Wikipedia so fast was a piece of software or "Wiki," which is a collection of hypertext documents that can be directly edited by anyone. The edit is then recorded and thus can be retraced by any other user. Each version of a document becomes available on Wikipedia's Web site, including the revision history so that it can be compared to other versions. The result of Wikipedia's open and egalitarian structure at the beginning was an increase in burlesque articles and vandal attacks, forcing Wikipedia to enforce a set of new regulations and rules to maintain the integrity and quality of its online encyclopedia.

While the technology contributed to the successful start of the online network, it is the social dimension that shapes the growth of the network. New members of an online network usually have strong motivation to participate in sharing or creating collective knowledge, often driven by some specific personal motive, such as wanting to solve a problem or sharing their expertise and experience in a particular field. Wikipedia, similar to other open-source projects relying on volunteers who share and create collective knowledge, faced a number of challenges. Foremost, these types of online network need a critical mass of people willing to share and contribute to keep a project alive. The result of poor involvement of editors or even inactivity of individuals can challenge the sustainability of an online network. Another issue is the credibility of the content; for Wikipedia it meant that inexperienced editors had to build credibility in the community and so attract others to join. A lack of credibility in the early stages of an online network lifecycle or delays in establishing creditability might result in not getting the network off the ground. The case of Wikipedia provides an example for an online network, with administrators and editors safeguarding the core that relies in part on how to promote participation and at the same time provide the infrastructure and social ties to nurture collaboration.

A recent study,[31] focusing on the sustainability and dynamics in online networks, provides evidence that online networks need to impose some form of structural control, otherwise the attractiveness, credibility, and, subsequently, content value of the network will decrease. The study claims, "to ensure sustainability, the network must be monitored, especially during the early stages of its evolution, so that rules and regulations that ensure value and validity can be selectively employed." The practical implications are that an open and egalitarian environment in an online network invites people to contribute during the early stage but in the long run, the network cannot exist without some form of structural control, through, for example, documents, terms, and policies governing how individuals interact. Removing boundaries or having too little control over who participates in the online network may cause a similar result, like the *Los Angeles Times*'s doomed experiment in unrestricted Internet comment, which had to be closed down after just two days under a bombardment of pornographic postings.

If boundary objects are an important structural dimension for online networks, there may be opportunities for organizations to encourage the growth of the network by creating initial boundary objects, using symbols (e.g., a brand), having the right instruments (IT infrastructure), or focal concepts (e.g., a theme), around which network members may congregate and interact. However, too much structure can easily result in the failure of an online community. The example of Wikipedia with its proliferation of rules for uploading and editing articles, suggests that the egalitarian and open environment from the early days is shifting into a more controlled and regulated construct, with the result that this may deter people contributing to the online encyclopedia. Indeed, Wikipedia's article base is increasing at a decreasing rate, while the rate at which articles are edited has also been on the decline.

While many factors, internal as well as external, may contribute to the success of an online network, it is suggested that in order to manage it successfully a network operator needs to make structural interventions at the different stages of growth to shape the network. Structural interventions can be defined as policies through which organizations can influence building or sustaining an online community. For example, establishing rules and regulation for people who contribute or share resources is a policy to maintain the quality and attractiveness of the network. So if someone wants to upload information to the online network, s/he must comply with the rules imposed by the organization or its governance body. Another policy is to provide an easy accessible environment at the early stage of an online network attracting enough individuals to collaborate and grow the network. When the network begins to grow, the focus should shift from openness into imposing rules and policies to maintain the quality of integrity of the network. The trade-off in establishing more rules and regulation is that the network might lose its attractiveness and openness. Although highly aggregated, a set of structural interventions could be established via three policy levers to help understand what cause and effect these policies will have on the sustainability of an online network.

In response to an increase in spoof articles or vandalism, a policy to increase "grid control" should be considered. The implication of this policy is that people who actively want to participate in an online network have to accept more rules and regulations to which they have to adhere. It is suggested, however, that if the network removes all rules and regulations, i.e., decreasing its grid control policy lever, people who are following rules of conduct may be deterred, but the changing environment would invite people with a high degree of self-responsibility (individualists). Individualists rely on their instincts and are prone to refuse accepting too many rules and regulations. The common feel among individualists is that each person is responsible for his or her own well-being and for whomever else s/he chooses. As result, a social environment with low-grid characteristics is one in which access to roles depends on the abilities, skills, and qualifications of an individual competing or negotiating for them. Consequently, this policy intervention will change the group cohesion and social characteristics of the online network. While an open egalitarian environment may appeal to individuals with their distinct characteristics, it may distract others. It is suggested that establishing an online network with an asymmetric distribution of social characteristics may not be sustainable.

At the beginning of its online encyclopedia, Wikipedia provided an open unrestricted environment, to enable a wide audience to edit or upload articles. As a result of the egalitarian and open environment, Wikipedia experienced an increase in burlesque articles and vandalism. To maintain the integrity and quality of its Web site, Wikipedia responded by changing its regulatory environment and imposing a set of new rules for people who wanted to edit or upload articles. For example, users who wished to upload an article to Wikipedia were required to complete a registration process and provide some basic personal information. Wikipedia also used its administrators as gatekeepers for quality and integrity—every edited article needed approval from an administrator before it was released. Those interventions were intended to address the problem observed in the *Los Angeles Times* online community experiment, where in absence of any control mechanisms the network lost its credibility and integrity and as a result vanished from the landscape. In using common sense one would assume that an open inviting environment should result in the fast growth of an online network. However, it is suggested that common sense is a notoriously poor predictor for time-dependent cause and effects of management interventions in a complex system.

The second policy intervention is concerned with "group commitment," suggesting that a network operator, e.g., Wikipedia, would not undertake any efforts to strengthen group commitment, i.e., focus on activities and incentives that may improve group cohesion. Following the Douglas framework, group strength is high when individuals dedicate significant time and attach great importance to interacting with other members in their unit. In turn, when individuals are acting in ways that only benefits them without being controlled or dependent upon others, group strength in the same social unit will be low.

A simple way to increase involvement of people in an online network is to acknowledge those who contributed and as a result reinforce the motivation to participate actively in the online community. According to the Douglas grid/group framework, such an intervention may change the social characteristics of the online network. While such a policy may appeal to people for whom group commitment is important, people who need hierarchical structure and boundaries may be repelled by such a policy. As a result, an online network may lose people who are guided by boundaries (hierarchists) by not having policies in place to guide and stimulate group commitment. An example for such a construct includes social environments where individual roles are based on seniority rather than on merit. Form a theoretical perspective, looking through the lens of the Douglas grid/group framework, not focusing on group commitment may marginally changes the size of the "egalitarian" cluster (individuals who are determined by "us" rather "them"[32]). In the real world, the online network would not make any effort to motive its members to pursue a common goal. Wikipedia, for example, is focusing on strengthening its user group by providing people who regularly make contributions and share knowledge with special privileges, e.g., faster upload to the Web site or giving access to better editing capabilities.

Changing the level of access to an online network is another policy intervention. Depending on the accessibility of the interface, a network operator could make it easier or harder for people getting into the online network. Wikipedia, for example, provided a high degree of accessibility with its browser-based interface to inspire users uploading or editing content to its online encyclopedia. Changing the level of accessibility may neither affect the social characteristics nor the group cohesion but only the frequency or scope with which people can exchange knowledge from an online network. As such, accessibility will affect the diffusion rate with which an online network will scale after interception.

CONCLUDING REMARKS

The "new economy," regardless of what the term really means, will definitely require new approaches to strategy, new organizational forms, and most assuredly new and different means for collaboration to facilitate the creation of collective knowledge. Whatever strategy a firm subscribes to, it must be one that enables the firm to learn and innovate. Because innovation has been shown to be the single most important factor in producing organizational wealth, innovating faster than the competition is essential to competing in the new economy. Similarly, new organizational forms will be required that will ensure flexible response yet stable systems and processes.

It is suggested that online networks can be an important architecture to share and distribute knowledge across different domains, from an online encyclopedia and open-source software development to a network of practices, connecting like-minded people for the benefit of the larger good.

The proposed Douglas grid/group framework described in this chapter should help to establish a better understanding of the effects of policy intervention in an online network. It may also provide insights into how policy changes can affect the social characteristics within the network, realizing that every network has at its core people. The use of the grid/group model to analyze cause and effect of policy interventions in online networks, however, is not without limitations. It is suggested that culture, a comprehensive social construct, cannot be easily depicted by a two-dimensional typology or any other simple framework for that matter.[33] As a result, the Douglas grid/group typology does have limited explanatory power.

On the other hand, having a framework to capture attitudes, beliefs, and values that are shaped, regulated, and controlled in an online network can help users to understand structural changes in the form of rules and regulations. For example, if a network operator is not imposing any control when building an online network, that network will experience a loss of credibility and integrity, and subsequently not have enough attractiveness to be sustainable. Subsequently, a network operator should carefully monitor the growth of its user base in the early stages and define rules and regulations as soon as the network begins to scale. Establishing an online network can help an organization to harness collective knowledge beyond the boundary of the firm. There are many examples of organizations that successfully added online networks to their business model as a way to reach out and make knowledge more accessible, whether it is a "not-for-profit" organization such as Wikipedia, an open-source endeavor such as Mozilla, or a "for-profit" enterprise, for example, Pfizer Inc. The critical success factor in pursuing an online network strategy, however, is to find the right balance between openness and control. Using a framework, like to Douglas grid/group typology discussed in this article, can help to improve our understanding of how policy interventions shape the social structure in an online network.

NOTES

    1. Peter Otto and Salvatore Belardo, "Managing in the New Economy: New Strategies, New Structures," in *Management-Konzepte fur die New Economy*, ed. Ralph Berndt (Springer, 2002).

    2. Michael Porter, *Competitive Strategy: Techniques for Analyzing Industries and Competitors* (New York: The Free Press, 1980).

    3. G. Hamel and C. K. Prahalad, *Competing for the Future* (Boston: Harvard Business Press, 1994).

    4. Alyssa Abkowitz, "Pfizer's Home Remedy," *Fortune Magazine*, August 18, 2009, http://money.cnn.com/2009/08/18/news/companies/pfizer_drugs _reorganizing.fortune/index.htm.

    5. A. McAfee, "Enterprise 2.0: The Dawn of Emergent Collaboration," *Sloan Management Review*, Spring 2006.

    6. P. E. Drucker, "The Network Society," *Wall Street Journal*, March 29, 1995.

7. R. M. Grant, "Prospering in Dynamically-competitive Environments: Organizational Capability as Knowledge Integration," *Organizational Science* no. 7 (1996): 375–88; G. Hamel, "Competition for Competence and Inter-Partner Learning within Interorganizational Strategic Alliances," *Strategic Management Journal*, no. 12 (1991): 83–104; T. Khanna, R. Gulati, and N. Nohria, "The Dynamics of Learning Alliances: Competition, Cooperation, and Relative Scope," *Strategic Management Journal*, no. 19 (1998): 193–210; B. Kogut, "Joint Ventures: Theoretical and Empirical Perspectives," *Strategic Management Journal*, no. 9 (1998): 319–322.

8. K. R. Harrigan, "Strategic Alliances and Partner Asymmetrics," *Management International Review*, no. 28 (1988): 53–72; M. E. Porter, "From Competitive Advantage to Corporate Strategy," *Harvard Business Review* 63, no. 3 (1987): 43–59.

9. R. K. Bresser, "Matching Collective and Competitive Strategies," *Strategic Management Journal*, no. 9 (1988): 375–385; see Hamel, "Competition for Competence," Note 7; A. C. Inkpen, 2000. "Learning though Joint Ventures: A Framework of Knowledge Acquisition," *Journal of Management Studies* 37, no. 7 (2000): 1019–1043.

10. J. A. Black and K. B. Boal, "Strategic Resources: Traits, Configurations and Paths to Sustainable Competitive Advantage," *Strategic Management Journal*, no. 15 (1994): 1331–148.

11. M. A. McDermott, "An Empirical Investigation of Core Competence and Firm Performance," Dissertation Proposal, State University New York, 2001.

12. G. Verona, "A Resource-Based View of Product Development," *Academy of Management Review* 24, no. 1 (1999): 132–142.

13. Ibid.

14. G. P. Huber, "Organizational Learning: The Contributing Processes and the Literatures," *Organizational Science* 2, no. 2 (1991): 88–115

15. Rebecca Henderson and Iain Cockburn, "Measuring Competence? Exploring Firm Effects in Pharmaceutical Research," *Strategic Management Journal*, no. 15 (1994): 63–84.

16. J. Lave and E. Wenger, *Situated Learning: Legitimate Peripheral Participation* (Cambridge University Press, 1991).

17. J. S. Brown and P. Duguid, "Organizational Learning and Communities of Practice: Toward a Unified View of Working, Learning, and Innovation," *Organizational Science* 2, no. 1 (1991): 40–57.

18. M. M. Wasko and S. Faraj, "Why Should I Share? Examining Social Capital and Knowledge Contribution in Electronic Networks of Practice," *MIS Quarterly* 29, no. 1 (2005): 35–57.

19. Ibid.

20. A. C. Inkpen and E. K. Tsang, "Social Capital, Networks, and Knowledge Transfer," *Academy of Management Review* 30, no. 1 (2005): 146–165.

21. M. Douglas, *Natural Symbols: Explorations in Cosmology,* (Barrie and Rockliff, 1970); M. Douglas, *Cultural Bias* (Barrie and Rockliff, 1978).

22. M. Thompson, R. Ellis and A. Wildavsky, *Cultural Theory* (Westview, 1990).

23. See Note 21.

24. T. Burns and G. M. Stalker, *The Management of Innovation* (Tavistock, 1961); R. R. Harrision, "Understanding Your Organization's Character,"*Harvard Business Review* (May-June 1972): 119–128.

25. See Note 21.

26. J. L. Gross and S. Rayner. *Measuring Culture* (Columbia University Press, 1985).

27. M. Bergquist and J. Ljungberg, "The Power of Gifts: Organizing Social Relationships in Open Source Communities," *Information Systems Journal* 1, no. 4 (2001): 305–320.

28. J. M. Dalle and P. A. David, "The Allocation of Software Development Resources in 'Open Source' Production Mode. Discussion," paper 02-27, Stanford Institute for Economic Policy Research, 2003.

29. N. E. Franke and E. von Hippel, "Satisfying Heterogeneous Use Needs via Innovation Toolkits: The Case of Apache Security Software," *Research Policy* 32, no. 7 (2003): 1199–1215.

30. R. A. Gosh, R. Glott, B. Krieger, and G. Robles, "Free/Libre and Open Source Software: Survey and Study," Working Paper, International Institute of Informatics, University Maastricht, 2002.

31. Peter Otto and M. Simon, "Dynamic Perspectives on Social Characteristics and Sustainability in Online Community Networks," *System Dynamics Review* 24, no. 3 (2008): 321–47.

32. Y. Altman and Y. Baruch, "Cultural Theory and Organizations: Analytical Method and Cases," *Organization Studies* 19, no. 50 (1998): 769–785.

33. S. A. Sackmann, "Culture and Subcultures: An Analysis of Organizational Knowledge," *Administrative Science Quarterly*, no. 37 (1992): 140–161.

7

HARNESSING THE POWER
OF THE OH-SO-SOCIAL WEB*

Josh Bernoff and Charlene Li

Companies are used to being in control. They typically design products, services, and marketing messages based on their own particular view of what people want. Keeping up with customers has meant conducting research on their needs and test marketing new products and services. Because the balance of power has favored large corporations with a lock on manufacturing, advertising, distribution, and other operations, the term "customer-centric" was mostly just a buzzword.

Now, though, many customers are no longer cooperating. Empowered by online social technologies such as blogs, social networking sites including MySpace, user-generated content sites such as YouTube, and countless communities across the Web, customers are now connecting with and drawing power from one other. They're defining their own perspectives on companies and brands, views that are often at odds with the image a company wants to project. This groundswell of people using technologies to get the things they need from one another, rather than from companies, is now tilting the balance of power from company to customer.

To understand the dramatic implications of this shift, consider what happened in 2006 when Brian Finkelstein, a law student, was having trouble with the cable modem in his home. A repairman from Comcast

Cable Communications Inc. arrived to fix the problem, but when the technician had to call the home office for a key piece of information, he was put on hold for so long that he fell asleep on Finkelstein's couch. Outraged and frustrated, Finkelstein made a video of the sleeping technician and posted it on YouTube. The clip became a hit, with more than one million viewings, and to this day the image continues to undermine Comcast's attempts to improve its reputation for customer service. Comcast is not alone. Another popular YouTube clip contains dialogue between a customer trying to cancel his subscription and America Online. What should have been a simple conversation becomes a battle as the AOL service representative stubbornly persists in trying to retain the customer, sorely trying his patience. Finally, the customer says, "I don't know how to make this any clearer for you: Cancel the account. When I say 'cancel the account,' I don't mean help me figure out how to keep it. I mean cancel the account." Apparently, the clip struck a nerve as hundreds of people posted comments on the YouTube page, many of them bashing AOL and relaying similar experiences with the company. CNBC even devoted a report to the whole flap. And the groundswell phenomenon is hardly limited to the United States, as shown in Figure 7.1. In April 2007, a blogger in South Korea posted a description, accompanied with photos, of what he described as unsanitary conditions at a supplier of Dunkin' Donuts. Other Korean blogs spread the word, and the story was eventually covered by *The Korea Times* with an article titled "Dunkin's Production Faces Sanitation Criticism."

WORKING WITH THE GROUNDSWELL

When we talk with executives about the growing groundswell of customer power, their reactions are mixed. Many are fascinated with the phenomenon but terrified that their companies might become the next Comcast, AOL, or Dunkin' Donuts. Some recognize the powerful potential of the groundswell but have no idea how that force can be turned to their advantage. Behind all of this is a significant cultural issue: Engaging with the groundswell means admitting that consumers are taking power and that corporations are not in control. It's a scary and difficult first step to take.

Consider, for example, the CBS television series *Jericho*. Based on life in a fictional town after a nuclear explosion occurs nearby, the show developed a moderate-sized but intensely loyal following after its debut in 2006. But in the spring of 2007, after a two-month hiatus, *Jericho* resumed airing in a new time slot—directly opposite Fox's hit *American Idol*. Not surprisingly, ratings dropped, resulting in the show's cancellation. But CBS and the producers of *Jericho* had created a forum on the network's Web site where followers of the series could interact with each other, and in the wake of the show's cancellation those fans decided that something had to be done. Led by Shaun Daily, a San Diego online radio talk

Participation in Online Social Activities Around the World

The percentages indicate the proportion of online consumers who participate in the indicated activity at least once per month.

	U.S.	U.K.	France	Germany	Japan	South Korea
Read blogs	25%	10%	21%	10%	52%	31%
Write blogs	11%	3%	7%	2%	12%	18%
Watch user-generated video	29%	17%	15%	16%	20%	5%
Visit social network sites (for example, Facebook)	25%	21%	3%	10%	20%	35%
Participate in discussion forums	18%	12%	12%	15%	22%	7%
Read ratings/reviews	25%	20%	12%	28%	38%	16%
Post ratings/reviews	11%	5%	3%	8%	11%	11%
Use Really Simple Syndication (RSS)	8%	3%	5%	4%	0%	1%

Source: Forrester Research Technographics consumer surveys from 2007

Figure 7.1

show host, people began to organize and devise ways to get CBS's attention. Taking their cue from a *Jericho* character whose favorite expletive is "Nuts!" they settled on a plan to send packages of peanuts to the person responsible for canceling the show: Nina Tassler, president of CBS Entertainment. Soon Tassler's office had received more than 20 tons of nuts.

Although this story of a consumer uprising might sound similar to what happened to Comcast, AOL, and Dunkin' Donuts, the ending is starkly different. Tassler and the rest of the management at CBS wisely recognized that the explosion of online support represented not a problem but an opportunity for relaunching the series. Culturally, television network executives have long dealt with their viewers at arm's length, through research and ratings. The easy thing for Tassler would have been to ignore the groundswell and reinforce her own ultimate power over programming decisions. But she instead engaged with *Jericho*'s online fans, requesting on their own message board that they rally their friends to watch the relaunched show in 2008 to help boost its ratings. Nina Tassler thus avoided the potentially costly mistake of canceling a TV program with an active, loyal fan base. And as a result, CBS has strengthened its connection with viewers, which will prove advantageous for future research and programming decisions.

MOVING BEYOND DABBLING

But tapping into the full power of the groundswell requires more than just a willingness to relinquish control to customers. To be truly effective, companies need a strategic framework for developing and implementing the right applications. A focus on objectives (and their corresponding metrics) is the best predictor of success. We identify these groundswell objectives with terms such as "listening" and "energizing" instead of "research" and "sales" to reflect how they differ from traditional organizational functions.

In the past, executives at most dabbled with social applications; their efforts were rarely strategic. But with the increase in social participation among consumers and the growing sophistication of the underlying technologies, it's now possible to put social applications on an equal footing with other business projects. That is, they can deliver measurable progress toward significant, strategic business goals. The following examples help illustrate how companies can harness the power of the groundswell for a variety of objectives with direct links to different departments.

Research and Development Applications ("Listening")

CBS was fortunate that *Jericho* fans took it upon themselves to voice their objections loudly after their show had been canceled. Otherwise, the network might have missed some crucial feedback. Other companies have made more systematic, concerted efforts to listen to their customers. Consider Salesforce.com Inc., a maker of online applications for customer relationship management. As with most software companies, Salesforce.com has tried to stay competitive by regularly issuing upgrades to its products, but by 2005, the process of determining what to include in future releases had become a daunting task. With 10,000 requests from customers, Salesforce.com's development and marketing staff often disagreed about which features to add and which to table.

Then, in 2006, the company hit on a solution: IdeaExchange, a groundswell application that enables customers not only to suggest feature ideas but to vote on them, with the most popular ideas eventually floating to the top of the list, while the less popular ones drift away. The application has been a huge success. Thanks to it, Salesforce.com was able to ship four new releases in 2007, in contrast to only two the year before. And recent releases now contain three times as many new features as in previous years.

Moreover, Salesforce.com has greater confidence in what it ships. Half the new features in each release now come from IdeaExchange suggestions that have been vetted by customers. Instead of holding big meetings to wrangle over features, developers can move forward knowing what the market truly wants. This makes for less wasted effort and a more efficient process. "We can help diminish the political pushing and make [development about] the quality of the ideas," says Steve Fisher, vice president in charge of the Salesforce.com platform. IdeaExchange, according to Fisher, "gave us back our velocity." That's a powerful statement in an industry where faster product development is a key competitive edge.

Marketing Applications ("Talking")

Marketers are used to crafting messages and interrupting customers with them in the form of television ads or online banners. When tapping into the groundswell, the key is to spur the interest of customers and let *them* carry the messages. In 2006, for example, Chevrolet wanted to increase awareness of the new Chevy Aveo among college students, a group notably difficult to reach with advertising. So the company and its PR agency, Weber Shandwick Worldwide, conceived the "Chevy Aveo Livin' Large Campus Challenge." In the challenge, Chevrolet recruited pairs of students on seven college campuses to spend an entire week living inside a Chevy Aveo, with breaks only for classes and occasional trips to the bathroom. The campaign was a success mainly because Chevrolet had encouraged the students to use the groundswell to publicize their experiences. The students wrote blogs, created and posted YouTube videos, and mobilized their friends by the thousands in groups on Facebook and MySpace. Weber Shandwick estimates that in the five days of the contest the students generated 217 million impressions and got more than one million college students connected to the contest through Facebook, MySpace, and other media. Not only was Chevrolet's challenge far less expensive than a traditional advertising campaign, it also helped establish a more powerful connection with the brand.

Sales Applications ("Energizing")

Other companies have gone beyond using the groundswell for just marketing, tapping into sales applications as well. Consider the crafts division of Fiskars Corp., a 350-year-old company best known for its high-quality scissors. Fiskars, which produces a wide variety of paper and crafting supplies and tools, wanted to grow its market among a predominantly female group of customers who identified themselves as crafters or "scrapbookers." But research revealed that the company's brand image within this market segment was bland—respondents said that if the company were a color, it would be "beige"; if it were a food, it would be "saltines." As Suzanne Fanning, head of public relations for Fiskars' craft division, explained, "Even though scrapbooking is an emotional craft, they were lacking that emotional connection to any of our tools."

So Fanning worked with Brains on Fire Inc., a brand consultancy, to address that deficiency by building an online program. First, Fiskars conducted a nationwide search and identified four enthusiastic crafters who were hired as part-time "lead ambassadors." These individuals would recruit others into an exclusive online brand community called "Fiskateers." All members of the community would receive a welcome kit that included a unique two-tone pair of scissors. In exchange, the company asked for their active online participation and social connection with as many other crafters as possible.

Fiskars launched Fiskateers in December 2006 with two specific goals: increase overall online discussion about the Fiskars brand by 10 percent and recruit 200 additional unpaid "brand ambassadors." But the company underestimated the enthusiasm of crafters, many of whom were already highly active social participants in an online groundswell. As one crafter put it, "Crafting isn't a matter of life and death; it's much more important than that." Indeed, just five months later, the online discussion of Fiskars products had surged by over 400 percent, and the number of ambassadors was more than 1,400. (It now exceeds 3,000.)

The seemingly boundless energy of those ambassadors has been a welcome boon for the company. Take, for example, Fiskateer number 99: Wendy Jo Avey, a 40-year-old woman who contributes to blogs on the Fiskateers site and helps to organize crafting events. At one such event, Avey gave hundreds of the attendees a gift that she had made: Using Fiskars products she had created magnets in unique shapes, each decorated with stamps and the Web address of the Fiskateers community. Such groundswell activities tie directly to sales increases. When one of the lead ambassadors visits a craft store—an event typically promoted within the Fiskateers community—the spike in sales at that location is substantial: typically triple the growth compared with other stores within the same time period.

Customer Support Applications ("Supporting")

Perhaps the best example of a company that has embraced social applications is Dell Inc. In many ways Dell was well prepared to embrace its customers in the groundswell. The company's original business model of allowing buyers to specify and customize their own PCs had already created a culture that was centered on customers (and not on engineers or marketers). And in the 1990s, Dell was an e-commerce pioneer, using its Web site to generate millions of orders long before its competitors had installed that capability. Furthermore, the company's online support forums had been in operation since the era of online bulletin boards, thus predating even the Web itself.

Even so, it took a crisis to get Dell better in touch with its customers. In the summer of 2005, Jeff Jarvis, a journalism professor and noted blogger, wrote a scathing entry in his blog. In a post titled "Dell lies. Dell sucks," Jarvis claimed the company sent him a defective machine and reneged on its promise of on-site service, telling him that he needed to send the machine back to Dell. As Jarvis's problems continued, he began to refer to the ongoing saga in additional posts as "Dell Hell," and his travails began to get covered not just by other blogs but also by the mainstream media.

Over at Dell, Jarvis's blog had gotten the attention of the top brass, and company founder Michael Dell called on Bob Pearson, the company's vice president of corporate group communications, to find a way to handle future problems before they fester. The result: a cross departmental "blog resolution" team that is trained to offer both customer service and technical support. The team actively tracks blog posts, and when it finds a disgruntled customer it reaches out to the individual, offering help to deal with the problem from start to finish, thus avoiding the painful "Please hold while I connect you with another department" experiences that have become all too common with telephone support.

Moreover, to communicate proactively with customers (whether they were content or not), Dell created its own blog, "Direct2Dell," which came in handy when the company had to recall millions of laptop batteries. Rather than hide behind a public relations wall, Dell acknowledged the issue in a straightforward post called "Flaming Laptop" even before the extent of the trouble was known. As soon as Dell had figured out the scope of the problem and had designed a solution, the blog became a useful channel for disseminating news of the company's battery replacement program. Dell thus minimized the impact of the problem, which by then was causing similar headaches for other computer manufacturers.

The blog-resolution team and Direct2Dell were designed to help Dell connect with its customers, but the company has learned through the years that consumers are often more than willing to help each other fix their problems—provided they have the means to do so. In fact, Dell's support forum has grown to four million posts, about a quarter of which are answers to questions about the company's products. In online surveys, 20 to 50 percent of visitors to the site say they found the answers to their problems on the support forum—which saves Dell the cost of customer support calls.

Operations Applications ("Managing")

Although groundswell applications with customers get much of the press, many businesses have found it much easier to start closer to home, with their employees. Best Buy Co. Inc., the huge electronics retailer, is a case in point. The groundswell within Best Buy began in August 2006 when Steve Bendt and Gary Koelling, two corporate marketers, wanted to tap into customer insights from the front lines. Using open-source software and parts salvaged from other projects, they started Blue Shirt Nation, a community and social network that focuses on the blue-shirted sales associates who work on the retail floor. Instead of making Blue Shirt Nation a top-down initiative, Bendt and Koelling hit the road, visiting stores to build enthusiasm for the project from the ground up. By October, the online site had grown to 14,000 members, mostly blue-shirt staffers, representing 10 percent of all full-time Best Buy employees.

As with so many other groundswell projects, Blue Shirt Nation evolved in directions beyond its original intent. Associates on the sales floor used the site to lobby for (and eventually receive) their own e-mail addresses, partly by proving how useful such contact channels could be in selling to customers. More importantly, Blue Shirt Nation has now become a useful support forum that helps improve the operational efficiency of the company. Through the site, employees often spontaneously help each other solve retail problems—for instance, a new store display that isn't working as designed—that in the past would have taken weeks to work their way up and down the management ladder.

Making Social Applications Work

In our research, we have interviewed managers and employees at more than a hundred companies that were rolling out social applications. These organizations ranged from media to health care, from financial services to consumer packaged goods. Some sold to consumers; others to businesses. They operated not just in the United States but in places as diverse as South Africa, Korea, France, and Canada. Regardless of the type of organization, the result of embracing the groundswell was the same: a cultural shift in a customer-centric direction.

But anything that changes culture tends to face resistance. This is especially true of groundswell applications because they require managers to embrace an unknown communications channel, one that responds poorly to attempts to control it. Based on an analysis of how companies succeeded or failed in deploying social applications, we derived these key managerial recommendations for any organization attempting to harness the power of the groundswell.

Accept the Loss of Control

Because they involve people banding together, social applications often move in unexpected directions. Consequently, in addition to careful planning (as for any advertising campaign or IT project rollout), social applications also require flexibility and nimbleness on the part of their creators. Within these newly formed communities, popular movements can arise that might make some executives uneasy (such as the uprising of Best Buy employees demanding e-mail). But managers should recognize that, if the desire and need are present, people will tend to find ways to connect in the broader Internet anyway. Companies are better off figuring out ways to manage that communication channel in-house so that the organization can reap its benefits.

Expect Pushback from Managers

Connecting with the groundswell tends to challenge internal boundaries. In fact, groundswell initiatives can easily reach across departments, including product development, marketing, customer support, and public relations. As such, they frequently elicit resistance from senior managers. Many groundswell projects have flopped not because of a lack of support from frontline employees, but because they were blocked by executives in traditional roles, including brand managers, chief marketing officers, CIOs, and corporate attorneys.

Line Up Executive Backing

To avoid such departmental turf wars, groundswell initiatives require the support of a senior executive with clout. At Dell Inc. it was Michael Dell, company founder and CEO, who helped ensure that managers were on board. "The tendency is to get wrapped up in the organization itself," Dell explains. "I didn't really tolerate a lot of resistance, to tell you the truth." Much of the change at Dell came from the hard work of Bob Pearson in corporate communications; Manish Mehta, who ran the support communities; and Lionel Menchaca, who was responsible for writing the company's blog. Michael Dell empowered those individuals and backed them up. At Best Buy, it was Barry Judge, chief marketing officer, who provided Steven Bendt and Gary Koelling with the resources and political cover to grow Blue Shirt Nation unencumbered. Without such sponsors, social applications face long odds of succeeding.

Start Small and Focus on Measurable Objectives

Groundswell projects that start small will seem less threatening to the powerful status quo within a company, and their limited budgetary impact will keep them under the radar until they have proven themselves. A focus on well-defined objectives will enable social applications to spread through the organization based on measurable successes that can be duplicated or extended. If a company is dead set against projects that tap into a customer groundswell, then the organization might consider commencing with an initiative that instead focuses on employees (such as the Blue Shirt Nation project at Best Buy).

Expand beyond Projects

Savvy managers know that any success with social applications will only strengthen their position for extending their work through the organization, and the learning and cultural change from such initiatives can spread from department to department *if* senior executives give the managers in charge of the groundswell effort the opportunity and resources to build on their success. With support from its president, for example, Fiskars was able to extend its online network by adding regular videos and a blog for crafters. Best Buy's internal social network now includes many of its senior executives.

Stay Focused on Culture, Not Technology

What's really changing at companies like Fiskars, Best Buy, and Dell? The applications might vary widely, as do the technologies used to implement them. But this is not about "embracing Web 2.0," as the technology-focused cognoscenti have put it. It's about embracing customers and their ideas. Although Michael Dell played a key role in providing the necessary support and political cover, the groundswell effort at Dell was hardly a top-down initiative—embracing a social application never is. The crucial thing to remember is that Dell always kept focused on the company's culture of engaging with customers and valuing their input. The technologies deployed were merely the means to achieve that goal.

WORTH THE EFFORT?

Groundswell customer applications can generate research insights, extend the reach of marketing, energize sales efforts, cut support costs, and stoke the innovation process. (And for companies like Best Buy that tap into employee groundswells, the result can be increased opportunities for collaboration across departments and geographical locations, as well as greater productivity and decreased inefficiencies.) But the greatest benefit might be cultural. At Salesforce.com, the product development and marketing departments fight far less about priorities, because both are now focused on the customers' needs, as defined by information from the IdeaExchange social application. That result is typical: As companies adopt social applications, political boundaries tend to weaken. Groundswell applications can change the culture of a company because they help weave two-way customer communications into the fabric of an organization.

This new way of thinking tends to spread. At Dell, the customer support forum, blog resolution team, and "Direct2Dell" blog were only the beginning. The company now has a blog for investors, where people can read and comment on the latest financial announcements. In addition, Dell has built on the success of its support forum by creating an idea community (much like that of Salesforce.com) that has already led to the rapid

Using Social Applications in Different Departments

Companies can deploy social applications in different departments to accomplish a variety of objectives.

Manager's role or department	Typical groundswell objective	Appropriate social applications	Success metrics
Research and Development	Listening: Gaining insights from customers and using that input in the innovation process	• Brand monitoring • Research communities • Innovation communities	• Insights gained • Usable product ideas • Increased speed of development
Marketing	Talking: Using conversations with customers to promote products or services	• Blogs • Communities • Video on user-generated sites	• Better market awareness • Online "buzz" • Time spent on sites • Increased sales
Sales	Energizing: Identifying enthusiastic customers and using them to influence others	• Social networking sites • Brand ambassador programs • Communities • Embeddable "widgets"	• Community membership • Online "buzz" • Increased sales
Customer Support	Supporting: Enabling customers to help one another solve problems	• Support forums • Wikis	• Number of members participating • Volume of questions answered online • Decreased volume of support calls
Operations	Managing: Providing employees with tools so that they can assist one another in finding more effective ways of doing business	• Internal social networks • Wikis	• Number of members participating • Increased operational efficiency • Decreased volume of e-mail

Figure 7.2

development of a line of Linux PCs. And Dell has given Bob Pearson a new title—vice president, communities and conversations—with a staff of 40 people dedicated to all of the various community programs. Pearson's charter is straightforward: expand how customers are involved in all of Dell's activities.

As a result of such groundswell efforts, Dell now has multiple social applications that provide a series of touch points with customers. By its own estimate, Dell now annually logs 100 million customer touches, or interactions, through all of its online initiatives. Managers in companies like Dell are becoming used to the practice of checking in with their customer communities to test new ideas, and for those that resonate, they're able to proceed with implementation more quickly. "I think being more closely connected with customers gives you deeper and better insights . . . and speeds reaction time," asserts Michael Dell. "I think it's had a very positive effect on the way our teams think about the customer."

Because of the newness of the technologies involved, few businesses have progressed far along the process of transforming themselves into becoming truly customer-centric, but more and more organizations are heading in that direction. The kind of direct, two-way contact that social applications create is infectious, and the benefits build as companies become more adept with these new ways of doing business.

But like all powerful forces, the groundswell has its share of risks. When Wal-Mart Stores Inc. created a social application for college students on Facebook, the application became a magnet for anti–Wal-Mart comments and discussion. When Chevy hosted a site where customers could edit clips to create their own commercials, environmentalists used that technology to post ads that dramatized how SUVs contribute to global warming. Managers should be aware of such risks, but perhaps the greater danger is to ignore the groundswell or to place too many restrictions on social applications, thus slowing down their adoption and possibly rendering them useless in the end.

The potential benefits of direct and intimate customer relationships that social applications can provide are just too compelling for companies to deny. Nevertheless, embracing the groundswell is certainly no panacea for whatever deficiencies a business might have. But as consumers around the world increasingly turn to social technologies, organizations can't pretend the phenomenon isn't occurring. Long term, engaging with the groundswell is the best possible way to promote customer-centric thinking within companies, because it confronts managers with very direct evidence of how customers think. There is no hiding from the groundswell.

8

Internet 2.0: A Dual-Edged Sword for Work-Family Balance

Cheryl L. Adkins and Sonya F. Premeaux

The introduction of the Internet, along with changes in communication technologies such as the increased use of cell phones, and personal data assistants (PDAs), such as the BlackBerry, have radically changed the ways that workers connect with both their jobs and their families. These devices have allowed work to be conducted outside traditional office settings and outside the traditional nine-to-five workday. They also allow workers to remain connected to family members more easily while in the traditional office setting during the traditional nine-to-five workday. This flexibility and change in connectedness has many, often contradictory, implications for workers' ability to balance work and family life. On one hand, the fact that workers may more easily work from home and after hours may facilitate work-family balance (WFB). For example, a worker may work in the evening after taking time out from the work day to attend a child's school play or sporting event, work from home while caring for a sick child, or routinely work from home in the afternoons after the end of a child's school day. Thus, the Internet and new communication technologies may greatly facilitate a worker's ability to balance work and family.

Paradoxically, however, connectedness may increase work-family conflict (WFC) as work can intrude into the home domain even more. Organizations may expect workers to be connected to work 24/7 even in jobs that traditionally have not required workers to be "on call." In some workplaces, informal norms may create expectations that workers check e-mail in the evenings and on weekends. Other organizations may provide cell phones or PDAs and require that workers be available after hours. In some instances, workers may even be expected to be connected to the workplace while on vacation.

In this chapter we will describe both the positive and negative implications of the use of the Internet and new communication technologies for workers' ability to balance work and family. This is an emerging area of interest in both the popular press and in scholarly research. As we examine the positive and negative implications of greater connectedness to the workplace brought about by the Internet and other communication devices, we will present information from scholarly research on WFC and technology use. We will also incorporate information from the popular press on the impact of the Internet and communication technologies on WFB. The topic has generated a great deal of interest in both arenas. We will begin by describing the boundaries between home and work, and how the Internet and communication technologies may facilitate crossing, and even blurring, the boundaries. We will then discuss factors associated with the use of the Internet and other communication technologies. Worker preferences, sex, generation or age, workplace policies and norms, and family norms and expectations are all examined as influences on the use of the Internet and other communication technologies to remain connected with the workplace. Finally, we will discuss the implications of the use of the Internet and other communication technologies for WFB for both employers and workers.

THE DOMAINS OF WORK AND HOME AND THE BOUNDARIES
BETWEEN THEM

To begin our discussion of the impact of the Internet and other communication technologies on workers' ability to balance work and family, we must first define WFC and discuss domains of work and home and the boundaries between them. WFC is formally defined as inter-role conflict that results when an individual's participation in the work role interferes with participation in the family role.[1]

Thus, WFC occurs when the demands of the workplace interfere with the worker's ability to respond to the demands of family life. Researchers have examined a range of factors that may lead to WFC (such as the number and ages of children, marital status, eldercare responsibilities in the family arena, and workplace policies and job responsibilities in the work arena) and a range of outcomes of WFC (including job satisfaction, satisfaction with family, and stress, to name a few).

Recently, researchers have examined the ways workers establish and maintain boundaries between work and home.[2] Individuals are described as creating boundaries between work and home that are defined by both time and location. Examples of temporal boundaries are the traditional nine-to-five work day, or the hours set apart by a manager to work at home in the evening or on a weekend. Boundaries of location are exemplified by an individual's physically going to an office away from the home, or by retreating to a home office. The boundaries between home and work may create an environment that is segmented, with the work environment distinct from the home environment in terms of time and location, or integrated with an employee working from home and perhaps interspersing family concerns with work.

The degree of segmentation versus integration is determined by the demands and policies of the workplace, and by individual preferences. For example, an employee who works predetermined hours in a workplace away from home, by definition, has a high degree of segmentation between the home and the work roles. If organizational policies prevent the employee from making or receiving phone calls or other communications from home during the workday, the degree of segmentation is higher. At the other end of the spectrum, the employee who works from home and who is able to interrupt the flow of work to respond to a child's needs has a high degree of integration between the roles. The Internet and other communication technologies may facilitate the transitions between boundaries or even blur the boundaries between work and home. In situations of high segmentation, for example, a worker may use a cell phone to call home on the way from work to ease the transition between home and work. In situations of higher integration, a worker may use e-mail to remain in contact with the workplace while staying at home with a sick child, or while working from home on a routine basis. However, in integrated roles, the use of the Internet and other communication technology may lead to blurring of the boundaries and ultimately to employee stress. For example, receiving e-mails or phone calls about work while engaging in a parental activity may cause anxiety and confusion, or even resentment.[3]

Similarly, Clark developed work-family border theory to "explain how individuals manage and negotiate the work and family spheres and the borders between them in order to attain balance".[4] Clark describes borders as the "lines of demarcation between domains" and notes that they can be physical (where), temporal (when), or psychological.[5] She notes that borders may vary in permeability, flexibility, blending, and strength. Permeability is described as "the degree to which elements from other domains may enter," and flexibility as "the extent to which a border may contract or expand, depending on the demands of one domain or the other."[6] Border-keepers, domain members who are influential in defining the domain and border (for example supervisors and spouses), negotiate what makes up the domain and its borders. Border-keepers impact border flexibility as they apply their own ideas of what constitutes work and family and as they protect domains and borders. Their awareness of the other domain and their commitment to the border-crosser impacts WFB, as do domain differences and communication patterns.

The Internet and other communication technologies may facilitate the crossing of these borders by facilitating communication with family during the workday or allowing an employee to work at home to attend to family demands. However, they may also increase the flexibility and permeability of the borders beyond the desire of the worker, for example when workplace rules or norms dictate that he/she check e-mail in the evening or on weekends, or be available by cell phone during vacations.

Scholars addressing boundary theory indicate that the degree of segmentation versus integration a worker faces stems from both workplace policies and norms, his/her own personal preferences, and the expectations and preferences of other family members.[7] Border theory similarly proposes that the extent to which an individual is a central participant in a domain will determine the influence he/she has over the borders of the domain. Border theory also proposes that the degree of domain members' awareness of the worker's other domains and commitment to the worker will influence WFC.[8] Thus, researchers believe that there are distinct borders and boundaries between work and home, and that the formal policies and norms of the organization, individual preferences, and family norms and expectations all influence the ease with which an individual may move between the domains and, ultimately, that individual's WFB. The Internet and other communication technologies may ease the individual's movement between domains, but when used to a high degree may blur the boundaries between home and work.

WORKER PREFERENCES

As noted previously, workers differ in their preferences for using the Internet and other communications technologies to remain connected to the workplace and in their actual patterns of connection. For example, Annis Golden and Cheryl Geisler investigated how workers used PDAs to manage the boundary between work and home.[9] Participants used their PDAs in very distinct patterns ranging from segregating work and personal life, with more focus on work for some and more focus on home for others, to integrating work and personal life. Their results indicate that individuals have diverse and sometimes contradictory goals for boundary management and these goals can vary even within individuals. At one time an individual may desire integration of home and work while at another time desiring segmentation.

Some individuals are more likely to use connectivity behaviors, and, thus, to have more fluid boundaries between home and work. Role integration preferences exert a strong influence on communication behaviors as do a tendency toward multitasking and personal innovative behavior with information technology.[10] Further, workers with high ambition and job involvement,[11] as well as those with strong role identity,[12] are more likely to use communication technologies that allow role integration.

Sex Differences in Technology Use

Empirical evidence suggests that there may be sex differences in the use of the Internet and associated communication technologies. Wendy Boswell and Julia B. Olson-Buchanan found that being male was positively associated with using the Internet and other communication technologies to connect with the workplace after hours.[13] Ellen Galinsky, Stacy S. Kim, and James T. Bond, in a study of employees' feelings of being overworked, found that the use of technology for connection to the workplace after hours was associated with feelings of overwork.[14] They found that men were more likely than women to be connected to the workplace after hours. Another workplace survey found that men were more likely to remain connected to the workplace during vacations than were women, although a sizeable proportion of women did also (33% of men and 25% of women responding to their survey).[15] Sabine Sonnentag noted the importance of recovery time, that is, leisure time to recover from the stresses of work, and found that men were less likely than women to seek recovery time.[16] Although she did not directly examine the use of the Internet and associated communication technologies, this finding is particularly striking when combined with the above findings that men are more likely to remain connected to the workplace after hours. This suggests that the increased connectivity may serve to exacerbate the lack of recovery time.

The impact of using the Internet and other communication technologies to cross the borders between home and work may reinforce (or be a symptom of) women's traditional role as the primary caregiver of children. Noelle Chesley found that the use of cell phones to cross the borders between home and work was positively associated with WFC for both men and women, but that it was associated with family-to-work conflict only for women.[17] Similarly, Lana Rakow and Vija Navarro found that for women the use of the cell phones has extended their family responsibilities into the workplace.[18] They described this phenomenon as "remote mothering" and "the parallel shift." They even noted that early marketing campaigns for cell phones were targeted at the "supermom."

Generational Differences in Technology Use

It is also likely that there are differences in preference for connectivity associated with generation and/or age. This may be due to generational differences in the adoption and use of new technologies, or it may be due to generational differences in work values. Karen Wey Smola and Charlotte D. Sutton found evidence to "suggest that work values are more influenced by general differences than by age and maturation."[19] They also found that across all ages, there is an increasing desire for a balance between work and personal goals. Conversely, as Chesley noted, younger workers, who have grown up using e-mail, cell-phones, and other communication technologies may simply expect to be connected "24/7" and see the blurred boundaries between home and work as the norm.[20] This perspective is reinforced by a recent blog on millennials at work.[21] Millennials are defined as the generation born between 1979 and 1994.[22] This perspective suggests that this generation prefers a high degree of integration between home and work, as illustrated by the following quote, "the thought is that work is something that you do, not a place that you go."[23] Colleen DeBaise noted that flexible scheduling is highly desired by younger workers (ranking right after higher pay as a desired workplace change).[24] Karol Rose, chief marketing officer for Flex Paths, a provider of Web tools for creating flexible workplaces, noted that younger employees who have grown up with the Internet and the ability to work anywhere and anytime "come in there demanding it (flexibility); they can't function without flexibility because they've been plugged in since they were born."[25] One participant in Schlosser's study discussing the use of the BlackBerry for work noted, "I don't let it control me—That's the difference I've seen in younger people at work. They let it control them—they never take it off."[26]

Ben Anderson and Tracey Karina examined individuals' patterns of Internet use (albeit general use, not use for work) and found that there were differences in the use of the Internet by age with the youngest participants in the sample (ages 16–24) using the Internet more for Web access and less for e-mail, and the oldest participants in the sample (ages 55 and up) showing the opposite pattern of use.[27] Thus, there appear to be generational differences both in expectations of flexibility and in patterns of technology use.

WORKPLACE POLICIES AND NORMS

Workplace policies and subjective norms about communication technology use also play a role in workers' connectivity behaviors. When companies provide workers with communication devices, they create the expectation that employees will be continuously available and quick to respond.[28] One Canadian Civil Service employee observed, "I believe that while technology has increased the ability to work from the home and outside regular business hours, it has also increased the expectation that you do so."[29]

Empirical research supports this argument. Katherine Richardson and Hannah R. Rothstein explored the impact of organizational distribution of wireless e-mail devices (e.g., BlackBerry™) and laptops on connectivity behavior, an individual's use of these devices to communicate with colleagues or coworkers during non-work hours.[30] Results show that when the communication device was provided by or paid for by the employer, employees used the device more often and for longer periods of time than they would have otherwise.

The study also explored the effects of subjective norms on connectivity behaviors. A subjective norm is "a person's perception that most people who are important to him think he should or should not perform the behavior in question."[31] In regards to connectivity behaviors, subjective norms guide workers in their beliefs about whether they should be accessible to colleagues both during the workday and at night. Richardson and Rothstein found that subjective norms about connectivity did positively impact both frequency and duration of connectivity behaviors.[32] When workers believed they were expected to respond to colleagues during non-work hours, they were more likely to do so. Further, workers have been shown to match their communication technology use to that of their supervisors and to their perceptions of organizational norms.[33] Moreover, supervisors' ratings of workers' performance seem to be positively influenced by workers' technology use.

FAMILY NORMS AND EXPECTATIONS

Perceptions about subjective norms extend to home border-keepers, making border-keepers' expectations important considerations in workers' boundary-spanning behaviors. While the use of communication technologies may lead to positive outcomes due to greater flexibility in work-life borders, if family members react negatively to these blurred boundaries or to the connectivity behaviors themselves, undesirable outcomes are likely. For instance, a public relations firm founder in New Jersey discovered the hard way that text messaging and e-mailing can cause conflict and tension during personal outings. She reports friends deserting her on the beach over these behaviors on one occasion and a family member actually taking and tossing her BlackBerry in annoyance on another.[34] These behaviors reflect one end of the tolerance spectrum of family norms for connectivity. At the other end is acceptance of connectivity, whether motivated by approval or resignation. One individual from Los Angeles confessed to using his phone extensively while on his honeymoon in Europe to forge deals with clients and host a Web conference. He states that he cannot relax when he is out of touch, but, luckily for him, his wife can appreciate that.[35]

These incidents are prime examples of the findings of a recent study on "work extending technology" including laptops, mobile phones, PDAs, BlackBerries, and home computers.[36] The majority of respondents in the investigation perceived that their families understand their need to use these technologies to work during family time. On the other hand, a substantial number also stated that their families did not like it. The mixed reactions are to be expected given the mixed results of technology's impact on participants' home lives. On a positive note, respondents identified benefits including their ability to keep in contact with family while at work, ability to work overtime at home rather than at work, ability to allow family members use of the devices, ability to work from home while meeting family responsibilities, and improved WFB. On the down side, they reported that time was given to work instead of family and the devices were seen as intrusive. Similarly, Rosemary Batt and P. Monique Valcour found that technology facilitates workers' ability to juggle work and family at the same time it increases disruptions in the family domain.[37]

When it comes to workers' home lives, communication technology devices are a dual-edged sword, both allowing workers more time to attend to family issues and allowing work to encroach more frequently on family time. Families are using technology to manage their complex lives even as BlackBerries, cell phones, and e-mail eat away at boundaries between work and other facets of life.[38] Technology allows families to stay in touch and increase their family time; however, some workers have a hard time disengaging from the office, checking their messages more than is really needed, even resorting to sneaking around behind their families' backs to check messages when doing so violates the family's established norms. Children of technology-obsessed parents have resorted to, in some cases, extreme behaviors to get their parents' attention off their gadgets and on them. Some kids have hidden their parents' BlackBerries and one young child even tried to flush her mother's BlackBerry down the toilet.[39]

As workers struggle with balancing the use of communication devices for work and being present while at home, employees and border-keepers alike have tried to regulate when and where connectivity is acceptable. Some families maintain strict boundaries between work and home, with workers turning their communication devices off while at home, leaving them at the office, not answering them, or putting them in a designated place when they arrive home until it is time to leave for work.[40]

SUMMARY AND RECOMMENDATIONS

As the previous discussion has highlighted, the use of the Internet and other communication technologies for remaining connected to the workplace have both positive and negative implications for WFB. On the positive, when used properly the use of the Internet and other communication devices allows workers a high degree of flexibility in terms of both the time and the place of their work. This can be beneficial to both the employee and the organization. In a study of IBM employees, Hill and colleagues found that not only did flextime and flexplace work arrangements, facilitated by the use of the Internet and other communication technologies, reduce WFC, it also allowed workers to work longer hours before experiencing WFC.[41] Additionally, they noted that it allowed workers to work at the time of day when they can be most productive. For example, a "morning person" could work at 5 A.M. when he/she is best at problem-solving and reasoning, while a "night owl" may choose to work at midnight when he/she is at his/her best. Thus, using the Internet and other communication technologies to facilitate work outside normal "working hours" and at different locations can have positive benefits for the organization in addition to facilitating WFB.

On the negative side, as noted above, some workers report more stress and higher levels of WFC when they are expected to be accessible to their employer after hours and on weekends. A major consideration in whether the Internet and other communication technologies facilitate or hinder WFB is the controllability of interruptions. The use of e-mail and other online features to remain connected to the workplace may be less intrusive than the use of cell phones and pagers. While the employee may easily check the former at a time of his/her choosing, the latter are thought to demand more immediate attention.

Recommendations for Employers

Despite the potential benefits of workers' ability to work anytime and anywhere, excessive intrusion of work into workers' personal lives can sometimes lead to undesirable outcomes. In addition to increased WFC, incessant work or working in nontraditional settings can have a detrimental impact on work quality and can lead to increased stress. Given these negative effects, organizations need to be aware of the signals they are sending through their policies and norms regarding expectations for connectivity while away from work and for work-family integration. Employers owe it to themselves, their workers, and other stakeholders to help workers recognize when enough is enough. Following are some recommendations on how employers can facilitate WFB through control of communication technology.

Companies should help managers and supervisors recognize the potential downside of employees being too tied to their jobs and the wisdom of supporting WFB. Although many companies have work-life benefits in place, workers are often fearful of using them because they perceive that doing so can have potential negative effects on their careers.[42] Research has demonstrated that managerial support is an important factor in mitigating WFC.[43] Extending these findings to communication technology, supervisors need to be made to understand the importance of workers' disconnecting and encouraged to support workers' attempts at juggling home and work, including not only using available work-life benefits but also tuning out on a regular basis. Supervisors themselves should model these behaviors. Formal policies limiting phone calls and e-mail after hours and on weekends or informal policies about how much of these types of behaviors are acceptable may be required.[44]

Research shows that flexible work policies that are fluid and adaptable to a wide variety of situations appear to work best.[45] One company, Best Buy, has taken flexibility to new heights with its results-only work environment. Employees who are eligible for this program may work on a fully flextime and flexplace model.[46] Supervisors and employees need to figure out what works for each of them so that both embrace and honor the arrangements. Workers with flexible supervisors will likely reciprocate with flexibility of their own.

Companies should also educate workers about the importance of turning off and tuning out digital devices that allow work to intrude at home. As mentioned previously, when organizations provide or pay for connectivity devices, workers use the devices more frequently and for longer durations.[47] Perhaps these devices should come with these words of caution, "Warning, excessive use of this device may be hazardous to your WFB." Managers at companies with successful flexible work programs indicate "that they have had to find a way to make the new way of working the *expected way of working.*"[48] It seems that if workers perceive the need to be connected 24/7 when their employers provide them with communication gadgets or through workplace policies and norms, employers' permission, and even encouragement, to turn the devices off may be required for workers to do so comfortably.

Beyond educating supervisors and workers on the wisdom of disconnecting from work on a regular basis, cultural values that support family and personal roles need to be developed and nurtured. A supportive work-family culture may increase workers' resources and decrease the stress of work-family interference. Research shows that individuals may actually welcome the blurring of boundaries between home and family because integration facilitates maintaining close communication ties with family and friends[49] and a supportive work-family culture contributes to lower levels of WFC.[50] However, if cultural norms prohibit workers from making or receiving phone calls or other communications from home during the workday, integration is unlikely. Establishing formal or informal policies about what is acceptable in terms work-family integration can help alleviate workers' fears associated with family spillover into work, but policies alone are not enough. Integrating work and life and controlling communication technology's impact may require a cultural change.

Recommendations for Workers

As the previous discussion has indicated, the use of the Internet and other communication technologies to span the boundaries between home and work has both positive and negative implications for managing WFB. It is imperative that workers, in conjunction with family members and employers, actively manage these devices to facilitate this balance.

Workers should reflect on their preferences for segmentation or integration between the home and work roles, and then structure their environment to best reflect those preferences. While workplace policies may define the location of work during the traditional nine-to-five workday, a worker may choose to designate a location such as a home office for work that is performed after hours or for regular telecommuting. Workers who desire a higher degree of segmentation may choose to work exclusively from the work location or to work from a "third place" such as a café or library. A higher degree of segmentation on the temporal dimension may be achieved by simply designating a specified time period, for example, a couple of hours after children are in bed, for working from home. This is especially important with respect to availability for receiving and returning phone calls. Calls and instant messages have been found to be more intrusive, and thus more detrimental to WFB, than e-mail simply because they seem to demand more immediate attention and are more likely to directly interrupt family time.[51]

Workers should also evaluate the necessity of connectivity after hours. Boswell and Olson-Buchanan, in a study of university employees, found that workers whose jobs did not require after-hours connectivity tended to check e-mail and other communication media after hours simply because the devices were available.[52] This suggests that some workers may stay connected simply because they can. Workers should evaluate the amount of after-hours work and connectivity that is necessary, and the amount that benefits WFB. Some jobs may require that the worker be available after hours, while other workers may benefit from the flexibility that the connectivity provides.

It is vital that the worker communicate with family members to negotiate the structure for managing work and work-related communications after hours. The preferences of spouses or significant others may be incorporated in setting the structure of when and where the worker is available to receive and respond to calls, e-mails, and other work-related communications outside traditional working hours. Once the structure is established, it should be communicated to family members so that they know when the worker has set aside time for work activities and whether he or she is also available to family members at that time. Family members may be much better able to cope with any intrusions of the work environment into the home environment when they understand the expected duration of such intrusions. For example, the worker may communicate to a child that he or she must have an hour without interruption to respond to a work-related call or attend to other work matters from home, but then the parent will be available to the child for an activity at the end of that time period. Similarly, when working from home to accommodate family issues, such as a child's weather-related school closing, it may be necessary to communicate that the parent is in "work mode" for a major portion of that time.

The worker's preferences for accessibility outside the workplace and working hours should also be communicated to others in the work arena. A worker who desires a degree of segmentation should communicate to supervisors, colleagues, subordinates, and clients when he/she is available to receive and respond to phone calls, e-mails, and other communications. As discussed in the previous section, managers should actively think about the impact of high levels of connectivity on workers' personal lives, evaluate the necessity of after-hours communications, and minimize such communications when possible.

CONCLUSION

In sum, the use of the Internet and associated communication technologies represents a dual-edged sword for employees in managing WFB. The use of such technologies offers workers the ability to work anytime and anyplace, and thus to better balance the demands of work with the demands of family life. Paradoxically, this increased ability to work anytime and anyplace has sometimes resulted in expectations that employees be connected to the workplace 24/7. As we have seen, these expectations are sometimes generated by managers, but sometimes they stem from the employees themselves. To realize the positive potential for the Internet and associated communication technologies in workers' quest to achieve WFB it is essential that employers develop policies and sustain a workplace culture that supports such balance. It is also essential that workers be proactive in defining when and where they are available to their employers outside the traditional workday, and in negotiating and communicating with both employers and family members to maintain WFB. With positive communication and cooperation between employers and workers the full potential of the Internet and associated communication technologies to facilitate both increased productivity and better WFB may be realized.

NOTES

1. Jeffrey Greenhaus and Nicholas J. Beutell, "Sources of Conflict between Work and Family Roles," *Academy of Management Review* 10, no. 1 (1985): 76–88.

2. Blake Ashforth, Glen E. Kreiner, and Mel Fugate, "All in a Day's Work: Boundaries and Micro Role Transitions," *Academy of Management Review* 25, no. 3 (2000): 472–491.

3. See Note 2.

4. Sue Clark, "Work/Family Border Theory: A New Theory of Work/Family Balance,"*Human Relations* 53, no. 6 (2000): 747–770, 750.

5. Ibid., 756.

6. Ibid., 756, 757.

7. See Note 2.

8. See Note 4.

9. Annis Golden and Cheryl Geisler, "Mobile Technologies at the Boundary of Work and Life," *Human Relations* 60 (2007): 519–551.

10. Katherine Richardson and Hannah R. Rothstein, "Examining the Situational and Individual Correlates of Workplace Connectivity Behavior," Paper Presented at the 2008 Academy of Management Annual Meeting, Anaheim, CA.

11. Wendy Boswell and Julie B. Olson-Buchanan, "The Use of Communication Technologies after Hours: The Role of Work Attitudes and Work-Life Conflict," *Journal of Management* 33, no. 4 (2007): 592–610.

12. Julie Olson-Buchanan and Wendy R. Boswell, "Blurring Boundaries: Correlates of Integration and Segmentation Between Work and Nonwork," *Journal of Vocational Behavior* 68, no. 3 (2006): 432–445.

13. See Note 11.

14. Ellen Galinsky, Stacy S. Kim, and James T. Bond. *Feeling Overworked : When Work Becomes Too Much* (New York: Families and Work Institute, 2001).

15. Deborah Rothberg, "BlackBerry on the Beach: You Call This a Real Vacation?" *EWeek*, June 9, 2006.

16. Sabine Sonnentag, "Recovery, Work Engagement, and Proactive Behavior: A New Look at the Interface between Nonwork and Work," *Journal of Applied Psychology* 88, no. 3 (2003): 518–528.

17. Noelle Chesley, "Blurring Boundaries? Linking Technology Use, Spillover, Individual Distress, and Family Satisfaction," *Journal of Marriage and Family* 67, no. 5 (2005): 1237–1248.

18. Lana Rakow and Vija Navarro, "Remote Mothering and the Parallel Shift: Women Meet the Cellular Telephone," *Critical Studies in Mass Communication* 10, no. 2 (1993): 144–157.

19. Karen Wey Smola and Charlotte D. Sutton, "Generational Differences: Revisiting Generational Work Values for the New Millennium," *Journal of Organizational Behavior* 23, no. 4, Special Issue: Brave New Workplace: Organizational Behavior in the Electronic Age (June 2002): 363–382, 379.

20. See Note 17.

21. J. F. Barrett, *Work-Life Integration = New Hotness*, May 5, 2007, http://millennialsatwork.wordpress.com/2007/05/05/work-life-integration-new-hotness/ (Accessed February 19, 2009).

22. See Note 19.

23. See Note 21.

24. Colleen DeBaise, "Work & Life: Flextime for Employees," March 25, 2008, in *SmartMoney*'s Small Business Site, http://www.smsmallbiz.com/bestpractices/Balancing_Work_and_Life_Flextime_For_Employees.html(Accessed February 24, 2009).

25. Ibid.

26. Francine Schlosser, "So, How Do People Really Use Their Handheld Devices? An Interactive Study of Wireless Technology Use," *Journal of Organizational Behavior* 23, no. 4, Special Issue: Brave New Workplace: Organizational Behavior in the Electronic Age (June 2002): 401–423, 416.

27. Ben Anderson and Tracey Karina, "Digital Living: The Impact (or Otherwise) of the Internet on Everyday Life," *The American Behavioral Scientist* 45, no. 3 (November 2001): 456.

28. Katherine Rosman, "BlackBerry Orphans," *Wall Street Journal Weekend Journal*, December 8, 2006, W.1.

29. Ian Towers, Linda Duxbury, Christopher Higgins, and John Thomas, "Time Thieves and Space Invaders: Technology, Work and the Organization," *Journal of Organizational Change Management: Space and Time and Organisation Change* 19, no. 5 (2006): 593–618, 615.

30. See Note 10.

31. Martin Fishbein and Icek Ajzen, *Belief, Attitude, Intention, and Behavior: An Introduction to Theory and Research* (Reading, MA: Addison-Wesley Publishing Company, 1975), 302.

32. See Note 10.

33. Jeanine Warisse Turner, Jean A. Grube, Catherine H. Tinsley, Cynthia Lee, and Cheryl O'Pell, "Exploring the Dominant Media: How Does Media Use Reflect Organizational Norms and Affect Performance?" *The Journal of Business Communication* 43, no. 3 (2006): 220–250.

34. Colleen DeBaise, "Balancing Work and Life: Goodbye Crackberry?" December 11, 2007, in *SmartMoney*'s Small Business Site, http://www.smsmallbiz.com/technology/Goodbye_Crackberry.html.

35. Ibid.

36. See Note 29.

37. Rosemary Batt and P. Monique Valcour, "Human Resources Practices as Predictors of Work-Family Outcomes and Employee Turnover," *Industrial Relations* 42, no. 2 (2003): 189–220.

38. Christopher Farrell and Ann Therese Palmer, "The Overworked, Networked Family," *Business Week* 3953, (October 3, 2005, 68–73.

39. See Note 28.

40. See Note 38, 28.

41. Jeffrey Hill, Alan J. Hawkins, Maria Ferris, and Michelle Weitzman, "Finding an Extra Day a Week: The Positive Influence of Perceived Job Flexibility on Work and Family Life Balance, *Family Relations* 50, no. 1 (January 2001): 49–58.

42. Marian Ruderman, Laura M. Graves, and Patricia J. Ohlott, "Family Ties: Managers Can Benefit from Personal Lives," *Leadership in Action* 26, no. 6 (2007): 8–11.

43. Sonya F. Premeaux, Cheryl L. Adkins, and Kevin W. Mossholder, "Balancing Work and Family: A Field Study of Multi-dimensional, Multi-role Work-Family Conflict. *Journal of Organizational Behavior* 28, no. 6 (August 2007) : 705–727; Linda Thiede Thomas, and Daniel C. Ganster, "Impact of Family-supportive Work Variables on Work-Family Conflict and Strain: A Control Perspective," *Journal of Applied Psychology* 80, no. 1 (February 1995): 6–15.

44. See Note 11.

45. Fred Van Deusen, Jacquelyn B. James, Nadia Gill, and Sharon McKecknie, "Overcoming the Implementation Gap: How 20 Leading Companies Are Making Flexibility Work," *Boston College Center for Work & Family*, 2008.

46. Frank Jossi, "Clocking Out: Best Buy's Novel Come-and-Go-as-You-Please Work Style Is Pleasing Employees and Catching on Elsewhere," *HR Magazine*, 2007.

47. See Note 10.

48. See Note 45, 6.

49. Judy Wajcman, Michael Bittman, and Jude Brown, "Families without Borders: Mobile Phones, Connectedness and Work-Home Divisions," *Sociology* 42 (2008): 635–652.

50. See Note 43.
51. See Note 17.
52. See Note 11.

SUGGESTED READING

Conley, D. *Elsewhere, U.S.A.* New York: Pantheon Books, 2008.

Frase-Blunt, Martha. "The Busman's Holiday." *HRMagazine* 46, no. 6 (June 2001): 76–80.

Galinsky, Ellen, Stacy S. Kim, and James T. Bond. *Feeling Overworked: When Work Becomes Too Much.* New York: Families and Work Institute, 2001.

Jossi, Frank. "Clocking Out: Best Buy's Novel Come-and-Go-as-You-Please Work Style Is Pleasing Employees and Catching on Elsewhere." *HR Magazine* 52, no. 6 (2007): 46–50.

Kossek, E. E., and S. J. Lambert, ed. *Work and Life Integration: Organizational, Cultural, and Individual Perspectives.* Mahwah, NJ: Lawerence Erlbaum, 2005.

Robinson, Joe.. An E-Tool Bill of Rights. http://www.fastcompany.com. December 19, 2007 (accessed December 10, 2008).

Van Deusen, Fred, Jacquelyn B. James, Nadia Gill, and Sharon McKecknie. Overcoming the Implementation Gap: How 20 Leading Companies are Making Flexibility Work. *Boston College Center for Work & Family.* 2008.

9

How Can Web 2.0 Help Increase Consumer Adoption of Sustainable Products?

Jason D. Oliver

Sustainable products are produced in a way that minimizes the negative impact of production, consumption, and/or disposal on the planet. The definition from SustainableProducts.com, a Web site designed to promote the understanding and usage of sustainable products, suggests, "sustainable products are those products providing environmental, social and economic benefits while protecting public health, welfare, and environment over their full commercial cycle, from the extraction of raw materials to final disposition."[1] Therefore, understanding how to increase consumer adoption of sustainable products is extremely important to long-term consumer welfare.

Companies are attracted to sustainable efforts because they have the potential to generate goodwill from consumers and profitability for shareholders. For example, following a third-quarter sales loss in 2007, Hershey's appealed to shareholders with an announcement they were moving away from specialty chocolates, like truffles, to invest in more sustainable product offerings.[2] Barneys New York has an eco-area in their store and sponsored an eco-fashion show in 2008. The goal of these and other efforts, including donations to help others or help the earth with every purchase, is to provide an added value or extra benefit to one's consumerism—the opportunity to benefit others.[3] In addition, Web sites like Greenopia serve those interested in sustainability by providing independent reviews of services and products based on the products' efforts to protect the planet and its inhabitants.[4] The demand for information about sustainable products is a testament to its importance to consumers.

However, there are challenges associated with getting consumers to adopt sustainable, or "green" products. According to a recent Mintel Reports, most consumers are interested in environmentally friendly and natural products but are willing to sacrifice sustainability when economic times are difficult.[5] In addition, despite manufacturer efforts to improve the performance of sustainable products, consumers are hesitant to buy them because they still perceive that buying sustainable products means paying more for products that have inferior quality.[6]

Consumers are also skeptical of company motives and claims regarding sustainability because companies have exaggerated their efforts to benefit the greater good in the past. In one case, Procter & Gamble's claims that Swiffer was an eco-friendly product came under attack on two popular environmental blogs (inhabitat.com and treehugger.com). Giofranco Zaccai,[7] the CEO of Continuum, a design consultancy, praised the Swiffer as an example of profitable sustainability because it saved millions of gallons of water, the energy needed to heat the water, and prevented detergents from being dumped into the earth. The blogosphere responded by calling Swiffer "the epitome of waste" because the disposable cloths leaked chemicals into the soil and water and take a long time to disintegrate, accusing Zaccai and Procter & Gamble of greenwashing, or trying to pass off an unsustainable product as eco-friendly.[8] Mixed messages are likely to increase consumer confusion and skepticism about the value of sustainable products.

Further, consumers are confused by sustainable product labeling practices. For example, Katy McLaughlin[9] indicated that although consumers felt it was trendy to buy sustainable products, they were overwhelmed by certifications and labels that range from "Fairly Traded" to "Fair Trade Certified" and from "Sustainable" to "Sustainable Certified." In addition, companies often publicize efforts toward sustainability without having to adhere to shared standards regarding what it means to be sustainable. Therefore, consumers are skeptical of how buying and using sustainable products will benefit them.

The latest iteration of the World Wide Web provides some unique opportunities for promoting sustainable consumption. The interactive component of Web 2.0 allows the audience to voice their concerns and validate information from companies in real time. Therefore, it is important to examine how Web 2.0 can help overcome challenges associated with the promotion of sustainable products and increase the rate of sustainable product diffusion.

DIFFUSION OF SUSTAINABLE PRODUCTS

As with any new type of product, different variables and other factors trigger product adoption. Thomas W. Valente describes the diffusion of a new product as "a communication process in which adopters persuade those who have not yet decided to adopt."[10] Consumers gain knowledge about the new product or idea, are persuaded or form attitudes toward the innovation, and make a decision to adopt or reject the innovation.[11] The Rogers theory on diffusion of innovations model has long been used to assess the likelihood of product adoption in the marketing literature. Thus, this framework, applied in Figure 9.1, is utilized as a means of understanding sustainable product adoption.[12]

The complete process of new product introduction from a few involved individuals to a general audience of consumers is usually associated with Rogers's diffusion of innovations.[13] Several key constructs have been demonstrated to influence product adoption. However, adoption patterns for sustainable products are different from adoption patterns for other types of products because existing perceptions about sustainable products are a source of resistance. Therefore, the role of selected constructs, related barriers in the context of sustainable products, and the ways Web 2.0 can be used to overcome these barriers are summarized in Table 9.1. Each construct will be discussed in the context of one type of sustainable product: an environmentally friendly product aimed at end-consumers.

ENVIRONMENTALLY FRIENDLY PRODUCT ADOPTION

Environmentally friendly products are designed to minimize the environmental impact when they are consumed.[14] Green products are important to firms because social responsibility and environmental issues are important to consumers. Although a poor environmental reputation will not make the average shopper avoid the latest must-have item, brands in mature markets with little product differentiation are vulnerable to competitors with a more responsible image. Generally, a company's efforts toward social responsibility and environmental sustainability receive more favorable product evaluations from consumers than less responsible organizations.[15]

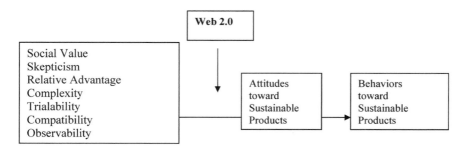

Figure 9.1 Sustainable Product Adoption Model

Table 9.1 Factors Affecting the Adoption of Sustainable Products

Factor	Effect on Adoption	Barriers in Sustainable Product Adoption	Web 2.0 Tools
Social Value	Increases Adoption	Social value changes locally as sustainable products fall in and out of style.	Use peer-to-peer networking to help potential adopters be influenced by a broader social network—and current users a platform to be recognized for their adoption.
Skepticism	Decreases Adoption	Many consumers believe that companies are not honest about sustainability efforts.	Consumers will use collective intelligence to verify or nullify company claims.
Relative Advantage	Increases Adoption	Consumers have the perceptions that they pay more for less (sustainable products traditionally do not perform as well and are more expensive).	Increase value with customized products and unique user experiences. Decrease perceptions of inferiority with customer reviews and dynamic product information.
Complexity	Decreases Adoption	Concerns about sustainable product performance increase complexity and fear.	Dynamic user help and live agent help can overcome concerns regarding product complexity.
Trialability	Increases Adoption	The difference attributed to sustainable attributes may be difficult to test or try in advance of usage.	Use podcasts and video casts to demonstrate the product or create simulated usage scenarios.
Compatibility	Increases Adoption	Sustainable products may require changes in usage behavior.	Increase compatibility with customized products that make behavior change desirable and convenient.
Observability	Increases Adoption	Many sustainable products are consumed privately.	Collective intelligence, peer-to-peer networking, podcasts, and video casts can increase observability of others who have adopted.

Despite the advantage of favorable product evaluations, environmentally friendly products have not been widely adopted. The barriers to adoption include higher prices and lack of consumer confidence that the green products will perform as well as traditional products.[16] In a 2002 Roper survey, 41 percent of consumers said they did not buy green products because they worried about the diminished performance of environmentally friendly versions. As a result, consumers perceive that if they want to consume in an environmentally friendly manner, they will have to pay more for a product that may not perform as well as its less environmentally friendly counterpart.

As with other sustainable products, environmentally friendly products have lacked economic viability because consumers fail to see the short-term gratification associated with "going green." Consumers have a difficult time bridging the gap between existing products, which provide high levels of satisfaction, and environmentally friendly products, which may ask them to sacrifice physical, emotional, or social satisfaction at a greater economic cost. Thus, when environmentally friendly products that actually provide a better solution are introduced, consumers may still be hesitant to adopt the product based on past perceptions. As a result, consumers fail to demand environmentally friendly products even though they pay lip service to the desire to protect the environment. The majority of consumers seem to continue to value disposable, low-cost, high-performance products.[17] Web 2.0 can be a useful tool for companies that offer environmentally friendly products to overcome these perceptions and to get consumers to buy their products.[18] The role of Web 2.0 is discussed in relation to social value, consumer skepticism, relative advantage, product complexity, product trialability, product compatibility, and product observability.

Social Value

Social value is important to the diffusion of innovations because consumers do not have fixed preferences.[19] Consumers are influenced by the consumption of neighbors, coworkers, opinion leaders, and other peers. According to Guillaume Deffuant, Sylvie Huet, and Frederic Amblard, individuals assign a social value to an innovation, and that value evolves during their interactions with others and with information.[20] Thus, individuals who feel the innovation has a high social value will look for information that helps them evaluate the benefits of adoption.

In Mark Granovetter's model, the social value is directly related to the proportion of adopters in the individual's social network, representing the diffusion as a contagion process.[21] Social contagion indicates that actors' adoption behaviors are a function of their exposure to other actors' knowledge, attitudes, or behaviors concerning the innovation. When the number of adopters increases in the consumer's network of peers, the pressure for adoption also increases. The threshold for adoption is the proportion of adopters in the individual's social network that is necessary to convince him or her to adopt. For example, Marco A. Janssen and Wander Jager indicate that consumers feel satisfied when they are consuming the same way as their neighbors.[22] Similar to other types of innovations, consumers evaluate their satisfaction with green products by comparing themselves with their social group or trying to satisfy their needs by imitating people in their social group. Therefore, social influences may serve as a catalyst for environmentally friendly product adoption.

The challenge is that the social value associated with adoption of an environmentally friendly product fluctuates. In many instances there is an external factor that affects the social value of a product's adoption. A recent example of this phenomenon can be seen with gas prices and automobile preferences. Before gasoline broke the $4 dollar per gallon amount, SUV sales were at record highs. When gas prices surged, the social desirability of owning a big SUV decreased. Consumers who continued to drive SUVs were judged as insensitive in terms of their environmental awareness. However, when gas prices decreased again, the social pressure against driving cars that consume more gas subsided. This is important because when consumers base their decisions on what others are doing, they may change their minds when the social situation changes, and the consumer may switch back while consumers who deliberate and figure out what they think on their own are more likely to be locked into existing consumption patterns.

Further, many environmentally friendly products are lower involvement. Unlike higher-involvement products, which often times are symbols of status, luxury, and personal identity, lower-involvement products are less likely to be consumed publicly. Thus, the way others perceive consumer use of products is likely to be a less important factor in lower-involvement environmentally friendly product-adoption considerations.[23] Because the social value affects whether or not consumers talk about the product, an innovation that has a high-perceived social value is more likely to be considered and passed along to others. Therefore, the adoption of lower-involvement environmentally friendly products is less likely to be motivated by social value, and the social value associated with higher-involvement environmentally friendly products is only useful when environmental issues are "in vogue."

The Role of Web 2.0

People who are less certain about what to do on their own are likely to focus their decision-making on the behaviors of others, even if it neither satisfies their own needs nor leads to the adoption of the most environmentally friendly option.[24] Web 2.0 can expand a consumer's social network so they are exposed to others who are adopting sustainable products. For example, Toyota launched a micro-site for hybrid drivers where they could share their experiences and reasons for driving a hybrid. This type of social network would be especially useful for promoting consumption of environmentally friendly products that are consumed privately or are not popular in a consumer's geographic region.

Thus, Web 2.0 can be used to develop peer-to-peer networking capabilities that help potential adopters reach a broader social network. These networks can also be used to provide current users with a platform to share their praises and concerns regarding a particular green product. Consumers may actively try to persuade non-adopters. In addition to providing potential consumers access to authentic advocates for adoption, existing consumers can be recognized for their adoption.

Consumer Skepticism

Another reason for lack of adoption of green consumer products is that consumers lack trust in environmental product claims. In fact, nonspecific environmental claims on packaging often scare consumers away.[25] Based on the results of a study by Les Carlson and his colleagues, this lack of trust may be justified.[26] Carlson and his colleagues found that 60 percent of environmental claims on products were either inaccurate or false. Some firms use environmental marketing and other forms of cause-related marketing as a form of sales promotion that happens to tie in with a social issue, leading consumers to question the firm's motives and the value of their effort.[27]

Other firms have been accused of "greenwashing," or publicizing environmental efforts to make them seem more important to consumers than they are. Living Green, a Boston-based consumer organization, nominates the top 10 greenwashers each year on April Fool's Day. Vague labels certifying eco-friendliness, falsely labeled organic goods, or trade policies that hurt the environment earn companies a spot on the list.

In addition, some companies use one environmental aspect of their product to overshadow other parts than might not be so environmentally friendly. Some examples include General Motors for their dichotomy of large SUV and hybrid models under the same umbrella brands, and low-involvement products like Herbal Essences shampoo, which has conflicting sustainability information.[28] The generalization of environmental claims, which are usually designed to promote something positive about the company, can backfire exponentially when claims are only partially true or over-exaggerated. Further, consumers often disbelieve information about a company's sustainability efforts due to poor experiences in the past.

The Role of Web 2.0

Web 2.0 can provide tools to activate collective intelligence. Consumers who contribute to collective intelligence can help verify or nullify company claims. Thus, companies doing the right things will be more effective in communicating about their efforts because word of mouth from another consumer is deemed more reliable than advertising from the firm. Companies can provide a platform for their consumers to validate their claims.

In contrast, and perhaps more threatening from a company perspective, consumers can uncover a false or incorrect sustainability claim and broadcast it like never before. Once posted, it doesn't take long for information, positive or negative, to disseminate throughout a company's target market. This activity is not in the hands of the company, and at best they can react to it, often well after the damage has been done. In actuality it is the presence of Web 2.0 that may force companies to verify sustainability claims before they are made and promoted. Ultimately, this benefits both efforts toward sustainability and companies who are being honest about their efforts to create environmentally friendly products.

Other Characteristics Affecting the Adoption of Sustainable Products

Rogers (1995) separated out the five perceived characteristics that constitute the perception of an innovation in an effort to explain the effect of perceptions on the adoption of the innovation.[29] The attributes are the following: relative advantage, complexity, compatibility, trialability, and observability.

Relative advantage is a better way to accomplish a goal (economic, social prestige, other benefits outweigh switching costs, learning costs, uncertainty). The aspects of relative advantage that matter the most to consumers depend on the nature of the innovation. For example, a new product based on a technological advance that reduces production costs may be evaluated as having a relative economic advantage. Potential adopters are motivated to understand whether a new idea or product is better than the existing alternatives. In the context of environmentally friendly products, they are likely to evaluate whether the car lowers their initial cost, lowers their ownership costs, increases their social prestige, saves them time and/or effort, or rewards them in another way. The challenge associated with the adoption of environmentally friendly products is that they are often perceived to be at a disadvantage relative to less environmentally friendly options. In spite of efforts by companies like Patagonia to improve quality and performance, consumers often feel they are sacrificing quality and paying more for an inferior product when they buy green.

Complexity is the degree of difficulty presented to the user based on their understanding of the innovation. It is important because the more difficult a product is to understand and use, the less likely consumers are to adopt the product. It has been shown to affect the rate of product adoption in the context of personal computers. Concerns about sustainable product performance can increase perceptions regarding the product's complexity and raise consumer fears, decreasing adoption. This fear may be higher for high-involvement product categories.

Compatibility is consistency with existing values, experiences, needs, and existing consumption patterns. It is important because if a product is not compatible with cultural values, the product will not be adopted. Compatibility with social values has been shown to affect the rate of product adoption in the context of agriculture, bar code readers, and fertilizer. Products have to be compatible with existing products and with consumer needs in order to be adopted. Increasing perceptions of compatibility increases the rate of adoption. If environmentally friendly product usage changes the way consumers need to behave, they are less likely to adopt the product.

Trialability is the ease with which the user can test innovation. It is important because when users can try an idea in small doses or ease into an innovation gradually, they are more likely to adopt the innovation. It has been shown to increase the rate of product adoption because it allows consumers to reduce their sense of risk associated with the adoption of the innovation. The difference attributed to sustainable attributes may be difficult to test or try in advance of usage.

This obstacle may involve availability. Toyota dealers often have limited shipments of the Prius (the most successful hybrid car in the world). As a result, it is difficult for a potential buyer to make an informed decision. Sustainable products may require changes in usage behavior. Many sustainable products are consumed privately. In contrast to buying a hybrid car, many sustainable product decisions involve low-involvement products. These include, but are not limited to, paper towels, tissue, soap, detergent, shampoo, and toothpaste. These products are not all around for potential consumers to try them in advance. Further, consumers may have habitual purchasing patterns for these lower-involvement products.

When products are easy to observe, it also lowers the perceived risk associated with product adoption. Observability is the degree to which results are visible to others or one can observe others using the innovation. Observability also increases the rate of adoption, and was a key driver in the rapid adoption of Nintendo game systems and cellular telephones. For lower-involvement and privately consumed environmentally friendly products, the inability to directly observe others using the product can be a barrier to adoption.

The Role of Web 2.0

The five characteristics described by Rogers are features that will influence the majority of a population to adopt a new innovation. The capabilities of Web 2.0 should enable the real-time communication that can enhance perceptions regarding the relative advantages of an environmentally friendly product, minimize concerns regarding complexity, provide virtual trial and demonstrations, provide dynamic and user-generated information regarding the compatability of the product with the consumer's lifestyle, and expand the consumer's social network and make typically unobservable product usage observable.

Marketers can use Web 2.0 to overcome perceptions that an environmentally friendly product does not have any advantages relative to alternatives. Marketers can increase the value a consumer associates with a product by offering customized products and/or unique user experiences. Web 2.0 storehouses make it easy to dynamically generate options that enable customization.

In addition, Web 2.0 can be used to provide forums for customer reviews. The interactive capabilities of Web 2.0 facilitate user posts of any product, including sustainable ones, which can convey advantages and disadvantages. A sustainable product can be compared to competing brands and allow potential customers to read through reviews. Web 2.0 can also be used to generate dynamic product information. This process should make the research process both quicker and easier. It is important that consumers who are engaged in active searches for product information find the right information when they are searching.

Web 2.0 can also help marketers overcome concerns regarding environmentally friendly product complexity using dynamic user help. Giving consumers the ability to drill down easily on frequently asked questions may alleviate concerns they will not be able to handle environmentally friendly version of a product. Similarly, live agent help can provide direct human contact, at a relatively low cost, to answer questions directly and overcome concerns regarding environmentally friendly product complexity. In addition, consumers can view and respond to posts to understand challenges other consumers have encountered.

Given the availability issues with sustainable products, Web 2.0 can use podcasts and video casts to demonstrate the product or create simulated usage scenarios. User feedback also provides observable feedback from others that may substitute for product trial. Dynamic content can include an online tour of an environmentally friendly product. It can also enable customization that can improve the fit, which may offset inability to gain direct experience with the product. A customer can obtain some useful indirect experience that should help them with their decision-making process.

Potential customers can research a variety of aspects concerning sustainable products and see if a particular product is substantially different from the products they are used to buying. They might look to see how other people with similar values are respond to a product they might be interested in purchasing. Increase compatibility with customized products that make behavior change desirable and convenient.

Because not all sustainable products are consumed publicly, Web 2.0 provides an opportunity that has been missed since the beginning of the environmental movement. Someone who just wants to find out about what sustainability is will have the opportunity to read and discuss both ideas and products that comprise a sustainable lifestyle. A simple online search could connect a person with people all over the world who can answer questions and recommend products. Collective intelligence, peer-to-peer networking, podcasts, and video casts can increase observability of others who have adopted the product.

CONCLUSION

Despite improvements in quality and reductions in price, consumers are not responding to sustainable products. Web 2.0 can help break down the barriers to sustainable product diffusion. When used properly, companies can provide information as well as create interactive product experiences. This will allow existing and potential customers to explore the sustainability aspects of any company. From a new product perspective, people can virtually handle and test the product before they actually see it in a retail setting. Consider this list of Do's of how to encourage sustainable product adoption using Web 2.0:

- Do provide an online outlet for customers to share experiences.
- Do, when necessary, use promotional or reward tactics to encourage customer conversations online.
- Do monitor online forums to gauge consumer perceptions in the marketplace.
- Do have all information related to the environmental impact of products available to consumers.
- Do, when possible, track customer experiences, both good and bad.
- Do incorporate customer feedback into product offerings whenever feasible.
- Do get out ahead of problems, whether from a public relations standpoint or product development perspective.

In addition, there are several "don'ts" that can benefit the firm seeking to practice enhanced sustainability.

- Don't use different or conflicting terminology to describe the environmental friendliness of a product.
- Don't let customers discover and then broadcast false environmental claims.
- Don't hide or make vague environmental claims (which can often be just as damaging as making false claims).
- Don't make environmental claims without validating them first. Validation should occur both in-house and from independent third parties.

- Don't forget to consider all aspects of the product when making an environmental claim. This includes raw materials, manufacturing, distribution, packaging, product usage, and disposal.
- Don't ignore online consumer conversations or buzz related to specific products or the company in general.
- Don't allow a mistake or oversight regarding an environmental claim to dampen the commitment to sustainable product development.

Web 2.0 empowers the consumer like never before; companies are finding out the hard way that it does not take long for consumers to research their sustainability claims and report the good or bad news. Consumers can communicate with each other online where sustainability claims are put to the test. Consumers are also helping each other learn about sustainability online. Companies can add their own tools and information to improve the diffusion process.

Past perceptions about green products, most of them negative, still linger in consumers' minds. This new online environment provides consumers the opportunity to talk about sustainable products with all kinds of users. Through Web 2.0 tools, questions can be answered, experiences posted, frustrations vented, and success stories shared in a setting that ultimately influences consumer decisions to adopt sustainable products.

NOTES

1. "What Are Sustainable Products?," Sustainable Products Corporation, http://www.sustainableproducts.com/susproddef.html.

2. Jonathan Birchall, "Chocolate Maker to Raise the Bar on Marketing," *Financial Times*, October 19, 2007, 17.

3. Vanessa Friedman, "Shopping for Absolution," *Financial Times*, March 22, 2008, 7.

4. Shivani Vora, "Are You Looking for an Environmentally Friendly Dry Cleaner? Greenopia Can Help You Out," *Inc.*, 30, no. 12 (2008): 34–35.

5. Mintel International Group, "Environmentally Friendly Cleaning Products," January 2009.

6. GfK Roper Consulting, "Green Gauge Report," 2002.

7. Giofranco Zaccai, "Matching Sustainability with Profits," *Business Week*, February 21, 2007, http://www.businessweek.com/innovate/content/feb2007/id20070221_603937.htm?chan=innovation_innovation+%2B+design_insight

8. *Business Week*, "A Debate Over 'Greenwashing'," July 16, 2007, http://www.businessweek.com/innovate/content/jul2007/id20070713_936726.htm

9. Katy McLaughlin, "Is Your Grocery List Politically Correct? Food World's New Buzzword Is 'Sustainable' Products," *Wall Street Journal*, February 17, 2004, D1.

10. Thomas W. Valente, *Network Models of the Diffusion of Innovations*, Hampton Press, 1995.

11. Everett M. Rogers, *Diffusion of Innovations*, 4th ed. Free Press, 1995.

12. Ibid.

13. Ibid.

14. Michael J. Polonsky, Les Carlson, Andrea Prothero, and Dimitri Kapelianis, "A Cross-cultural Examination of the Environmental Information on Packaging: Implications for Advertisers," *New Directions in International Advertising Research*, 2002, 21–30.

15. Tom J. Brown and Peter A. Dacin, "The Company and the Product: Corporate Associations and Consumer Product Responses," *Journal of Marketing* 61, no. 1 (1997): 68–84.

16. Ajay Menon and Anil Menon, "Enviropreneurial Marketing Strategy: The Emergence of Corporate Environmentalism as Market Strategy," *Journal of Marketing*, no. 61 (January 1997): 51–67.

17. See Note 6.

18. Arnt Meyer, "What's in It for Customers? Successfully Marketing Green Clothes," *Business Strategy and the Environment* 10, no. 5 (2001): 317–330.

19. Jennifer L. Aaker, "The Malleable Self: The Role of Self-expression in Persuasion," *Journal of Marketing Research*, 36, no. 1 (1999): 45–57.

20. Guillaume Deffuant, Sylvie Huet, and Frederic Amblard, "An Individual-based Model of Innovation Diffusion: Mixing Social Value and Individual Benefit," *American Journal of Sociology*, no. 110 (2005): 1041–1069.

21. Mark Granovetter, "Threshold Models of Collective Behavior," *The American Journal of Sociology* 83, no. 6 (1978): 1420–1443

22. Marco A. Janssen and Wander Jager, "Stimulating Diffusion of Green Products: Co-evolution between Firms and Consumers," *Journal of Evolutionary Economics*, no. 12 (2002): 283–306.

23. Jane Hickie, Ellen Konar, and Steven Tomlinson, "Aligning CSR with Power: Two Pragmatic Strategies for Transformational Change," *Center for Responsible Business Working Paper Series*, Paper 26, March 1, 2005, http://repositories.cdlib .org/crb/wps/26

24. See Note 11.

25. Joel J. Davis, "Strategies for Environmental Advertising," *Journal of Consumer Marketing* 10, no. 2 (1993): 19–36.

26. Les Carlson, Stephen J. Grove, Norman Kangun, and Michael J. Polonsky, "An International Comparison of Environmental Advertising: Substantive Versus Associative Claims," *Journal of Macromarketing* 16, no. 2 (1996): 57–68.

27. P. Rajan Varadarajan and Anil Menon, "Cause-related Marketing: A Coalignment of Marketing Strategy and Corporate Philanthropy," *Journal of Marketing* 52, no. 3 (1988): 58–74.

28. Shirlee Deen, "Don't Be Fooled: America's Ten Worst Greenwashers," *Valley Advocate*, August 29, 2002.

29. See Note 11.

10

CONVERSATIONAL MEDIA

Scott Sherman

Consumers are evolving at the same time advertising media are evolving. However, the two evolutions are not working in tandem. Meanwhile, the Internet continues to revolutionize communications. The result is a new era in brand communications. One of the resulting opportunities is that consumers are talking with consumers about brands (companies, products, and services) in new and exciting ways—and brands need to know how to communicate in this new era.

MEDIA'S PERFECT STORM

Immediately after the dawn of commerce, there was the dawn of commercial communication—also known as advertising, public relations, and "branding" (a new term). From the moment of the first commercial pitch, without a mere moment to come up for a breath, there has been a growth in the amount of advertising. Year after year and century after century, consumers have accepted the increase in branded messages. Sure, there's been an outcry when advertising invades a new space (such as when ads started to be played before motion pictures in the movie theater). But for the most part, the public has accepted more and more advertising. That is until recently. Consumers finally have reached their limit; they are oversaturated with advertising.

Consumers now are better than ever before at ignoring ads. A TV show's audience was at one time the advertiser's captive audience. Now, every TV comes with a remote giving channel surfers the ability to avoid ads by simply moving one digit of their thumb. With cable and satellite TV, channel surfers received a plethora of places to wander during commercials. Then came TiVo and people could watch hours of primetime TV without seeing a single ad. DVRs, devices (like TiVo) that allow viewers to skip TV ads, are in 29 percent of homes in the United States in 2009. That's up 7 percent from the previous year.[1] This ad avoidance phenomenon is happening in other media, too.

And, if this weren't bad enough, people are just getting better at ignoring ads that they are exposed to. Consumers' level of disdain for seeing ads has reached its highest level ever. I don't even like advertising interruptions, and the ad business has given me a good career. So I can't blame the general public for their disdain.

There was never a time when people believed everything they saw in advertisements. Audiences have always been skeptical of ads and rightly so. However, today's consumers are more cynical and unbelieving than every before. This makes it harder for brands to make a connection with consumers.

Media fragmentation and media multiplication make for media complication. Traditional ways to advertise include the five traditional media—TV, radio, newspapers, magazines, and outdoor (billboards). The popularity of the Internet has added a sixth media channel (online advertising) to the mix. Only 25 years ago, there were three major TV networks. There was an era when advertising during prime time on those three networks could reach 80 percent of the households in the United States. Back then, most households got a newspaper delivered to their doorstep every day. The University of Southern California reports that 80 percent of Internet users (age 17 and older) consider the Internet to be an important source of information—higher than television (68%), radio (63%), and newspapers (63%). Hence, newspaper subscription numbers are dropping.[2] In the last 25 years the number of magazines has gone the other way; it has doubled. Instead of general, broad-appeal magazines like *Life* and *Reader's Digest*, today's magazines focus their editorial toward specific audience interest. Now three different national magazines are dedicated to crocheting. Now, homes with a satellite dish can receive hundreds of channels. Cable homes don't get that many, but the options are plenty. With satellite radio, iPods, video games, Netflix, and Blockbuster, the American public simply has a lot more home entertainment options that involve consuming media without advertising.

At the same time, advertisers are having a hard time getting noticed by consumers, brands are having a harder time standing apart in the marketplace. It's more competitive than ever for brands. The relative cost to bring a product to market continues to drop. Distribution is relatively easier and cheaper than ever so it's easy for regional brands to expand into new territories. It is cheaper today simply to knock off a successful product as compared to designing and engineering a totally new one. This phenomenon creates low product differentiation among competitors. There are more and more product options for consumers. Visit a supermarket and count the brand options for basic things like mayonnaise and ketchup (or catsup). Stroll down the aisle to salad dressing and the options can be overwhelming. The options for beverages (sodas, juices, beer and wine) are mind blowing. The marketplace today is full of competitors having a harder time communicating with consumers.

Meanwhile the scope for common people to communicate has grown enormously. Just 20 years ago if a company wanted to tell a million people about their product, they used one of the traditional media (TV, radio, newspapers, or magazines). There were only a few people who had access to these media because the cost was too high for the average citizen to afford it. So if a normal citizen wanted to tell a lot of people about something without spending a fortune, they could write a letter to the editor or post a sign along a busy street, but that was about it. With the Internet, people have recently been given the tools to easily communicate with millions of other people.

Citizen communicators now have an unlimited reach, and the time needed to create communications now is just seconds. People can communicate on experiences within moments. By using a cell phone, *citizen reporters* send news around the world as it happens—stories, photos and video. Disgruntled customers can air their grievances within moments of a dispute. And, happy customers can share their stories as they happen. An avid blogger, Chris Brogan, tells of a time when he was traveling to give a speech at a conference.[3] Just before leaving for New York City, he mentioned on Twitter that he was on his way. (Twitter is a social networking Web site that allows people to quickly post short messages called tweets.) Within moments two different friends suggested that he stay at the Roger Smith Hotel because it had a special offer. Then moments later the hotel's marketing coordinator sent him a note to say they'd love to have him at their hotel at a discounted rate, and he offered Brogan an upgrade to a bigger room. Then the hotel took it one step farther. Brogan describes it on his blog: "They throw a tweet up for all the Twitter folks who want to come by. This is hosted by the hotel's other social-media star, Brian Simpson, who between the two of us, gathered up quite a crowd of folks to an event where they bought the drinks, and where we had a little space just for us." Why did the Roger Smith Hotel do this? Brogan says, "Where will I stay the next time I go to New York? Who did I talk about every time someone asked me where I'm staying?" Brogan says that he mentioned the hotel during his presentation the next day, and he posted a video of the hotel on his blog. That could not have happened 15 years ago.

Chris Brogan's story demonstrates the speed with which communication happens now. And it demonstrates the possible geographic reach available at everyone's fingertips. Brogan's blog has nearly 20,000 subscribers.

A clear change is happening in media. There are new ways for companies to communicate with consumers, for consumers to communicate with companies, and for consumers to communicate with other consumers. Media evolution or revolution; media democratization or saturation; media fragmentation or multiplication? It doesn't matter. What matters is that changes in media mean changes in conversations.

CONVERSATIONS

Last month my friend's car broke down . . . again. Sarah didn't want to spend any more money fixing it . . . again. It had too many miles, and it was costing her a lot to keep it on the road. Plus, she wanted a car that was more reliable and got better gas mileage. She had been sort of thinking about a new car for quite a while, so she had done a little research online. Now that it was decision time, Sarah did something that many of us do . . . she phoned a friend. She called Leon (another friend of mine).

A few years ago Leon purchased a hybrid car, a Toyota Prius. Hybrids had been on the road for a few years, but they were still a new phenomenon. Before buying it, Leon was skeptical about the ROI on a hybrid—the extra cost versus the higher miles per gallon. Leon did a lot of research, and eventually took a leap of faith. For the first several months, he was doubtful that he made the right decision—buyer's remorse. Over two years and 26,000 miles later, Leon is now very happy with the car.

Sarah knew that Leon drove a hybrid. She also knew that Leon is not a motor head (he doesn't even rotate his own tires). I'm sure Sarah knew that Leon couldn't give her any real specifics about the car, its engine, the interior space, or the number of horsepower. But she called Leon anyway. And Leon, in all of his mechanical ignorance, influenced Sarah's car-purchase decision more than any of her research, more than any of the ads, and more than the salesperson's pitch. Within a day of talking with Leon, Sarah owned a brand-new Prius.

What if companies could motivate happy consumers (like Leon) to talk to potential consumers (like Sarah) about the company's products?

There are two ways to get people to talk about a company. One is to cross your fingers and hope that people will talk. The story about my friends and their hybrid cars is an example. The other way is to help spark the conversation, to encourage a discussion, and to make it easy for people to talk about your company.

Is Starbucks coffee so much different from other coffee brands that it commands the conversation it gets? Compare a Harley Davidson motorcycle side-by-side to the rest of the pack of motorcycle brands and see if the Harley deserves all of the attention. To make something that people want to talk about doesn't take a national distribution. Local companies and local brands all across the nation have loyal followers who sing their praises. Think of the best restaurants in your neighborhood or town. Think of the restaurants that are always pretty full. Are they all national chains with hundreds of locations? Likely not. Some (if not all) of the best restaurants are locally owned and operated, and they aren't advertising on the TV. To make something that people want to talk about doesn't take a national advertising campaign. (Please note, many of the examples used in this book are national brands only because everyone is familiar with those brands. If I talked about Ukrop's Super Markets, the Byrd Theater, and the Jefferson Hotel you would only be familiar with their work if you were from Richmond, Virginia. And if you are from Richmond, you know that these are companies that locals talk about.)

How does Harley get talked about more than Honda, BMW, and Ducati? Simply put, they make something that people want to talk about.

WHAT SPREADS?

How can brands develop an effective brand conversation that will lead to something bigger called conversational media?

If you want to get your consumers to talk about your company, you need to listen first. What do consumers think about your brand? What do they think about your competitors? Traditional media create a one-way conversation—a brand is talking *at* a potential consumer. This model was fine when it worked well, and this model is still fine if you can afford to use the traditional media.

To get your consumers to talk about you, they need to feel a connection to your brand. People don't care about a brand unless it connects with them. It's not enough to satisfy the consumers' material needs with a good or service. Satisfying a material need will work for a short while, but soon a competitor will come along and offer the same good or the same service for a cheaper price. Then your company has entered the dismal swamp of price competition—a lose-lose situation for you and your competitor. Sooner or later, a competitor will come along and do more than provide an adequate service or an adequate product to satisfy the consumers' material needs. That competitor will create an emotional connection between their brand and the consumer.

People don't buy Starbucks coffee because they are thirsty or need a hit of caffeine. There were many places for consumers to get hot coffee. In fact, 7-Eleven serves coffee that performs well in blind taste tests. There's too much competition in the marketplace for products to merely serve customers on the material-need level. Today's customers expect more than that, and the competition is offering it. Customers today want to connect emotionally with the things they buy.

Customers weren't feeling a connection to 7-Eleven and the coffee it offered. Customers want to spend their money with brands that offer the consumer a sense of identity, and they are willing to pay a premium for it. This is where Starbucks fits in.

People shop at certain grocery stores because those stores make them feel a certain way; it's grocery fashion. People buy certain brands of beer so that others can see them holding the bottle in their hand; it's beer fashion. In the same way, Starbucks is coffee fashion. And, when you can turn your company, your service, or your product into a fashion, then your customers will "wear" your brand like a fancy outfit to a party. They will proudly sing the praises of your brand. Developing a fashion-like brand experience can be done for plumbers, roofing companies, financial analysts, adult diapers, and law firms. Virtually any product or service can turn its brand into a fashion-like brand for a segment of the market. Building this connection with consumers will allow you to leverage the relationship to gain more consumers and to charge a premium price for it.

Like the whims typical in the fashion world, styles come and go. No matter how practical, logical, and functional a fashion piece is, it sometimes doesn't catch on and become mainstream. The mainstream, mass-marketed consumers are not the goal. Mass marketing is very expensive. Mass-market consumers are good at ignoring mass-media messages. The era of mass-market media is becoming a harder and harder place to do business. It has been replaced by targeted marketing. Focus on the narrow market that knows your product and is interested in it.

The best way to build this kind of a deep connection with customers is to talk with them (not at them). As mentioned earlier, the first step is to listen, really listen. Smart companies now have people in the marketing department whose job is to listen to the online conversation—what people are saying. Most national consumer brands have full-time listeners to monitor conversations on Twitter, in blogs, and in other social-media Web sites. The listeners' job isn't to boast about the brand in the typical, traditional-media, one-way-conversation method. The listeners' job is primarily to listen to the conversation. Sure, if there is incorrect information being sent around the world, a listener will add to the conversation to right the wrong.

A *BusinessWeek* article calls Comcast's Frank Eliason "the most famous customer service manager in the US, possibly in the world." In early 2008 Eliason searched for "Comcast" and "Comcrap" in Twitter and found that Comcast customers were complaining about the company and its service.[4] Through tweets (those short messages on Twitter) Eliason began using this online platform to hear what customers were saying. Then he began a dialogue with unsatisfied Comcast customers. He has since handled over 26,000 messages on Twitter (and counting). When discovering an unhappy message online about Comcast, Eliason usually sends a simple note, "Can I help you?" The Comcast Cares page on Twitter features a nice photo of Eliason and this intro, "Hi, my name is Frank Eliason. I am the Director of Digital Care for Comcast. We look forward to listening to your feedback and helping when we can." Many technical problems are handled outside of Twitter because of the limited dialog (Twitter only allows messages of 140 characters per tweet), but Twitter is a great way to open a dialog with customers. For Comcast, there's a clear benefit from listening to people on Twitter—better customer service. However, there's another benefit of having a director of digital care. What do a lot of satisfied customers do after Eliason fixes their problem? They tell the world about their positive Comcast experience through Twitter and other online media.

GETTING PEOPLE TO TALK

Using social media like Facebook, Twitter, blogs, and chat rooms is not the simple answer to getting consumers to talk about your great product. In fact, brands that jump into social media are in danger of alienating the very consumers with whom they want to engage. Brands are used to talking at consumers and controlling the conversation. Brands need to learn to listen and speak with consumers in new ways.

The conversation needs to be genuine. It needs to be credible from the consumer's point of view. It cannot feel like an advertising message. Visit Comcast Cares and watch how Frank Eliason ends the conversations. He simply says, "Glad I could help." Genuine. How would it feel if Eliason ended each successful interaction with this phrase, "Thank you for choosing Comcast. We hope that you will choose Comcast for all of your TV, phone, and Internet needs. Please tell a friend that Comcast cares." I feel dirty just writing it. As Eliason wrote on Comcast Cares (as a response to a customer inquiring about his marketing role), "I try not to really have a marketing message, although servicing customers is a marketing message by itself."

To get consumers to spread a message about a company to others, the feeling of advertising needs to be nearly nonexistent. This also means that the company cannot sensor negative messages. In fact, some negative messages add to the authenticity of the site. Watch Comcast Cares and you'll see some colorful language from customers who are clearly angry with Comcast.

It's okay to have an advertising aspect to the conversation, but the consumer needs to be comfortable with it. How much of a brand message is too much and alienates the audience? It depends on your consumers' comfort zone and it depends on the payoff they receive from the message. Netflix, the online DVD rental site, gave subscribers one free month of service for each subscriber they recruited. As an added bonus, the new subscriber got a free month, too. This was a successful promotion especially when the service was new. Netflix recruited their current customers to recruit new customers by offering each a free month of movies.

At a party recently, a friend of mine was telling a group of us about Clear, a company that verifies the customers' identities and credentials. Clear takes images of members' irises and fingerprints so members are allowed to go past long security lines at airports. Andy is a frequent traveler, so this service is perfect for him, and he loves it. Clear also has a "Refer-A-Friend" program where the referrer and the referred earn an extra month membership (just like Netflix). In the middle of the party, Andy was using his BlackBerry to e-mail all of us his referral code to secure his extra free months of membership. Clear motivated Andy to tell many of his friends about the service. In fact, Andy was acting more like a salesperson motivated by commission. Was Andy interested in helping his friends zip past the long lines in airports or was he interested in the free months? A little bit of both, and that's what really made this an effective campaign. Andy was genuinely interested in telling friends about this new service (because Clear is a cool new product and it makes Andy look cool), but each free month gave him the incentive to e-mail everyone right then.

Companies need to be creative to find the balance to allow their customers to be genuine while at the same time to spread the word about the brand. If Andy were *not* a frequent flyer or a casual user of Clear, would he have sent e-mails to his friends while at a party? Probably not. Andy is clearly an evangelist—a brand ambassador for Clear.

Examine your customers and pick out people like Andy; they are your strongest advocates—people who genuinely love your products or services. Approach those evangelists with premiums or special offers to refer new customers to you. Most customers, regardless of how much they love your brand, will not promote your brand without a payoff. Remember Leon (the Prius owner) was willing to tell Sarah about his hybrid car after she asked him about it. What could Prius have done to motivate Leon to talk with friends (like Sarah) *before* she asked him about his car? What would it take to make Leon an evangelist for Prius just like Andy is for Clear, the airport security service? Successful payoffs depend on the consumer, the coolness factor, and the brand fashion.

Some customers like to receive early releases of your new products to try or to demo. Take that idea further, and give these select few customers a platform to discuss these products in public or on your Web site. Leverage these relationships as advertising opportunities. How can you make your customers be your evangelists for your brand? Customers will want to talk about your brand if it makes them feel privileged, feel ahead of the trends, feel successful, and feel other positive emotions. This is what fashion is all about. Apple has successfully used this method many times. Steve Jobs, Apple's charismatic CEO, invites 100,000 fans from all over the world to go online and watch him introduce Apple's newest product in front of 5,000 people live. This allows the tried and true Apple fans to be the first to know all about the newest Apple gadget. It's fashion.

When there's a new Harry Potter book or a new episode of Star Wars released, it's the same thing. Fans enjoy being the first to get the book or to see the movie even if it means standing in line outside of a store at midnight. They know the book will still be available on the store shelves in the morning. That's not the point. This experience gives them a wonderful way to connect to the brand, to be part of the select tribe, and it gives consumers something to brag about for at least a couple of weeks.

Jorge is the technology manager in my company, and he loves technology fashion. When a new software program is being tested, he receives a beta version to test out before it hits the market. He loves talking with his friends and colleagues about versions of software that aren't out yet. Version 2.4 is so passé; version 3.0 is much more fashionable. Jorge's free beta copy is a good investment because Jorge tells everyone about the new version. When the real version of the software is ready to hit the streets, who gets a free copy? Jorge—this gives him another reason to tell everyone about the product. "I got the new X Software 3.0 last week. I had the beta, and the street version is a little better." This makes Jorge really cool—software fashion.

Software companies have connected with Jorge because he buys a lot of software. He makes purchase decisions for his employer. Jorge also has a circle of influence beyond his coworkers. He is a member of a broad and informal technology community of people who enjoy computer hardware and software. Humans are social beings, and social creatures like to be part of a pack, a flock, or a community. We like to associate with like-minded people. These groups help us make sense of our lives and our priorities. They reinforce our decisions and confirm our identities. Gathering into his community is natural for Jorge, and it's a common trait for all consumers.

To be most effective, these groups or communities must have an aspect of distinction or uniqueness because it tends to generate more conversation. People don't brag about being a mammal (not exclusive), but they do wear tattoos proudly telling the world that they served in the U.S. Marine Corps (not everyone has the guts to do that). Consumers of Macintosh computers make up about 20 percent of the U.S. personal computer market. They are rare in the ubiquitous PC world. You'll see Mac users proudly wear the little apple logo on their T-shirts and car windows. One might expect to see 80 percent more T-shirts and stickers for Dell, HP, and Toshiba, but it doesn't work that way. Those brands have not developed a sense of tribalism like Macintosh.

Jorge aspires to be a leader and an influencer in his high-technology peer group. He craves acknowledgment from other members of the loosely defined group. Technology companies who connect with Jorge have secured an unpaid sales person, and they have initiated a conversation about their products.

What Spreads?

A few years ago someone discovered that dropping a Mentos candy into a two-liter bottle of Diet Coke creates an explosion. Immediately from the top of the soda bottle, brown foam shoots two-stories high into the air. It's an amazing sight. A couple of guys in Maine decided to create something interesting by dropping Mentos into many bottles of Diet Coke.

They call themselves EepyBird, created a Web site (www.eepybird.com), and got to work on The Extreme Diet Coke & Mentos Experiments (that's what they call it). "Our first video . . . went online at EepyBird.com on Saturday, June 3, 2006. We told one person. He told some friends . . . They told some friends . . . Within hours, thousands of people were coming to see the video. That Monday morning, the *Late Show with David Letterman* called. It was that quick. Three weeks later, we were headed to New York to appear on Letterman, the *Today Show,* and more!"[5] According to Eepy-Bird's Web site, Mentos sales increased 15 to 20 percent and traffic to Coke.com doubled. As EepyBird shows us, one of the key elements to creating conversational media is a WOW! factor. What spreads is something worth talking about. Dropping Mentos into Diet Cokes is interesting. Doing it with 200 liters of Diet Coke and 500 Mentos in a choreographed display is worth talking about. One video alone has had more than 8 million viewers, and they have many videos. This is a great example of the WOW! factor—one of the key elements to making conversational media that spreads. To get the biggest bang for your buck with the WOW! factor, you need to have something unexpected. Unfortunately these types of surprises don't maintain attention for a long period of time. For long-term attention, we must do things to develop curiosity and to generate interest. The trick to long-term interest is to continuously develop curiosity in the audience. Tell them things that interrupt their continuity of knowledge. Throughout a lecture many effective speakers (especially college professors and preachers or ministers) will pose problematic situations to their audience as a way to interrupt the audience. This unexpected break in knowledge (and subsequent solutions) engages audiences over the long term.

The folks at EepyBird clearly made something that grabbed our attention long enough to watch their three-minute video. Go to their Web site and see what they are doing to generate interest for long-term attention.

There are a few other basic ingredients to making stuff about your product (branded content or conversational media) that people want to talk about and want to hear about. In order to make something that millions of people want to know about, it needs to be easily tellable—a simple idea that can easily be told in a story. The best kinds of stories are emotional and tangible. The story about Mentos and Diet Coke shows the power of the WOW! factor. The story is easy to understand and easily told to another person. It was tangible and it was emotional (funny and amazing). Let's look at these other factors in spreading information: core ideas expressed in tangible, tellable, and emotional stories.

Tellable and Core

If you want one of your customers to talk about your brand, you need to make it easy for them. The best way to do it is to put it in the form of a story with a clear, core idea that the audience can relate to. A clear, core idea is a simple idea, but not ideas only for the feeble minded. The story Al Gore tells in *An Inconvenient Truth* is about a scientific and technical subject (global warming), but he digested the technical data and scientific complexity down to the essence of the idea. Then he makes it tellable by presenting it in a series of stories that nonscientific people can relate to. Stories are important because they are memorable. Stories allow our minds to group somewhat unrelated facts together so that our memory can recall them easier. One way to remember a person's name is to put it into a story. I learned this trick from Ray Herder, a man I met only once over 15 years ago. He used his name to develop a story about a cowboy that used a ray gun to herd his cattle. I remember thinking that Ray Herder is a space cowboy. Regardless, I still remember that guy's name (but I don't remember what he looks like).

If we ask 10 people to remember three facts and recite them to others, chances are all ten people couldn't do it perfectly. If we wrap a story around these three facts and ask 10 people to retell the story, most people would be able to remember the three key elements of the story. The details of the story will change, but the key elements of the story would remain. Stories are easy to remember and better yet, stories are easy to retell to others.

There's a well-known adage that if you say three things, you say nothing. So edit the big ideas of your brand down to their essence by focusing on their most important parts. Wrap those core elements into a tellable story that your customers can tell. This will be something that your consumers will understand, remember, relate to, and spread to others.

Tangible

This is one of the hardest aspects for many business people to execute. Talk about your ideas in terms that relate to people's senses (smell, touch, see, hear, and taste). Business people tend to talk in abstract terms, and customers tend to react to real, tangible things. Instead of saying that the goal is to become the market leader, say that you need to sell 100 shoes every day. Analogies and comparisons are often used to take something from abstract to something more tangible. It's common for people to describe the size of a tumor in terms of fruit. Saying that the tumor was 63.47 cubic inches means nothing to many people so a doctor might say that the tumor was the size of a grapefruit. The grapefruit description is less accurate than 63.47 cubic inches because there are big grapefruits and little grapefruits, but grapefruits are tangible and cubic inches are not. Hurricane Katrina caused enough damage for Federal disaster declarations to 90,000 square miles or an area twice the size of Ohio. The concept of two Ohios isn't very tangible, but it's more tangible than 90,000 square miles.

Abstract things are harder to remember than tangible ones. Without looking in the previous paragraph, can you remember the size of the tumor? Did you remember it in terms of fruit or could you remember the number? Another benefit of tangible terms is that they tend to make things sound more realistic. People are more familiar with things they see, hear, and touch. Tangible descriptions will make your stories and your brand more realistic, more believable, and more authentic. Consumers gravitate to brands that are more authentic to their lives. Talking in tangible terms will help make consumers remember your brand and connect to your brand.

Emotional

One cannot watch a TV show (without TiVo) without noticing the use of humor in advertising. Funny ads make people feel good things about the brand, and that makes it easier for consumers to connect to the brand. People like to be entertained, and funny ads get noticed. The use of humor represents about a quarter of the TV ads in the United States.[6] Humor is just one of the effective emotions used to make communications more interesting: fear, guilt, jealousy, love, sex, attractiveness, hate, anger, happiness, and many more. Depending on the brand, the audience, and the message, it's possible to use any emotion effectively in your communications. Emotional messages make quick connections to people. They grab the audience's attention, and they make them care about your message. There's a saying in nonprofit advertising that if you want people to care, talk about one victim; people are less emotional about groups of victims. That's why we see only a few dogs on ads for animal shelters. That's why children's charities often feature one child in need. In the ad we learn her name, what she likes to do, and where she lives. The more we know about the girl in need, the more we care about her, and the more we'll donate to help her. Emotions make the audience care. Several notes of caution about the use of emotions:

- Don't use humor unless it's really funny, and most people aren't really funny.
- They say that sex sells, but it's not always appropriate. Tread lightly here.

The goal is a simple one: Design your brand so there's something to talk about and there's a connection to your loyal consumers. Then develop a story that is about the core ideas told in tangible, tellable, and emotional terms. Add in a WOW! factor and you'll have a story that can spread. Find out who your die-hard customers are (your evangelists) and get them to tell your story to everyone they know. Give your evangelists a payoff and the platform to talk about you and they will.

BUILDING CONNECTIONS

The audience, the message, the communicator, and the media are core elements in all communications. They work together in advertising differently from one campaign to the next. Likewise they work together differently in advertising as compared to public relations, and as compared to consumers' conversations. In conversational media (the advertising of the future with smaller budgets and targeted audiences), we spread the message through our brand evangelists (our loyalist customers). We need to compensate our evangelists with premiums, status, or a little fame. In advertising, the message in consumer conversations often needs to be designed to encourage catching on and spreading. Not all consumers will connect to your brand or embrace your brand message, but that's how it works with the big-budget ads, too. In advertising, companies spend a lot of time and money to learn about the audience. We need to know about the audience in consumer conversations, too. In advertising, creative people spend a lot of time figuring out what to say and how to say it. The message needs to be well designed or engineered to be successful in consumer conversations, too. Back in the days of mass-media advertising the most important thing was to build a connection from your brand to your audience. As media evolve, consumers evolve, and brands evolve, building connections continues to be paramount.

So the next time you're watching a TV show or a sporting event and it's interrupted by a commercial, don't reach for the remote. Just ignore the expensive ads talking *at* you, and use those two minutes to think of ways you can build connections with your customers.

NOTES

1. Joanne Ostrow, "Network TV Is Going down the Tubes," *Houston Chronicle*, February 16, 2009.

2. University of Southern California Annenberg School for Communication, "The World Internet Project: International Report 2009," www.digitalcenter.org.

3. Chris Brogan, "Café Shaped Business—The Roger Smith Hotel," www.chrisbrogan.com/cafe-shaped-business-the-roger-smith-hotel.

4. Rebecca Reisner, "Comcast's Twitter Man," *BusinessWeek*, January 13, 2009.

5. "EepyBird Experiment 137," EepyBird, http://eepybird.com/dcm1.html.

6. John Philip Jones, *The Advertising Business* (Thousand Oaks, CA: SAGE, 1999), 238.

SUGGESTED READING

Cesvet, Bertrand, Tony Babinski, Eric Alper, and Sid Lee. *Conversational Capital: How to Create Stuff People Love to Talk About.* Upper Saddle River, NJ: FT Press, 2008.

Godin, Seth. *Tribes: We Need You to Lead Us.* New York: Penguin Group, 2008.

Li, Charlene, and Josh Bernoff. *Groundswell: Winning in a wWorld Transformed by Social Technologies*. Boston: Harvard Business School Publishing, 2008.

Micek, Deborah, and Warren Whitlock. *Twitter Revolution: How Social Media and Mobile Marketing Is Changing the Way We Do Business and Market Online*. Las Vegas: Xeno Press, 2008.

Vollmer, Christopher, and Geoffrey Precourt. *Always On: Advertising, Marketing, and Media in an Era of Consumer Control*. New York: McGraw-Hill, 2008.

11

BRAND FANS: WHEN ENTERTAINMENT + MARKETING INTEGRATE ONLINE

Robert V. Kozinets

FANS ARE FREAKS

There's just no getting around it.

Fans are freaks. They're nerds and geeks, outsiders on the margins, losers and weirdos, lonely, awkward, deviant pocket-protector-wearing young men stumbling around with nothing better to do with their time and their lives. Get a life, fanboy. That's just the way it is.

But if that's the case then *why should companies want people to be fans of their brands*? Think about it. Who would want cretinous creeps to be their key consumers or losers to be their main users or misanthropes as the main market mavens? Does an insufferable eccentric make a good influential? What kind of marketing is that? Sure, there's an emotional attachment. But is it really of value when the attachment is to someone no one wants to be like or be around?

The first argument I'm going to make in this chapter to answer that question is that consumer culture and pop entertainment culture have collided and intermingled, and so fans—a certain kind of fan, at least—aren't on the margins anymore, if they ever were at all.

Fans, the fanatics, the word deriving from *fanaticus*, the one who belongs heart and soul to a particular temple but applied, more generally, to the Church of Mass Culture, are important. They are important because what is commonly dismissed as popular and trivial is important. How many people have watched a Shakespearean play in the last year? How many watched an episode of Australian or Asian or Indian Pop or American Idol? How much money was spent mounting ballets and operas? How much creating Hollywood blockbusters? Which, then, is more "important" to our current culture? Economically, socially, culturally—in terms of the devotion and reception of resources?

Entertainment fans aren't on the margins. On the contrary, they have been the cultural mainstream for over a half-century. And the commercial culture of corporations selling products and services and the entertainment culture of Hollywood glitz and glamour are like the peanut butter and chocolate of the old Reese's Peanut Butter Cup commercials. They are just two great consumer tastes that go great together.

Soap and soap operas, commerce and commercials, these old pals have been smeared into a tasty admixture for a long time. And they're getting closer all the time. Procter & Gamble sponsored the early daytime television serials, and automotive companies would sponsor entire television shows. Television advertising bankrolls television production, and often contains the endorsements of celebrities within it. Movies contain product placements, often not very subtle. Selling beer, soap, Big Macs, and toothpaste goes great with *ER*, *Die Hard*, Green Day, or the Super Bowl. And television and radio advertising tells a short but complete story, a culturally influential and meaningful form of entertainment in and of itself.

In order for there to be sports events, large theatrical productions, or musical concerts, not only advertising but corporate sponsors are often necessary. They play a major part in the promotion of these entertainment events. Not only that, but the entertainment industry has become very much like any other product-based industry, with sophisticated and rapid turnover marketing dictating the moves of inventories of package and shrink-wrapped disks from retailer shelves. Entertainment is marketed like a consumer good, and consumer goods are marketed using entertainment.

Soda pop and pop culture. Marketed together, and marketed the same ways. Why wouldn't we be able to be a "fan" of both?

Inextricable Internet Intertwining

The second argument fits this book like a glove. That argument states that the Internet is playing a key role in upgrading and sophisticating the media consumption of fan communities. Not only that, but the Internet and its connectivity is absolutely complicit in the social phenomena we see turning consumers into fans, creating the phenomenon of brand fandom—not mere consumers, but not quite a regular brand or other community, either. Something a bit different: a group of people who see themselves as fans of marketplace offerings.

This intertwining of material and popular cultures has important macro and social implications on our world, trends that ramify on a global scale. As soon as one communicates, one is affecting—in however large or small a way—culture.

Popular culture is, then, by definition, amazingly influential.

Think about the influence that Hollywood and music celebrities have always had on fashion for clothing and hairstyles. There's no escape from the idea that mass communications leads to mass cultural change, and little doubt that our expanding development of information and communications technologies over the last six decades has greatly accelerated the rates of change affecting our consumer culture. Now, with the rise of the Internet age, the question becomes what happens when we allow 1 billion more people into this mass communications party, and how is it affected by the continuing intermix of popular and commercial cultures? As interested people, as marketers, as managers, and as citizens, there seem to be a number of lessons we can start to learn, some trends we can anticipate, and some tendencies we can watch out for.

This chapter is going to start with a necessarily brief overview of some essential concepts of cultures, communities, and fans, before broadening out to link media fans with the fans of brands. From there, the discussion will weave in the role of online communities and Internet connectivity, and show its place in the phenomenon. The chapter will link to some ongoing streams of theory on media and consumption, and suggest some implications for managers, marketers, and scholars.

CRACKED SYMBOLS

What exactly do we mean when we talk about consumer culture or entertainment culture? The anthropologist Clifford Geertz[1] defined culture as "an historically transmitted pattern of meaning embodied in symbols, a system of inherited conceptions expressed in symbolic forms by means of which [people] communicate, perpetuate, and develop their knowledge about and attitudes toward life." As I have written elsewhere,[2] consumer culture is related to this concept, but is more specifically an interconnected system of *commercially produced images, texts, and objects* that various types of groups use to make collective sense of their environments and to orient their members' experiences and lives. The way that they achieve this sense-making is through the uniquely cultural construction of overlapping and even conflicting practices, identities, and meanings. These meanings become embodied and negotiated by consumers when they act in particular social situations roles and relationships. Consumer culture is therefore linked to a particular historical and social configuration, a certain institutional set and setting.

Relating as much to the notion of popular culture as to the everydayness of all culture, Paul Willis[3] declared that culture is "the very material of our daily lives, the bricks and mortar of our most commonplace understandings." We can think of culture as the communicative basis for our lives. Like fish in water, we live in culture, but it is largely invisible to us. But like fish in water, the ocean contains everything that is significant to us. When we think our most private, secret, individual thoughts, we still do it in the shared language, with the common terms, and the embedded historical, social, emotional, and embodied connections of our culture. And, as we suggest here, we swim in another ocean: the intermingled symbols of consumer and popular culture.

Consumer culture is directly related to "the consumption of market-made commodities and desire-inducing marketing symbols" and that this consumption and these images are "central to consumer culture."[4] Furthermore consumer culture is a dense network of global messages and relationships through which transnational capital and the global mediascape penetrate and shape local cultures.[5]

Baked into the very notion of consumer culture is this sense that consumers consume things that are commercially produced and marketed through pervasive and persuasive mass media symbologies—not just symbols, but interlocking and systematic systems of symbols. These cultural meaning are not monolithic or total, but always fragmented and incomplete. They invite improvisation, and a vast range of types of participation. Consumer culture and its various marketplace and other incorporated ideologies may impel movement toward one dominant set of actions, interpretations, and feeling, but they can not compel it.[6] Oftentimes, this compulsion creates a corresponding resistance, sometimes playful, other times deadly serious, which, in itself, can create new forms of culture.

Pop Fragments

It is this fragmentation that should fascinate us. It should quickly becomes obvious when we contemplate terms such as "French culture," "Asian culture," or "world culture," that, as soon as we talk about any sort of culture, we're really dealing with complex interconnections of various sets of meanings, practices, and identities, which don't adhere in any simple way or form any necessarily coherent pattern. I can envision consumer culture or world culture as an almost infinite set of overlapping circles, a multihued Venn diagram stretching out to the horizon in all directions, composed of the various different groupings and elements of each individual culture.

It's in this sense that we need to think about fan culture. Fan cultures themselves contain sets of shared meanings. Fan cultures link to interconnected systems of commercially produced images, texts, and objects—as well as to all of the ancillary material produced by various corporate and other social actors and by consumers themselves relating to, expounding upon, and expanding that system.[7] These images, texts, and objects are symbols that groups of people use to make collective sense of their situations, to orient themselves, and to bring meaning to their lives on a short-term, moment-by-moment basis as well as over the long haul of life: that biggest of the big enchiladas.

One individual Madonna fan is not necessarily going to orient herself in relation to Madonna, or to other Madonna fans in the same way as another individual fan. However, we can think of groups of Madonna fans—for example her fashion-forward followers—who might tend to read Madonna and interpret her in a stylistic fashion that affects their clothing choices more than, say, the followers of Madonna who emphasize her children's books or her spiritual connection to the Kabbalah Center. Each cultural grouping might emphasize different elements of the commercial production of the entity known as Madonna. There would be enough commonality among the members who shared these meanings for them to be meaningfully considered groupings of their own. And, on a wider level, because they all had a connection to Madonna, they would all be united in the Madonna fan culture on that similar level, and probably other ones as well.

Amassing Culture

Mass media build culture. Fans of *True Blood* or *Torchwood* possess a common vocabulary of actors, incidents, languages, and episodes that allows them to instantly communicate—and even achieve rapport—with one another, even though they may never before have met. On a larger sense, our shared knowledge of key texts such as the sport of football or *Survivor*, or our knowledge of "what movies have you seen lately?" allow us common cultural ground for conversation, discussion, and communion. We can feel an instant sense of shared culture when we are rugby fans attending an All Blacks event at a stadium or sports bar, or fans of the Red Hot Chili Peppers lining up for tickets or attending a concert. Why? Because we are all partaking in the *social spoils of culture-bearing and meaning-making*. We are united in the significance of the event and the phenomenon, the significance—however allegedly and admittedly "trivial"—of its substance for our personal and collective meaning-making.

So, although the popular image of the fan is of a lonely, isolated, pathetic individual watching a television or computer screen alone in his room, this exploration of culture points out that even though the connection to a commercially produced media property may be developed on one's own, it is actually an act of cultural participation. That culture might be widely shared. It might be held closely in small groups. But because those meanings are shared, watching YouTube alone in your room or listening to music on your iPod is an inherently social activity. The vision of the loner, loser fan is not only outdated and naïve, it's wrong. If popular culture is the sea we swim in, then partaking in it in all of its forms is necessary for full social participation. Any tween or teenager in the industrially developed world almost intuitively knows this to be a fact.

Mass Comm(unity)

So how does culture then connect to community? How does fan culture become fan community? Anthony Cohen[8] states that "community is that entity to which one belongs more immediately than the abstraction we call society [or culture]." Although there are probably more definitions of community available than there are sociologists alive today, I'm going to act very unacademic, go out on a limb, and actually (over)simplify the idea by stating that, for my purposes, community exists where there is a sense that one's identity is recognized, that there is some repeat contact, some remembrance and familiarity. Community requires sharing something about your identity (and this can be a pseudonymous identity, it doesn't have to be one's actual, "real" name and face) as well as sharing cultural referents, meanings, and language—the content of the symbol system. Thus, communities tend to refer more to associations of individuals engaged in relationships involving ongoing contact, and this contact can be in-person, computer mediated, or of course both. Communities contain the personal, dyadic, or multi-player communications that people hunger for—the physical and symbolic places to connect in, build relationships, and express with other people, in an active way.

It should be obvious that community today has become much more than a shared space or place—it has morphed into a common understanding of a shared identity. Railroads, telegraphs, national newspapers, magazines, telephones, television, and national commerce fractured the previously narrow notions of community and social consciousness over the last century. Through the twenty-first century, the notion of community continues to broaden and grow as mass communications technologies and the Internet unite geographically dispersed communities and individuals and enable them to infuse one another with common purposes and identities, to share common rituals, practices, and, of course, brands.

The term "brand community" was popularized by Albert M. Muñiz, Jr., and Thomas C. O'Guinn[9] who suggested that communities based around brands possessed a number of characteristics, including that they are "stable," are "committed to both the brand and the group," are "explicitly commercial," possess a "mass-media sensibility" as well as a sense of moral responsibility, are identity-centered, have their own rituals and traditions, and can be briefly defined as "a specialized, non-geographically bound community, based on a structured set of social relationships among admirers of a brand." Although "non-geographical boundedness" seems to emphasize the virtual lack of in-person contact in these groups, many of Muñiz and O'Guinn's[10] examples are of in-person meetings and gatherings. In addition, it is questionable how structured and stable is the set of social relations that governs the brand community, how strong are their members' commitments to one another, and how pervasive are their moral sensibilities.

Many sociologists have speculated that symbolic communities such as these are a response to the breakdown of traditional structural communities such as families, religions, nation-states, and neighborhoods. Further, the loss of community allows, or perhaps even compels, people to choose to figure, refigure, and transfigure their own identities through membership in a succession of temporarily meaningful symbolic communities. We can therefore envision consumer tribes, consumption communities, communities of consumption, commercial communities, virtual communities of consumption, brand communities, product communities, service communities, retail communities, and a range of other commercially related communities coexisting with one another in a multifaceted tapestry of overlapping consumer and popular cultures, all powered by the profound and fundamental need of human beings to connect with one another. In this tapestry, we can see the patterns of brand fans emerging, a thread woven throughout all of these constructs. Contemporary society is often portrayed as deeply individualized, unstable and inauthentic, furthering a sense of alienation and disconnectedness. In such a world, the hunger for belonging, situated in the sweet spot on Maslow's hierarchy of needs, turn out to be a key driver impelling people to find new ways to connect with one another—whether through sports, at concerts, using brands, or over television shows. The medium is not only the message, the community is the message's meaning.

BEING, EXISTENCE, FANDOM

What does it mean to say that one is a fan? What can all managers and marketers learn from the study of fans? As I noted above, the word "fan," derives from a religious meaning but now is colloquial for a person who is enthusiastic about a specific sport, hobby, leisure activity, or performer. These meanings are fluid; they continue to shift—from devotees of religion to enthusiast of popular culture and leisure pursuits to followers of consumer culture, marketing, managers, companies, and brands, these are not major steps, but the following of the spreading of commitment and attention from one center of cultural endeavor to another.

Academic attempts in the field of media studies to distinguish the elements of being a fan have resulted in several defining characteristics, which are highly debatable and widely debated. These investigations link being a fan to at least five different characteristics, which are discussed in the sections that follow.

Emotional Engagement

The first and most fundamental characteristic of fandom references the enthusiastic relationship between an individual and some consumption object, such as a television. "The most obvious and frightening thing about contemporary popular culture is that it matters so much to its fans," says cultural studies scholar and rock fan researcher Larry Grossberg.[11] Attempting to define the essence of what a fan is, he considers the state of being a fan as an "affective sensibility," locating its essence in the powerful relationship between the pop culture "object" or "text" and the social and emotional life of a person. Being a fan means that a particular text matters—it is used to navigate one's way into and out of moods, relationships, life stages, issues, problems—it is a beacon for dreams and desires, a focus point for avoidances and fears. If you are a fan, the thing you are a fan of speaks to you in an authentic way. It helps to guide you to what is important in your life. It sets emotional and intellectual priorities and directs the investment of energy and effort. These investments and priorities can be big or little, major or minor, profound or superficial. But at the core of the relationship, the cultural object or text is has real impact and consequence to its fans. It matters.

Collectively, individual fans share some, or many, but by no means all, of the meanings associated with their "core texts" or "central" or "canonical" "myths." These "core texts" or "canonical myths" are the basis for the community, and they are also commercial products and/or services. A core text might be the music of the Rolling Stones, the content of the *Saw* movies, or the complete *Nip/Tuck* television show. There are considerable differences among fans in terms of how expansive these core texts can be. For example, most Rolling Stones fans will recognize "Gimme Shelter" but hardcore Stones fans may have several dozen bootleg versions of the song, recorded over four decades of concert touring. Similarly, some *Lord of the Rings* fans may love the motion picture, own all of the boxed sets versions, making-of books, and related materials, but have never read the books. Conversely, some *Lord of the Rings* fans may consider reading all of Tolkien's major works, not simply the core texts, to be essential to an understanding of *Lord of the Rings*.

Much fan activity consists of comparison and rating, considering the body of work of the object, as well as rumor-starting and news-spreading about the future: Guess what television show Britney is going to cameo on next? Guess which director is going to develop the Hobbit into a major motion picture? As well, fans often enjoy filling in the "gaps" in meaning left by the authors of the cultural text. What is Burton from Survivor really like? Was Madonna's divorce a publicity stunt? Are the survivors of Oceanic Flight 815 in purgatory? What happened to George Castanza between episodes 110 and 111 of Seinfeld?

Different fan communities may be separated by many such themes. In the *Star Trek* community, a particularly well-developed example, clubs might specialize in one species of fictional alien, one actor, one type of Starship, or one particular Star Trek series, as well as having national, regional, and local inflections. They might also be separated by level of formality and ethos. Some engage in orthodox, militaristic rituals. Others are more like drinking clubs. Others still are loose grouping of individuals who merely post messages on the same electronic forums. Yet, invariably, despite their differences, members of these fan organizations feel themselves to be connected to one textual universe and its world of fans: *Star Trek* "fandom."

Self-Identification as Fan

The symbolic interconnection of self and community in the word "fandom" points to the next distinctive characteristic of fans, namely, their personal identification with a community of like-minded fans. *Jericho*, U2, and Pittsburgh Steeler fans identify themselves as members of a distinct social group, partaking in at least some of the generalized consumption characteristics of that group, as well as regarding the community's collective resources and experts as a pool of legitimate knowledge. Cultural studies scholar John Fiske[12] emphasizes fans' investment in aesthetic textual criteria as a particular instance of accumulating "cultural capital," thus linking communal self-identity with consumption knowledge. The more cultural or subcultural knowledge one has accumulated, the more one can gain resources—investments of attention, things, time, and money—from members of that culture or community. If I am a hardcore Li'l Wayne fan with a deep knowledge of the man and his music, I can navigate his fan community and the people in it will pay attention to me and grant me status, which will allow me access and privilege.

Cultural Competence

In discussing the nature of media fandom, John Fiske[13] emphasizes the third characteristic: the "cultural competence" of fans of popular culture, where this competence "involves a critical understanding of the consumption object and the conventions by which it is constructed, it involves the bringing of both textual and social experience to bear upon the program at the moment of reading, and it involves a constant and subtle negotiation and renegotiation of the relationship between the textual and the social." For Fiske and other scholars, a "program," "text," or "object" can be defined very widely: a TV program, a band, a motion picture, a commodity such as cigarettes or blue jeans, *or a brand*. We can therefore think about the cultural competence of fans of a brand, such as Dr. Pepper, the Apple iPhone, or the Corvette Stingray. These brand fans would delve into the product itself, its history, its manufacturing, its management, and its marketing, taking "consumption" into a symbolic domain far beyond the basic utilization of the functionality of the product.

Auxiliary Consumption

Cultural competence requires knowledge and practice, qualities honed both individually and collectively. The conception of cultural competence leads fans and other consumers to want to gather information and experiences beyond the "core" audiencing or consuming event. Why would people collect Coca-Cola memorabilia and merchandise? Why would people buy coffee table books dedicated to fast food restaurants? Why would people buy T-shirts with breakfast cereal logos and characters? For media fans, the purchase of ancillary merchandise is a way to deepen the relationship between the individual and the media text, its characters and meanings, and perhaps the wider fan community. The use of symbolic goods such as coffee mugs or T-shirts can serve as reminders of the importance of the text, while the use of books, magazines, and other reading material serves to deepen the intellectual and ideological understanding of the core text, its authors and actors, its production, and its social and cultural significance.

Production

Finally, "being a fan involves active, enthusiastic, partisan, participatory engagement with the text."[14] Cultural competence, the fan's depth of knowledge and skills, sometimes along with auxiliary consumption, enables the next characteristic of fandom: the fan's participation in the production of new "texts." Again, "texts" can be interpreted widely. Fiske[15] posits that fans' "fandom spurs them into producing their own texts. Such 'texts' may be the walls of teenagers' bedrooms, the way they dress," the "gossip of soap opera fans," the predictions of sports fans and their "what if" imaginative scenarios, the lip synching of Madonna look-alikes, the production of fan photos or videos and posting to Flickr or YouTube, the writing and performance of fan songs, or the authorship of literally new texts, such as new *Moonlight* stories or scripts.

According to Derecho,[16] the production of "fan" fiction may have a very long history, beginning "as a medium of political and social protest in the seventeenth century." More contemporary manifestations of the fan fiction phenomenon occurred in the 1920s with the Jane Austen and Sherlock Holmes fan societies, as well as in the late 1960s with the publications of the first *Star Trek* fanzines.[17] And, according to Busse and Hellekson[18], fandom changed dramatically with the widespread adoption of the Internet.

FANDOM 2.0

Before the Internet, "fandom was a face-to-face proposition," where fans met at fan clubs, attended conventions and wrote newsletters, fanzines, and add-on circuit newsletters called APAs.[19] The Internet radically changed the nature of being a fan and gave fans many more ways to participate in fandom. "Fans may write and post fan fiction, for example, without even knowing what it is or knowing that there are forums to do this in, and such fans naturally have no idea that they are part of the wider community. In turn, fans can remain lurkers who consume fannish artifacts without interacting with other fans."[20] The rules of participation in fan communities have changed. Because it is so easy to share and distribute writing online, the economics of fan production have radically shifted. Financial resources have become less important as the only necessary investment is in computer hardware and broadband access. Demographics have shifted to younger fans, and international participation has been facilitated.

This is a key point: *because of information and communications technologies, more people of more ages from more places around the world are able to participate in more ways in more fan communities than ever before.* And, increasingly, they are doing so.

There are now widespread blogs relating to fan literature, and these blogs blur the communal boundaries of fandom. Whereas newsgroups, forums, and lists tended to focus on particular media properties, blogs focus on individual fans and partake in an idiosyncratic, individualized discourse.[21] However, balancing some of this individualistic orientation, other forms of fan community are emerging, among them the wiki form.

LOST ON THE NET

To illustrate this development, I introduce and analyze an important fan wiki dedicated to the popular ABC television series *Lost*. *Lost*, which debuted in 2004, is a serial dramatic television series with a paranormal twist. It concerns the lives of the survivors of a plane crash on a mysterious tropical island located somewhere in the South Pacific. The key to the series' popularity seems to be in its complexity. It has a large (and growing) ensemble cast, with constantly shifting and developing friend and romantic relationships. The main characters' personalities and motivations are detailed in flashbacks (and also flash-forwards) to key points in their lives, leading to richly developed story lines. Added to this are the many continually unfolding mysteries of the island, the survivors, and the crash. These supernatural and paranormal mysteries include: seemingly random appearances of dead people on the island; a group of inhabitants termed "The Others" who live in relatively modern and developed quarters; Polar Bears on the tropical island; a strange and advanced research organization called "the Dharma Initiative"; a cyclonic monster; a number sequence that recurs on the island and in the lives of many of the characters; as well as many odd, apparently coincidental connections between the lives of crash survivors in their past, present, and future.

Because of the quality of its production and writing, *Lost* has become a cult television hit and the show subsequently has been exploited by ABC/Disney and its producers on multiple platforms such as novelizations, video games, comic books, numerous toys and games, "official" Web sites, an official "licensed" fan club, and an alternate reality game.

The show has gathered a devoted international community of fans who often call themselves *Losties* or *Lostaways*. Lostaways have already gathered at various conventions, developed numerous forums, and built fan Web sites dedicated to activities such as producing and sharing fan fiction, podcasts, and videos, following character relationships (or, turned into a fannish verb, "shipping"), compiling episode transcripts, and collecting and reviewing auxiliary merchandise.

With at least 14 major characters, past and present plot lines, and a heap of major mysteries to keep track of, it is easy for ordinary viewers and even devoted fans to become a little bit confused. But this is where the hive mind of the fan community enters in, enabled and, in some sense, created by the (r)evolutionary power of the Internet and its wiki form. "*Wikis* are a specialized, collaborative form of web-page in which the page is designed so that it is open to contributions or modifications of its content."[22] *Lostpedia* is a wiki dedicated to helping *Lost* fans keep collective track of, debate, and assess the complex, cross-media platform or "transmedia" plot lines and character developments of the fictional *Lost* universe.

Lostpedia helps us to understand the changing nature of media fandom in the age of increasing Internet connectivity. Today, as I investigate *Lostpedia*, it has 5,119 distinct articles, many of them detailed and extensive, exploring various elements of the television series. *Lostpedia* contains a new community blog, a forum, a community portal, and an Internet relay chat (IRC) domain. *Lostpedia* is an online community dedicated to all things *Lost* and offering community members various ways to interact. But it is also, first and foremost, a constantly evolving encyclopedia that fans used to keep track of the show, its production, its complex plot, and character development.

If I want to learn about *Lost* characters, I have my choice of main characters, supporting roles, flashback characters, flash forward characters, The Others, members of the Dharma initiative, and crew of the ship Kahana. Regarding the world of *Lost*, there are interviews with cast and crew, podcasts, two alternate reality games, and the videogame. Various aspects of the site are available in various languages, including German, Spanish, French, Hebrew, Italian, Japanese, Dutch, Polish, Portuguese, Russian, and Chinese.

Some of the most important features are contained in the main pages of the online encyclopedia. Here we find a complete and up-to-date listing of all *Lost* episodes, descriptions of the seasons and the major events occurring in them. We have a complete timeline. Transcripts, complete fan-generated scripts of each and every episode, are also provided. We also have analysis and listing of the cultural references in the television show, the literary techniques used, and recurrent themes. We can find a listing of the mysterious occurrences of the island and classifications of them as unsolved, partially solved, or solved.

In the Mysterious Happenings portal of *Lostpedia*, for example, we have a listing, with photographs, of 15 "Island Mysteries" (four of which are solved, five of which are partially solved, and six of which are unsolved). This is followed by 15 "Island History Mysteries," 12 "Character Mysteries," 15 "Dreams and Visions Mysteries," 13 "The Others Mysteries," 8 "The Kahana Mysteries," 11 "The Dharma Initiative Mysteries," 12 "Dharma Stations Mysteries," and 10 "Off the Island Mysteries." In total there are 112 mysteries, of which 20 are solved, 38 are unsolved, and 46 are tantalizingly close and yet not completely solved. For the average *Lost* viewer, that is a whole lot of mystery.

Clicking on each of these mysteries leads to a separate page with comprehensive referenced and cross-referenced descriptions. To consider just one example, we can click on the very first mystery, which is the mystery regarding the island's "monster," also known as the "smoke monster" or "Cerberus." We learn from *Lostpedia* that we first encounter the monster in the pilot episode of *Lost* and that it has killed and spared various characters ever since. We get a description of the smoke monster as well as numerous pictures of it and learn the opinions of various lost characters regarding its origins and purpose. There is an analysis of the characteristics of the monster, such as its "polymorphism," the sounds it makes, the control that some characters have over it, its relation to a mysterious "Cerberus system" relating it to comments made at a comic book convention (among other comments by producers and writers), an official lost jigsaw puzzle, an Xbox 360 game, and Greco-Roman mythology.

Encounters with the monster are then carefully explicated and tabulated from all five seasons of the television series, and there is a listing of the monster's known victims. Next, there are appearances of the monster from "non-canon" sources, i.e., those that are not in the actual television show itself. These "transmedia"[23] appearances include those in the videogame, those in "the semi-canon *Lost* novel *Signs of Life*," the alternate reality game and related podcast, and *Lost: The Mobile Game* for iPods and mobile phones. Finally, a listing of "trivia" about the monster is provided, including general trivia, possible explanations, appearances, sound effects (including the pitch of the howling sound made by the monster), production notes, the series producer's "favorite fan theory" regarding the monster, and cultural references regarding the monster. The final sections are unanswered questions that remain about the monster, as well as links to fans theories about the monster, and external links to videos portraying the monster.

As I read through the history of the monster and trace the various discussions regarding the various entries about it, other mysteries, characters, and plotlines, I'm struck by the role of technology. Networked computing technology enables these pages to evolve out of the intense collaborative efforts of hundreds and thousands of devoted fans. And it enables me to slow down, run that evolution backward and forward,

watching how it has developed, in fits and starts, from the earliest page
that simply separates out "facts" from "theories" to this detailed, cross-
linked and hyperlinked article. In stop-and-start fashion, with attacking
hackers intent on creating mischief and mayhem, with corrective comments and conversations shared, with careful aggregation of information
over time, this group of fans creates an incredibly valuable tool for all to
enjoy and learn from, one whose capabilities forever alter the way I will
watch, process, and enjoy the television series. And this new set of abilities is enjoyed and empowered not only by technology, the Internet,
and the wiki form, but by the preexisting presence and nature of fandom
itself. As Weinberger[24] notes regarding Wikipedia, "Wikipedia is to a large
degree the product of a community, not just of disconnected individuals."
And this is not a run-of-the-mill community, either, but a community
of thinking, intelligent fans, devoted keepers of the flame: accounters, col-
lectors, theorists, solvers of mysteries. What fans do, indeed, is academic.
They are producing a collective work on *Lostpedia* that is analogous to, even
indistinguishable from, academic work—indeed, in many case I would say
these articles are written more lucidly and reasoned more coherently. It is
perhaps unsurprising that research conducted by *Nature* magazine found
that the accuracy of "amateur-produced" Wikipedia was not significantly
different from that of the professionally commissioned *Encyclopedia
Brittanica*.[25]

This phenomenon of collective communities developing and maintaining ambitious creative projects online has been the subject of a number of
influential expositions in the last few years. James Surowiecki's[26] *The
Wisdom of Crowds* is one of the better known of these expositions, where
he discusses the superiority of collective over individual decision-making.
On the business front, Don Tapscott and Tony Williams's[27] *Wikinomics*
explores the various creative strategies used by online communities and
their value to industry. The origins and forms of this important phenomenon of online community creativity, and its specific implications for
marketing and macromarketing thought are also explored by Robert V.
Kozinets, Andrea Hemetsberger, and Hope Schau.[28]

Renowned media scholar Henry Jenkins[29] draws on Pierre Levy's[30]
notion of collective intelligence and applies it to fans' "spoiling," or
guessing the winner of, the reality television *Survivor* series. Jenkins[31]
describes collective intelligence as the ability of online fan communities
"to leverage the combined expertise of their members." There are close
ties between the sociality of online groups and their knowledge activities
and exchanges: "What holds the collective intelligence together is not the
possession of knowledge—which is relatively static—but the social
process of acquiring knowledge—which is dynamic and participatory,
continually testing and reaffirming the group's social ties."[32] Furthermore, these types of "emerging knowledge cultures [are] defined through
voluntary, temporary, and tactical affiliations."[33]

It seems sensible to conclude that the more mysteries and puzzles that tantalize a community, and the more facts and factors they have to gather and weave together, the longer-lasting and, perhaps, the closer and more binding might be the social ties they spin. Fans want to prolong their contact not only with an engaging series and its engrossing, expanding universe but also with an enjoyable and friendly community—the informational and the social components of consumption blending effortlessly into one another in the virtual community of consumption.[34] Now, we turn to an analysis of how these interacting components, described in media fandom and its highly engaged online manifestations, also manifest through online "fan" communities devoted to product, services, and brands.

FACEBOOK'S BRAND FANDOM: ONLINE AND ON DISPLAY

Can we establish that consumers of products want to self-identify themselves as "fans," borrowing the metaphor of media fandom and applying it, for example, to beverages or restaurants? We need look no further than the popular social networking site Facebook for examples. On Facebook, you can become a "fan"—that's what they call it—of just about any "thing" commercial. Not only celebrities, television shows, hip-hop artists and classic rockers, politicians and pundits, but also Puma shoes, Kit Kat chocolate bars, M&M's candies, Starbucks coffee, the Levi's store, Casper the Friendly Ghost, Jack Daniels whiskey, the Hard Rock Café, the Sony PSP, and so much more.

Just as we saw with *Lostpedia*, the depth of these individual fandoms runs deep. There is not only a fan club for "McDonald's restaurants" (boasting 208,180 fans), but also fan clubs for McDonald's Café, McDonald's Breakfast, McDonald's Opportunity, McDonald's Coke, McDonald's Clown, Generazione McDonald's, McDonald's WiFi, McDonald's Australia, McDonald's Columbia, McDonald's French Fries, McDonald's Sweet Tea, Monopoly at McDonald's, McDonald's Prosperity Burger, Eurodeals au McDonald's, McDonald's First Love Commercial, McDonald's Thanksgiving Parade, McDonald's LPGA Championship, and dozens more.

Now, what exactly does it mean to be a fan of McDonald's or some other service or product on Facebook? If we look at a popular product or service fan page, what do we see? Reconnoitering the Coca-Cola fan page, a fan club that, on the day in the winter of 2009 that I examined it, has 2,905,381 fans, it becomes apparent that this is a different type of fan relationship, a different type of "consumption" or "brand" "community" than academics have previously written and theorized about. The page is dominated by a gigantic graphic of a cold-and-sweaty classic red and white Coca-Cola can. Underneath it is the information that Coca-Cola was founded in 1892 by Asa Griggs Candler. Off to the right hand side are thumbnail pictures of six fans, out of the nearly 3 million people who have connected and identified as Coke fans. If one chooses to dig deeper, most of these fans have pictures showing their faces and most of them are, following Facebook custom, using what appear to be their real names. You can click on their names and access a larger photograph. You also have the option to send them a message or attempt to connect with them and make them a part of your social network. Identifying as a fan of the brand of Coca-Cola therefore opens up, almost immediately, a world of socially connective possibilities. Connected by Coca-Cola and Facebook, we still seem, to me, to have remaining at least five degrees of separation between us. If one is motivated, and one would want to connect with all of these quasi-anonymous people, then maybe one could broaden one's online social network through the simple act of reaching out and sending a message: "Hi, I like Coke too. Do you want to be my friend now?"

More food, or drink, for thought, are provided by the 640 fan photos posted below the fan IDs. People have posted photographs of themselves with Coca-Cola memorabilia, drinking Coca-Cola, with Santa Claus, with the Coca-Cola polar bears, and at stadiums, as well as pictures that they have taken of various areas and items such as Atlanta's World of Coca-Cola,[35] Coca-Cola trucks, Coca-Cola bottles and cans, Coca-Cola memorabilia collections, scanned and captured images of Coca-Cola advertising both classic and contemporary, animals drinking Coca-Cola, and art using Coca-Cola, such as a Valentine's heart made out of an arrangement of Coca-Cola cans.

There are a few fan-posted videos, constituting street scenes where noisy Coca-Cola trucks pass by while blaring music to the accompaniment of shouts from passersby, YouTube-style amateur cinema productions using displays of Coca-Cola bottles, Times Square advertising time lapse photography, retrospectives of old print advertising set to the popular 1960s anthem/jingle "I'd Like To Teach The World To Sing," or, mainly, reposted Coca-Cola television commercials from around the world in various languages. In fact, one is struck by the international orientation of so many of these brand-related fan pages.

This international orientation continues as we move down the Facebook fan page to the social content sharing "Wall." On the wall, people have a chance to post messages that are viewed by the general public. On the Coke fan page these messages tends to be extremely short and oftentimes practically inarticulate. People from Hong Kong, Chile, Uruguay, France, Indonesia, Malaysia, Turkey, and Tennessee post sets of asterisks, insightful "AUGHs," the comment "RRRRRR," and repeat ad campaigns such as Always Coca-Cola.

In addition, posters offer up a number of pithy sayings and questions. Do people like the taste of Coca-Cola Zero? Does Coca-Cola own Pepsi-Cola? Confessions such as "I'm addicted to Coke," "I always drink a Coke first thing in the morning," or "I am very brand loyal and only drink Coke and would never drink anything else" are well-represented. Or the commonplace, quintessential, and in its own way rather profound, "I love Coke, don't you?" appears in many forms. There are 2,873 wall posts on display, the vast majority of them fewer than 10 words in length. They are not commentaries or communal discussions so much as short individualistic call outs. "Hey, I'm here, I'm connected to Coke," is all they seem to want or need to say. Part of this may be the nature of Facebook communications, but the other part may well be the nature of this new form of brand fandom.

Below this are discussion boards, based on the classic discussion board/forum/Usenet form that has populated the Internet, and Internet fan communities, since well before the World Wide Web opened up online communities to the global masses. On the date the fan page was checked, Coca Cola had 29 discussion topics, most of which had only one or two postings. Only 5 had more than 10 posts, and the most popular one had 42 posts. In places, the Coca-Cola Company seemed to be experimenting with using the forums as a location to hold informal public focus groups, posting questions such as "What did you think of the Mean Joe/Mean Troy commercial?"

These numbers, which hold up fairly well across many of the product, brand, service, store, and restaurant fan groups that I scouted, indicate that far more people are willing to join the community than to contribute to it. About 1/10 of 1 percent of the people will write on the wall, and tiny fractions of this number will post photos or videos or reply to discussion topics. Are they fan communities in the older sense, in the same sense as *Lostpedia* makers, *Battlestar Galactica* Convention organizers, or *True Blood* fan fiction writers? Or is this a more superficial and fleeting affiliation, an instant badging that to signify a common habit like one smoker nodding to the other with a shy smile, an acknowledgment of the inhabitance in a common consumption place, a focal area of the material world and a linkage of meanings—however fleeting or evanescent—to its prevalent symbols? We don't know the answers, of course. Are these true brand communities, or perhaps something else—semi-quasi-not-quite-communities or consumers collected for the moment in an easy acceptance of material culture, a momentary playfulness, a fleeting willingness to click a button and virtually associate to a new section of the world: a brand fandom?

REALIZATIONS OF BRAND FANDOM

We are only beginning to explore the sources and implications of this convergence of fan communities and brand cultures. How did this convergence come about? How did it emerge out of the cultural kernel of expanding fandom that began in the seventeenth century?

I've been trying to decipher that glyph for over a decade. I now believe that the notion of "the story" is the Rosetta Stone of translation between these two sets of communities. Along with Stephen Brown and

John F. Sherry,[36] I argue that powerful brands, those capable of being reanimated, possess their own detailed story: "Our study thus suggests that Aura (brand essence), Allegory (brand stories), and Arcadia (idealized community) are the character, plot, and the setting, respectively, of brand meaning. Antinomy, the final element of our 4As abbreviation, is perhaps most important of all, for brand paradox brings the cultural complexity necessary to animate each of the other dimensions."

In other research that my colleagues and I have conducted regarding the American Girl brand, we find that its marketers have used well-researched, moralistic, value-rich, historical stories to attach profound levels of complexity and meaning to the dolls, their clothing, and their accessories.[37] The dolls are storied brands, each with her own Aura, Allegory, Arcadia, and Antinomy. The stories have been so successful that the doll franchise has had its brand extended into a successful magazine, a set of made-for-television movies, and a major motion picture release.

Clotaire Rapaille[38] discusses the early childhood imprinting of sensations and emotions attached to product use; the smell of coffee and its association to homeyness and motherhood as one example. But what do we know about the imprinting of stories, media content, technologies, and brands? What do we know of a common mythology that links us as social beings, the deep collective well of archetypes upon which all of our stories, all of our imprints—whose origins may be much more cultural than Rapaille's sociobiological orientation suggests—draw?

Branding science is still learning that storytelling is the key to consumer engagement and involvement. Branding and marketing are continually working with the entertainment industry to develop and hybridize new forms of advertisement/entertainment. On the other side are entertainment brands that become products, such as *Duff's beer*, the fictional lager enjoyed by Homer Simpson and later licensed, produced, and successfully marketed by England's Daleside Brewery. Another popular example is the *Bubba Gump Shrimp Company*, a 31-chain restaurant named for a fictional company in the 1994 hit movie starring Tom Hanks, *Forrest Gump*.

Alongside these developments, multiplying and altering their effects, is the dynamism and interconnectedness of information and communications technologies. We are seeing the results, as popular consumer culture and fan culture merge effortlessly one into the other, their capabilities and possibilities continuously expanded and technologically accelerated. As television properties launch motion pictures, and have, for a long time, become action figures, puzzles, and games, they now also are spawning cross-media empires that reach from mobile games and videogames to alternate reality games, virtual worlds, and social networking sites.

Online, forum posters, denizens of virtual worlds, and bloggers are continually representing, parodying, and communally reworking their status as brand fans. In my analysis of the Barq's blog—The Blog With

Bite!—Michael Marx's now-defunct blog about an American root beer, I find a depth of fan relationship that fits perfectly the classic definition of the fan.[39] Reading this complex and multimodal fan text, I have as much deep symbolic material to work with as I would from practically any projective technique, such as the Zaltman Metaphor Elicitation Technique (ZMET). Fan texts online provide deep, rich data to fuel and impel our development of a new, digital generation of motivation research.

Brand Obama's campaign teaches us that nothing—not politics, not social policy, not religion, not nation or city-state—is out of reach of the online networks of brand fandom, as our society increasingly churns every species of role, social construct, and concept into an attractive and packageable brand and into diverting, engaging entertainment populated by likeable protagonists, in particular times and places, undergoing character-building challenges and confronting their antagonists. And now that he is in office, what has President Obama done with his online community network of supporters and enthusiasts? With radical revisions to the WhiteHouse.gov Web site, he has helped to turn volunteers and voters into a standing army of supporters that he can draw on when he needs popular support. Just as the ongoing relationship with the consumer, not the purchase, is becoming recognized as the rightful end goal of the marketer, so too has Team Obama recognized that the ongoing committed and engaged relationship with the American citizen, and not their mere quadrennial vote, is the true leader's campaign end goal.

We have had some speculation already about wikibrands[40] and wikinomics.[41] But what would brand wikis look like if they took the example of the *Lostpedia* wiki to the world of brands? What would be required of marketing managers in order to build corresponding levels of engagement and involvement? Would the wiki follow the company and the managers—the marketing decisions and decision-makers—as well as the brand and the advertising itself? Would this be a brand journalism of the highest order? What would its challenges be? Where would its central mysteries inhere? My research into *Star Trek* fans[42] and Muñiz and Schau's[43] research on Apple Newton communities suggests that these communities and individuals curl themselves around profound mysteries, those with inspiring spiritual and religious implications.

So fans aren't really freaks at all. Instead, they are, frankly, freakishly fascinating, phenomenal forecasters of the futures of marketers and marketing. For marketers, opportunities abound not only to work with the efforts, energies, and enthusiasm of brand fans expressing themselves online in forums such as the fan groups on Facebook or other forums[44], but also to work in partnership to create new sites and forms of marketing with these fans and with the converging trends of technology, marketing, and entertainment. The core qualities, the entertaining and engaging essences of these relationships, are tantalizingly close. And yet there is still so much more to know—and to do.

Notes

1. Clifford Geertz, *The Interpretation of Cultures* (Basic Books, 1973).

2. Robert V. Kozinets, "Utopian Enterprise: Articulating the Meanings of *Star Trek*'s Culture of Consumption," *Journal of Consumer Research*, no. 28 (June 2001): 67–88.

3. Paul Willis, *Learning to Labour: How Working Class Kids Get Working Class Jobs* (Saxon House, 1977).

4. Eric J. Arnould and Craig J. Thompson, "Consumer. Culture Theory (CCT): Twenty Years of Research," *Journal of Consumer Research*, no. 31 (March 2005): 868–882.

5. Ibid.

6. Ibid.

7. Robert V. Kozinets, "Inno-tribes: Star Trek as Wikimedia," in *Consumer Tribes*, ed. Bernard Cova, Robert V. Kozinets, and Avi Shankar (Oxford and Burlington, 2007), 194–211.

8. Anthony Cohen, *The Symbolic Construction of Community* (Routledge, 1985).

9. Albert M. Muñiz, Jr., and Thomas C. O'Guinn, "Brand Community," *Journal of Consumer Research*, no. 27 (March 2001), 412–432.

10. Ibid.

11. Lawrence Grossberg, " 'Is There a Fan in the House?': The Affective Sensibility Of Fandom," in *The Adoring Audience: Fan Culture and Popular Media*, ed. A. Lisa Lewis (Routledge, 1992), 50–65.

12. John Fiske, *Television Culture* (Routledge, 1987).

13. Ibid.

14. John Fiske, *Understanding Popular Culture* (Routledge, 1991).

15. Ibid.

16. Abigail Derecho, "Archontic Literature: A Definition, a History, and Several Theories of Fan Fiction," in *Fan Fiction and Fan Communities in the Age of the Internet*, ed. Karen Hellekson and Kristina Busse (McFarland & Company, 2006).

17. Ibid.

18. Kristina Busse and Karen Hellekson, "Introduction: Work in Progress," in *Fan Fiction and Fan Communities in the Age of the Internet*, ed. Karen Hellekson and Kristina Busse (McFarland & Company, 2006).

19. Ibid.

20. Ibid.

21. Ibid.

22. Robert V. Kozinets, *Netnography: Doing Ethnographic Research Online* (Sage, 2010).

23. Henry Jenkins, *Convergence Culture: Where Old and New Media Collide* (New York University Press, 2006).

24. David Weinberger, *Everything Is Miscellaneous: The Power of the New Digital Disorder* (Times Books, 2007).

25. Jim Giles, "Special Report: Internet Encyclopaedias Go Head to Head," *Nature*, no. 438 (December 15, 2005): 900–901.

26. James Surowiecki, *The Wisdom of Crowds: Why the Many Are Smarter Than the Few and How Collective Wisdom Shapes Business, Economies, Societies and Nations* (Random House, 2004).

27. Don Tapscott and Anthony D. Williams, *Wikinomics: How Mass Collaboration Changes Everything* (Portfolio, 2007).

28. Robert V. Kozinets, Andrea Hemetsberger, and Hope Schau, "The Wisdom of Consumer Crowds: Collective Innovation in the Age of Networked Marketing," *Journal of Macromarketing*, no. 28 (December 2008): 339–354.

29. See Note 23.

30. Pierre Levy, *Collective Intelligence: Mankind's Emerging World in Cyberspace*, trans. Robert Bononno (Plenum, 1997).

31. See Note 23.

32. Ibid.

33. Ibid.

34. Robert V. Kozinets, "E-Tribalized Marketing? The Strategic Implications of Virtual Communities of Consumption," *European Management Journal* 17no. 3 (1999): 252–264.

35. Candice R. Hollenbeck, Cara Peters, and George M. Zinkhan, "Retail Spectacles and Brand Meaning: Insights from a Brand Museum Case Study," *Journal of Retailing* 84, no. 3 (2008): 334–353.

36. Stephen Brown, Robert V. Kozinets, and John F. Sherry, Jr., "Teaching Old Brands New Tricks: Retro Branding and the Revival of Brand Meaning," *Journal of Marketing*, no. 67 (July 2003): 19–33.

37. Nina Diamond, John F. Sherry, Jr., Mary Ann McGrath, Albert Muniz, Jr., Robert V. Kozinets, and Stefania Borghini, "American Girl and the Brand Gestalt: Closing the Loop on Sociocultural Branding Research," *Journal of Marketing* (May 2009); Robert V. Kozinets, John F. Sherry, Stefania Borghini, Mary Ann McGrath, Nina Diamond, and Albert Muniz, Jr., "I'm an American Girl " (color videography, VHS, 20 minutes), exhibited at the *2003 ACR Film Festival*, October 2003.

38. Clotaire Rapaille, *The Culture Code: An Ingenious Way to Understand Why People around the World Live and Buy As They Do* (Broadway Books, 2006).

39. Robert V. Kozinets, "Netnography 2.0," in *Handbook of Qualitative Research Methods in Marketing*, ed. Russell W. Belk (Cheltenham, UN and Northampton, MA: Edward Elgar Publishing, 2006), 129–142.

40. Leyland F. Pitt, Richard T. Watson, Pierre Berthon, Donald Wynn, and George Zinkhan, "The Penguin's Window: Corporate Brands from an Open-Source Perspective," *Journal of the Academy of Marketing Science* 34, no. 2 (2006): 115–127.

41. See Note 27.

42. See Note 2

43. Albert M. Muñiz, Jr,. and Hope Jensen Schau, "Religiosity in the Abandoned Apple Newton Brand Community," *Journal of Consumer Research*, no. 31 (March 2005): 737–747.

44. See Note 22.

12

Growing Up "Virtual": The Impact of Interactive Technologies on Adolescent Consumer Behavior

Natalie T. Wood

Jenny unlocks the front door. She throws her backpack on the sofa (barely missing the table lamp), grabs a juice box from the kitchen and kicks off her shoes. As she heads to the den she glances at the clock on the wall—4:17 P.M. That leaves about 1 hour of "play" with just enough time to complete her chores before her parents arrive home at 6 p.m. She eases into the leather chair and flicks on the screen and disappears into another world.

Every day thousands of American kids and teens like Jenny find themselves home alone. If this were 1985, the electronic baby-sitter keeping Jenny out of mischief would be the television. But it's 2010 and even though television is still popular, evidence suggests that its hold on, and perceived importance in, the lives of young people is slowly eroding. The television is experiencing fierce competition from the Web. In 2007, 93 percent of youth ages 12 to 17 reported using the Internet, up from 87 percent in 2005, and 73 percent in 2000.[1] Forty-six percent of them reported the Internet as the most essential medium in their live compared to television at 31 percent.[2] But the popularity of the Web is not just confined to the tween and teen market. As many as 75 percent of kids aged six to eight are also accessing online content on a regular basis.[3]

So what is it that draws them to the Web? The answer is online interactive technologies including social networking sites (e.g., Facebook), file sharing services (e.g., YouTube and Flickr), chat rooms, blogs, and virtual worlds. As the youth of today spend more time with online technologies they spend less time interacting with traditional media. Eighty-three percent of 10- to 14-year-olds spend at least one hour online everyday.[4] Virtual world Cartoon Doll Emporium (CDE) surveyed over 10,000 of its members and found that 64 percent of them spent more time on CDE than watching TV and 89 percent of them spend more time in the virtual world than reading magazines. A new user joins CDE every 10 seconds, and a new blog is created every 95 seconds.[5] Given the decline in use of traditional media, marketers and advertisers are often left struggling with the best way to reach young consumers in these new environments.

This chapter explores why young people are drawn to interactive technologies. Next it discusses the growing popularity of virtual worlds and how they impact adolescent consumer behavior. It concludes by offering suggestions for marketers wanting to reach this virtual generation.

GENERATION V (VIRTUAL)

Interactive technologies—those that allow content to be modified and customized in real time and shared with others—have fast become a popular form of entertainment and a staple of twenty-first-century communication. They are particularly popular with young people, especially those the Gartner Group calls Generation V (Virtual). Born after 1991 into a digital world, Generation V are active consumers who embrace all forms of technology, both as a means of communication and as a form of entertainment. Whether it is updating their *Facebook* profile, chatting with a friend from class (or one whom they just met online) in a Jonas Brothers chat room, hanging out in *Virtual Laguna Beach*, or reading a blog discussing the trials and tribulations of Lindsay Lohan's love life, Generation V are, at an increasing rate, choosing to log out of traditional forms of real-world entertainment and log into those that exist online. So what is it about these technologies that kids find so compelling? Research shows that young people are drawn to interactive technologies as a means of satisfying their need for social interaction, immediate and constant entertainment, self-expression, discovery, and creation.[6]

The Need for Social Interaction

Without a doubt, the most common reason young people use the Internet is to interact with others. Ninety-three percent of teen Internet users treat the Web as avenue for building and maintaining social relations.[7] While a parent may struggle to understand why her son would prefer to talk to his friend online rather than in person it is important to remember that kids today have never known life without the Internet. Whereas previous generations have grown up listening to radio or in front of the television, the youth of today are growing up virtual. For them the "virtual" and the "real" are not distinct spaces. The Internet is a part of everyday life. It is simply a tool that has the ability to enhance their social life and create new forms of connection and social exchange.[8]

Identity Creation and Expression

"Child's play" is an important part of self-development.[9,10,11] It is that time in life when one has the opportunity to imagine, pretend, and experiment without little to no risk or consequence. Today, the Internet affords adolescents many new and exciting opportunities to experiment with their identities in a relatively safe environment.[12] Social networking sites permit young consumers the opportunity to express their actual or aspirational self. Blogs, Vlogs and sites such as YouTube permit them to share their opinions with potentially hundreds of thousands of like-minded people.

Immediate and Constant Entertainment

Kids have shorter attention spans than adults. As a result they are often drawn to technologies that employ flash technology and animation and those that require them to be active participants rather than passive observers.[13] As a result, television is just not that exciting to them. Furthermore, their insatiable appetite for stimulation often results in their using multiple media at once. In 2005 it was reported that approximately one quarter (26%) of the time young people aged 8–18 years are using media, they are using more than one medium at a time.[14] For example, they are surfing the Web while instant messaging a friend and listening to a podcast. In a typical day these kids are cramming 8.5 hours worth of media into less than 6.5 hours of time. As children age, their exposure to and experience with different media increases, as does their ability to multitask, with girls more likely to than boys to use more than one medium at a time.[15] This makes it difficult for advertisers to capture and maintain their attention.

Discovery, Creation, and Recording

Unlike traditional offline media, the Web "is not scheduled, it demands discovery."[16] In order to utilize the Web the user must be an active participant. Discovery can be both deliberate and accidental. In terms of deliberate discovery, young consumers, just like adults, use the Web to search for information about products and services. Four out of 10 young consumers use the Internet for this purpose.[17] But a lot of discovery is also accidental. Young people are big Web surfers, scouring sites such as YouTube for whatever grabs their attention. The result is a more tailored and potentially more rewarding experience for each user.

But searching for information or entertainment is not the only reason for spending time online. Creating and recording are two popular activities of Generation V. By the end of 2006, a reported 64 percent of online teens ages 12–17 participated in one or more content-creating activities on the Internet, up from 57 percent in 2004.[18] Thirty-three percent of teens create or work on Web pages or blogs for others, 27 percent maintain their own personal Web page, 26 percent report remixing content they find online into their own creations, and 39 percent share their own artistic creations (e.g., artwork, photos, stories, or videos) with others online.[19]

To satisfy these needs, many young people turn to social networking sites such as Facebook, MySpace, Hi5, and Friendster. At least 65 percent of American teens have a profile on one or more of these sites. Through these profiles, young people have the ability to express their identity, voice their opinions, share their creations, and interact with others. Despite the popularity of social networking sites, analysts predict that virtual worlds eventually will replace or subsume these platforms.[20] Within the next three years the number of teens in virtual worlds will more than double to 20 million.[21] By then, an estimated 53 percent of children and 80 percent of all active Internet users will be using virtual worlds.[22]

VIRTUAL WORLDS

A virtual world is an online representation of real-world people, products, and brands in a computerized environment.[23] Users inhabit these virtual worlds and interact with others through the use of an avatar—a digital persona that they construct. When in-world these individuals (through their avatars) socialize with others from around the globe, play games, watch videos, shop, and tryout different personas. There are six characteristics that define these worlds:[24]

- **Graphical user interface**. Virtual worlds use 2D or 3D digital imagery to visually create environments and user avatars. Some of these environments are replicas of real-world places (e.g., Virtual Lower East Side, New York), others present a fantasy world (e.g., Club Penguin) and others yet again a hybrid of the two (e.g., Teen Second Life). Over the years as animation technology has advanced, so too has the quality of the graphical images of people and places. In some cases these representations are so good that it is difficult to determine whether what we are viewing is real or fake. This level of realism is part of the attraction of virtual worlds.
- **Shared space**. Virtual worlds allow for large numbers of people to meet in the same space simultaneously. It is not uncommon for tens of thousands of young people to be online and in-world at the same time. On a social networking site a user can tell if one of their friends is online, usually by a flashing beacon (or other icon) next to his name, but they cannot actually see him. In a virtual world, users have the ability to see each other by way of their digital doppelgangers—their avatars. Being able to see the digital representation of a person creates *telepresence* (the feeling of being there), but even more powerfully a feeling of *co-presence* (the sense of being there with others). Both factors are important for holding users' attention.

- **Interactivity**. In a virtual world the user is allowed to alter, develop, build, or even submit customized content to the environment. The majority of worlds allow users to customize their avatars' appearance (height, weight, facial features). Some even allow the user to create items for his virtual life by using in-world building tools. For instance *Habbo Hotel* allows users to decorate their own room with items that are available for free or for purchase from one of their many in-world stores. On social networking sites, friends are not part of the creation process they only see the end result. In a virtual world the experience is shared. Users can create, modify, or shop for items on their own or in the company of friends.
- **Immediacy**. As in the real world, in a virtual world all interactions take place in real time. There is little to no lag effect. Communication is instantaneous.
- **Persistence**. A virtual world continues regardless of whether an individual user is logged in or not. Activities and events will continue to develop without the need for any one individual to be present. Not only does this add to the realism but it also creates a compelling reason to spend as much time as possible in-world—so that users don't miss out on anything.
- **Socialization/Community**. A virtual world is essentially a virtual community—a group of individuals who connect and interact online for the purpose of personal and shared goals. Within each teen world there are hundreds of clubs that users can join. Whether you are looking for people who share your taste in music, have similar political views, are committed to a particular social cause, or simply are fans of your favorite television show, within these environments you can easily find communities of like-minded people.

While it is true that other interactive technologies (e.g., social networking sites and blogs) do present a number of these characteristics, they unfortunately do not offer them all. When all six characteristics are combined into one platform, as they are in virtual worlds, they provide a more compelling experience. It is this unique experience that facilitates users' engagement and often creates a flow state. A flow state is a mental state in which the user becomes so immersed and involved in what he is doing that he loses all sense of time and space. And why is flow important? The answer is simple—flow results in Web site stickiness. If the environment, in this case the virtual world, is sticky, then users will spend more time in it.[25] Recent reports suggest that young people are already engaging in virtual worlds upward of 16 hours each week.[26] This presents great possibilities for marketers attempting to reach this generation.

A World for Everyone

With over 150 virtual worlds either live or currently in development, it is fair to say that there is a world to satisfy everyone.[27] Worlds are often segmented by user age. For example, there are worlds that are designed for and appeal to young kids (under 7 years), tweens (8–12 years), teenagers (13–19 years) and adults (20+ years). The content of each world, including the activities that take place, are closely aligned to the interests of each age group. To illustrate, the number one reason kids are drawn to virtual worlds is to play games. As a result, in kid worlds there are a variety of games for kids to play either on their own or with others (e.g., tic tac toe and scavenger hunts).

As kids age they gravitate to worlds that contain content and activities more relevant to their interests. For instance, MTV created a number of virtual worlds based on their popular youth-oriented television shows such as *The Hills* and *Laguna Beach*. In these worlds, teenagers have the opportunity to shop for virtual clothing created by real-world designers, attend virtual events, meet the stars, listen to the latest music, watch current episodes, and socialize with others their own age.

As teenagers become adults their motivation for participation is less about game playing and shopping and more around escaping life and experimenting. The activities and events that take place in these worlds are more in line with the interests of older consumers. For instance, users can attend virtual book launches, participate in political discussions, or take educational classes.

Whereas much of the media attention to date has been on adult virtual worlds such as Second Life, the real action is taking place in those that target younger consumers. Kid and teen worlds surpass adult worlds both in total membership numbers and the number of visitors per month. For example, as of February 2009, Habbo Hotel, which targets 13–18-year-olds, boasted over 121 million registered users and over 11.5 million unique users each month. The popular adult world Second Life pales in comparison with only 16.7 million registered users and approximately 940,000 log-ins per month. With so much of young people's free time consumed by immersive environments, the question that is often asked is "how does participation in a virtual world effect consumer behavior?"

How Virtual Worlds Influence Consumer Behavior

These environments influence adolescent consumer behavior in three key ways: (1) They encourage identity experimentation; (2) They help users form virtual friendships and social support systems that may be missing in their real world; and (3) These virtual peers often serve as a reference group for in-world and potentially real-world purchases.

The Virtual Me

The somewhat anonymous nature of the Web provides young users with the confidence to try out new experiences, engage with different people (and products), and experiment more freely than in the real world. One popular and important area of experimentation is that of self-identity. These environments offer users the opportunity, through their avatars, to experiment with personas that are often far from their real self. In fact it is not uncommon for users to have more than one avatar, each one representing a different self.[28] One world in particular, The Virtual Hills, challenges teenagers to "come as you are and become what you want to be."

But not everyone is drawn to these virtual worlds to create alter-egos. Kids and tweens are attracted to virtual worlds for both entertainment and as a novel way to communicate with others. These young users are more concerned about their real-world identity than creating new ones. Reports indicate that in some youth-oriented virtual worlds such as Wee-World at least 50 percent of users chat with their real-life friends as their real selves.[29]

But for adolescent users, virtual worlds are a tool for defining who they are and experimenting with who they (may) want to be. Identity exploration is an essential developmental task for adolescents.[30] Virtual worlds offer them the ability to "try on" new personas without the pressure to conform to norms that exist within the real world. Often experimentation begins with altering the appearance of the avatar so that it looks more like the adolescent's ideal and less like his real self. Once the avatar has been altered the places visited, the conversations discussed and the activities (including shopping) are altered to match this new identity.[31]

On one hand, this is perhaps the greatest attraction of virtual worlds—young people have the freedom to choose how they represent themselves to other people. On the other hand, it is also the feature that leaves advertisers and marketers pondering "To whom am I talking?" The outgoing, flamboyant, 17-year-old from Paris, France, you are chatting with may in fact be a mousy, modest 12-year-old from Punxsutawney, Pennsylvania. But this may not be as much an issue as one might think. For it has been suggested that whereas users have the ability to manipulate who they are in-world, deception may not be the user's purpose, rather the intent is to present a more honest presentation of the real-world persona.[32] In other words, regardless of their avatars' appearance, virtual-world residents are often more "virtually" honest than they are in the real world.[33] This premise may provide marketers with a more accurate insight into consumer desires.

Virtual Peers

The *Global Habbo Youth Survey 2008*, a survey of over 58,000 young people (aged 12–18) from 31 countries, revealed that the most important value uniting teens is the desire to gain acceptance from their peers.[34] Beyond experimenting with their identity, young people are also drawn to these environments as a way to develop and strengthen relationships with others.[35] For adolescents, acceptance and popularity are often measured by the number of virtual friends. As such, in an effort to increase one's popularity it is not uncommon for teenagers to accept the friendship of people that they barely know, and it is rare for them to "un-friend" people they no longer keep in regular contact with. This suggests that definition of "friend" in virtual environments may be very different from that in the real world. So what are the implications of these online friendships and what influence (if any) do virtual friends exert on behavior?

Virtual-world friendships can offer adolescents positive social support and connection that may be missing in their real world.[36] Over half of the Cartoon Doll Emporium users surveyed said they felt closer to their CDE friends than real-life friends.[37] Many of these in-world relationships mimic those we typically find in the physical world. Avatars form friendships with other avatars, they discuss real life problems, they argue, and even go on dates, but often without ever meeting in the real world or in some cases knowing the real life identity of the other person/s. Whereas these virtual friendships can be helpful at satisfying unfilled real-world needs they can also be fraught with complications.

Anonymity in virtual worlds allows users to engage in deception and maliciousness.[38] Whereas kid-oriented virtual worlds are highly monitored for inappropriate behavior and language, adolescent worlds do not appear to be as tightly controlled. Some of these teen virtual playgrounds are ripe with bullies who relish insulting and ridiculing others. One exploratory study of a popular teenage world found that just as in the real world, in the virtual world a social hierarchy exists.[39] At the basic level there are two groups of users—the virtual-world veterans and the new kids who are often referred to as "Noobs." Veteran members are those users who have been in-world for some time. They are extremely skilled and knowledgeable on the intricacies of virtual-world life, but they can be intolerant of new inexperienced members. The new kids— the Noobs—are instantly recognizable by their uniform appearance and standard-issue wardrobe. They are the frequent targets of verbal abuse.

Being accepted by others is important in virtual worlds. Without friends, the virtual space can be a very lonely place. Gaining acceptance in these environments is not all that different from the real world. The first step is usually to alter your avatar's appearance so that it conforms to the norms of the environment.[40] Changing an avatar's appearance includes altering the body shape, facial features, and clothing. Many worlds provide a certain amount of avatar customization free of charge. But to create a truly unique appearance usually requires spending real-world dollars on your virtual self. Most virtual words operate their own in-world currency. For instance, There.com uses There Bucks and Teen Grid Second Life uses Linden Dollars. Users convert their real-world Dollars, Euros, Yen, and many other currencies into the relevant in-world currency and use it to purchase virtual products. In the real world, a make-over may be time consuming and expensive, but in virtual world it is instantaneous and inexpensive. Virtual items sell for only a fraction of their real-world asking price—many items sell for less than $1, but the potential for sales is huge. In mid-2007, Charles River Ventures proclaimed that the virtual goods market was worth approximately $1.5 billion (real-world dollars) and growing rapidly.[41] Whether it is for some new clothing, a virtual pet, a car, or a beach house, avatars are spending big. So how do users know what to spend their money on? They know by observing other avatars and seeking the input of their virtual peers.[42]

Virtual Reference Groups

Traditionally, in the real world, it was family and friends who served as a reference for identity exploration and purchase decisions.[43] In the virtual world, experimentation and decision-making often occur both in the presence, and with the aid of, people they have never and may never meet in the real world. Early reports reveal that the dynamics of social influence of peers that are so well documented in physical contexts has the ability to transfer to virtual relationships as well. Furthermore, if virtual peers have the ability to influence in-world purchases, then there is also the potential to spur sales of real-life items.[44]

Peer-to-peer marketing is nothing new. For years marketers have been recruiting young people to help spread the word about products. In 2000 Proctor and Gamble (P&G) founded the company Tremor to create and manage buzz in the teen market. Today the company counts more than 200,000 teens among its members and boasts non-P&G companies such as Hershey's, Ford, and Hallmark as clients. Teen members are offered free products and services, *in exchange*, not compensation, for participation. If members like the products they are encouraged to spread the word to peers. Another company specializing in peer-to-peer and word-of-mouth marketing is Big Fat Institute. Big Fat recruits kids to help generate buzz about brands via the Internet. A potentially more persuasive technique for generating buzz involves "seeding." Seeding is the process whereby the company gives away merchandise to some of the more popular kids in the hope that products popularity will extend to those who aspire to be part of the in-crowd. It won't be long before peer-to-peer marketing and seeding moves from the real world into virtual worlds—if it has not already done so.

REAL BRANDS IN VIRTUAL ENVIRONMENTS

The popularity of interactive technologies has forced marketers to rethink how they reach today's youth. When virtual worlds first entered the market, companies rushed to stake their claims in this unchartered land.

When results failed to live up to expectations, many of them retreated. The result was a slew of negative press, and virtual worlds were discounted as a passing fad. So why did the marketing efforts of these companies fail?

Virtual-world failures often occur for a variety of reasons including poor planning, timing, and execution. But perhaps the underlying problem is that many companies do not understand how to harness the unique characteristics of the environment to offer a satisfying experience to customers.[45] For instance, some companies make the error of replicating real-world strategies in-world, only to have residents flatly reject them. To illustrate, American Apparel was the first real-world company to open a virtual-world clothing store. Unfortunately their efforts were short-lived. The mistake they made was that their in-world store was an exact replica of their real-world store. In short, the store was boring. After the initial visit there were was no motivation to return. American Apparel failed to create a space that appealed to the needs of young people. Their virtual store did nothing to encourage discovery, creation, or interaction. Simply replicating real-world strategies in virtual worlds is not the key to success. The rules of engagement are different online, and until marketers accept that there are likely to be more failures than successes.

But for all the failures, there are examples of success. To date over 200 brands including Coke, Pepsi, Kraft, and Pizza Hut have chosen to engage with kids and teens in interactive environments.[46] What sets many of these companies apart from those that have failed is that they recognize, appreciate, and utilize the unique characteristics of the environment to craft interactive product experiences. To illustrate, JCPenney chose to place virtual representations of their back-to-school outfits on the Yahoo Avatars page. During a seven-week experiment, 5 million outfits were tried on and 1.5 million Yahoo avatars opted to wear JCPenney clothing. In another example, Kohl's department store opened a boutique in Stardoll, a virtual world that boasts over 20 million members. In this boutique are pieces from the real-world Abbey Dawn collection designed by singer Avril Lavigne. In the first 16 days the boutique logged 2.2 million visits and sold 1.8 million virtual items. Furthermore, Kohls was successful in luring 97,000 visitors to its Web site (www.kohls.com), visitors who clicked through from the boutique site. In an effort to achieve similar success, Sears department store has since entered Stardoll, hosting daily virtual fashion shows.[47] There is no doubt that real-world brands and advertising are a crucial part of the virtual-world experience—they help make the environment more realistic. Marketers just need to understand how to market in these environments.

MARKETING IN VIRTUAL WORLDS

Unfortunately in these early days there are still no best practices for marketing in virtual worlds. But with an understanding of what motivates young consumers to engage in these environments coupled with the findings of those who have had success (and of those who have failed), marketers can employ some factors to increase their chances of success. These factors are referred to as the *4 C's of Virtual World Marketing Communications*: Content, Collaboration, Conversation, and Community. These four factors are by no means mutually exclusive, but for the purpose of discussion they are explained separately here.

Content

Choose your virtual-world content carefully. As we have seen, what works in the real world does not necessary work in the virtual world. In the real world we know that product integration in television shows and movies is more successful than simple product placement. Likewise in virtual worlds, passive marketing communications such as billboards are not likely to generate positive feelings and will have little effect at motivating residents to purchase the virtual- or real-world product. Virtual-world residents are more likely to have positive attitudes toward and interact with brands that are integrated in the environment, rather than those that are merely decorative advertising.[48] For example, L'Oreal USA decided to promote its cosmetics in virtual worlds. To do so they created four real-world makeup looks in the forms of skins (cosmetic masks that fit the avatar's face like a second skin). During the three-month campaign they distributed 34,000 makeup skins, an average of 2,428 per week.[49] CosmoGirl decided to host a virtual prom in the virtual world There.com. Avatars came dressed in their finest attire for an evening of music and dancing. There were photograph opportunities and even a prom king and queen. During the event ABC Family showed video trailers for its reality series *America's Prom Queen* and avatars were treated to virtual makeovers—Acuvue Contact Lenses gave away free colored lenses for avatars attending the event. In both of these examples the product was integrated into the environment to provide a more meaningful virtual experience.

Collaboration

No longer satisfied with being a passive recipient of marketing messages, consumers today want to be able to interact with the brand and in some cases aid in its creation.[50] Therefore, marketers should provide opportunities for residents to work with the brand rather than just use it. For example, Toyota allowed people to decorate and customize (virtual) Scions that they could drive, share, and sell to other residents in There.com. But involvement should not be limited to just customizing products; rather marketers should involve consumers early on in the innovation process. Coca-Cola was the first company to launch a virtual-world partnership with their consumers. It invited the general public to submit designs for a virtual-world vending machine that would help them dispense not cans of Coke but the "essence of Coca-Cola" in virtual worlds—after all avatars can't drink! The final product was a series of "Puzzle Bottles" that dispense cool interactive experiences and Coke-branded virtual gifts. The opportunity for consumers to co-create with their favorite brands in this manner can be very successful in generating positive buzz. This type of collaboration also appeals to the community element of virtual worlds and promotes dialogue among consumers and between consumers and marketers.

Conversation

In virtual communications individuals are only too willing to exchange knowledge about personal experiences with products.[51] Interactions and conversations with others in virtual worlds can influence customers' attitudes toward the product and the company.[52] Therefore, the selection of the source is essential for success. In the real world, an advertiser painstakingly selects a spokesperson to promote a product. For the spokesperson to be persuasive she needs to be credible, attractive, and someone with whom the target audience can identify. Companies are equally careful when it comes to selecting the popular kids, the trendsetters, to help generate positive word of mouth. The same due diligence needs to be undertaken if selecting a virtual-world spokesperson (avatar) or brand ambassador to promote a product in-world.

Identifying and recruiting appropriate opinion leaders may be paramount for success. As a starting point, companies may want to solicit the help of in-world guides. In-world guides are individuals who volunteer their time to help new users navigate and master the world. These guides, having logged many hours in-world, are usually extremely knowledgeable and equally friendly. When a new user arrives in a new world they are often greeted by a guide who offers them assistance. When new users have questions they typically turn to these guides for help. As such, these guides serve as a reference group and have the potential to be great brand ambassadors.

Community

Individuals join virtual worlds primarily for the opportunity to interact with others. Not unlike in the real world, in the virtual world both formal and informal reference groups exist. These reference groups function as a virtual community, and they can potentially impact opinions and behavior both in-world and in the real world. Embracing and facilitating the community element of virtual worlds should be an important goal of any company wanting to reach young people. To succeed, advertisers need to identify which groups are the most influential and determine how they can be enlisted to advocate the advertiser's product or service.[53]

If an appropriate group does not exist, then it may be necessary to create one. Either way it is important that advertisers become part of the community and join in the conversations.

Conclusion

Harvard Business Review predicts that by 2013 virtual environments are likely to emerge as *the* dominant Internet interface. In addition to corporate Web sites, companies will also operate virtual stores and will interact with customers in these environments.[54] Within the first 6 months of 2008 alone, investors poured $345 million into this space, suggesting that the technology is gaining momentum.[55] But with all the possibilities that virtual worlds have to offer, it is important to remember that it may take time to see real-world results. Companies need to keep in mind that it took decades for marketers to learn how to effectively and efficiently create advertising messages for television. Companies now need to master the learning curve to these new environments, because soon they will become an indispensible tool for any company intent on reaching out to the virtual generation.[56]

After an extensive and lively discussion with her friends, Jenny decides to buy the Gucci sunglasses. Everyone agrees they definitely give her that Hollywood look she has been craving. A couple clicks of her mouse and they are all hers. As she and her shopping posse leave the store and head down to the beach, the compliments from passersby helps to reaffirm her choice, and she feels good. She settles down on a beach towel and starts to drift away to the latest song from Alicia Keys. Somewhere in the distance she hears a door open and the sound of two familiar voices. In the blink of an eye warm sunny Laguna Beach is gone and she back in cold dreary Pittsburgh. The time on the clock reads 6:15 P.M. Oops!

Notes

1. Watching television, 2009, http://www.childtrendsdatabank.org/?q=node/149.

2. Victoria Rideout, Donald F. Roberts, and Ulla G.Foehr, "Generation M: Media in the Lives of 8–18 Year Olds," The Henry J. Kaiser Family Foundation, 2005, http://www.kff.org/entmedia/entmedia030905pkg.cfm.

3. "Toy Industry Association Study on Kids and Online Play, 28% of Kids Who Use SGE's Have Purchased Products," Virtual World News, 2008, http://www.virtualworldsnews.com/2008/07/toy-industry-as.html.

4. Young Consumers Research Purchases Online, eMarketer, 2008, http://www.emarketer.com.

5. "64% of Cartoon Doll Emporium Users Spend More Time on Site than Watching TV," Virtual World news, 2008, http://www.virtualworldsnews.com/2008/07/64-of-cartoon-d.html.

6. Damien Arthur, Claire Sherman, Dion Appel, and Lucy Moore, "Why Young Consumers Adopt Interactive Technologies," *Young Consumers* 2 (2006): 33–38.

7. Amanda Lenhart, Mary Madden, Alexandra R. Macgill, and Aaron Smith, *Teens and Social Media*, Pew Internet & American Life Project, 2007, http://www.pewinternet.org/PPF/r/230/report_display.asp.

8. Brian Simpson, "Identity Manipulation in Cyberspace as a Leisure Option: Play and the Exploration of Self," *Information & Communications Technology Law* 14 (2005): 115–131.

9. Erik Erikson, *Childhood and Society* (New York: Norton, 1963).

10. Susan Harter, *The Construction of the Self: A Developmental Perspective* (New York: Guildford Press, 1999).

11. J. E. Marcia, *Ego Identity: A Handbook for Psychosocial Research* (New York: Springer, 1993).

12. James E. Katz and Ronald E. Rice, *Social Consequences of Internet Use: Access, Involvement, and Interaction* (Cambridge: MIT Press, 2002); Howard Rheingold, *The Virtual Community: Homesteading in the Electronic Frontier* (Reading: Addison-Wesley, 1993); Kaveri Subrahmanyam, David Smahel, and Patricia Greenfield, "Connecting Developmental Constructions to the Internet: Identity Presentation and Sexual Exploration in Online Teen Chatrooms," *Developmental Psychology* 42, no. 3 (2006): 395–406.

13. Conrad Bennett. "Keeping Up with the Kids," *Young Consumers* 2 (2006): 28–38.

14. Ulla G. Foehr, "Media Multitasking among American Youth: Prevalence, Predictors and Pairings," The Henry J. Kaiser Family Foundation, 2006, http://www.kff.org/entmedia/upload/7592.pdf.

15. See Note 2.

16. See Note 6.

17. See Note 4.

18. See Note 7.

19. Bill Rose and Joe Lenski, "Internet and Multimedia 2006," Arbitron, 2006, www.arbitron.com/downloads/im2006study.pdf.

20. Amy Nowak, "Big Media Muscles In on Virtual Worlds," CableFax, 2008, http://cablefax.com/cablefaxmag/other/Big-Media-Muscles-In-on-Virtual-Worlds_29346.html.

21. Stephanie Olsen, *What Kids Learn in Virtual Worlds*, Cnet, 2007, http://sympatico-msn-ca.com/What-kids-learn-in-virtual-worlds/2009-1043_3-6218763.htm.

22. Debra Aho Williamson, "Kids and Teens: Virtual Worlds Open New Universe," eMarketer, 2007, http://www.emarketer.com/Reports/All/Emarketer_2000437.aspx.

23. Natalie T. Wood and Michael R. Solomon, "Virtual Worlds, Real Impact: Advertising in Immersive Digital Environments. Handbook of Research on Digital Media and Advertising: User Generated Content Consumption," ed. Neal M. Burns, Terry Daugherty, and Matthew S. Eastin (Information Science Publishing, forthcoming).

24. "What is a Virtual World?" Virtual Worlds Review, http://www.virtualworldsreview.com/info/whatis.shtml.

25. See Note 23.

26. See Note 3.

27. "150+ Youth-oriented Virtual Worlds Now Live or Developing," Virtual Worlds News, 2008, http://www.virtualworldsnews.com/2008/08/virtual-world-5.html.

28. Natalie T. Wood, Lan Nguyen Chaplin, and Michael R. Solomon, "Virtually Me: Youth Consumers and Their Online Identities." Paper presented at Advances in Consumer Research, San Francisco, 2009.

29. See Note 27.

30. See Note 9, Note 10, and Note 11.

31. See Note 28.

32. See Note 8.

33. Adam Broitman and Jack Tatar, "How to Reach Real People in a Virtual World," iMedia Connection, 2008, http://www.imediaconnection.com/content/19487.asp.

34. Global Habbo Youth Survey (Lahti, Finaland: Sulake Corporation, 2008).

35. Janis Wolak, Kimberly J. Mitchell, and David Finkelhor, "Escaping or Connecting? Characteristics of Youth Who Form Close Online Relationships," *Journal of Adolescence* 26 (2003): 105–119.

36. Ibid.

37. See Note 5.

38. See Note 35.

39. See Note 28.

40. See Note 28.

41. See Note 23.

42. See Note 28.

43. See Note 12.

44. See Note 23.

45. See Note 23.

46. See Note 34.

47. Cheryl Lu-Lien Tan, "Retailers 'Sell' to Young Virtually," *The Wall Street Journal*, August 19, 2008.

48. Michelle R. Nelson. "Recall of Brand Placement in Computer/Video Games," *Journal of Advertising Research* 42 (2002): 80–92.

49. "K Zero Distributes 34,000 L'Oréal Paris Items in Three-Month Campaign," Virtual World News, 2008, http://www.virtualworldsnews.com/2008/04/k-zero-distribu.html.

50. James H. McAlexander, John W. Schouten, and Harold F. Koening, "Building Brand Community," *Journal of Marketing* 6 (2002): 38–54.

51. Robert V. Kozinets. "E-Tribalized Marketing?: The Strategic Implications of Virtual Communities of Consumption," *European Management Journal* 17, no. 3 (1999): 252–264.

52. Nambisan Satish and Robert A. Baron, "Interactions in Virtual Customer Environments: Implications for Product Support and Customer Relationship Management," *Journal of Interactive Marketing* 21 (2007): 42–62.

53. See Note 23.

54. Miklos Sarvary, "Breakthrough Ideas for 2008," *Harvard Business Review* (February 2008): 17–45.

55. "$345 Mill Invested in 39 Virtual Worlds-related Companies in First 1/2 of 08," Engage Digital Media, 2008, http://www.virtualworldsmanagement.com/2008/q2.html.

56. Jonathon Richards, "McKinsey: Ignore Second Life at Your Peril," Times Online, 2008, http://technology.timesonline.co.uk/tol/news/tech_and_web/article3803056.ece.

SUGGESTED READING

Palfrey, John, and Urs Gasser. *Born Digital: Understanding the First Generation of Digital Natives*. Philadelphia: Perseus Group, 2008.

Tapscott, Don. *Growing Up Digital: The Rise of the Net Generation*. New York: McGraw Hill, 1998.

Wood, Natalie T., and Michael R. Solomon. *Virtual Social Identity and Consumer Behavior*. Advertising and Consumer Psychology Book Series. New York: ME Sharpe, 2009.

Wood, Natalie T., and Michael R. Solomon. "Virtual Worlds, Real Impact: Advertising in Immersive Digital Environments," in *Handbook of Research on Digital Media and Advertising: User Generated Content Consumption*, ed. Matthew S. Eastin, Terry Daugherty, and Neal M. Burns. IGI Global (forthcoming).

13

COMMUNITY DEVELOPMENT IN THE VIRTUAL SPACE

Ellen Kolstö

Virtual worlds and online social spaces have given rise to a new type of community—the virtual community when people come together to share similar interests, mind-sets, or learning opportunities. The key to turning virtual spaces into active communities is making sure these places have things to do and people to share things with. Virtual worlds can become "real" places where people come together as avatars or icons to have shared experiences, whether as simple as having conversations or as involved as playing games, taking classes, viewing art, or watching films. These shared experiences give users a reason to come back to the space, and then the space itself becomes the foundation for a community. Just as in the real world, virtual communities develop out of shared experiences with others. However, development of such communities must start with an understanding of the elements needed to attract and keep users in your space. This means that creating a virtual community from scratch does take ongoing work and perseverance. In the early days of virtual worlds, especially for the virtual world of Second Life, it was not clear to users or brands and companies that community building should involve more than simply creating the space itself. Many felt that no one came to visit their space due to lack of interest in overall virtual spaces or because users didn't care to visit places with sponsors on brands. In fact, real-world and virtual brands have found success in building communities in virtual spaces. Orange Island in Second Life (sponsored by Orange Telecom in France) as well as Glass Earth (neko gear and clothing) and Toyota Scion in There.com have all attracted engaged visitors to their virtual locations, and these visitors continue to be active in their communities. Successful in-world brands such as Kyoot Army Head-quarters and Paper Couture (both Second Life clothing brands) have also developed a strong following for their goods and have fan groups who sign up for notices of their latest releases.

Early brand sponsorship and community failures in the virtual space suffered from a lack of understanding of how to develop a virtual community and even how to develop a truly meaningful product for virtual users. Many did not realize that, just like the real world, ongoing events and activities are key to keeping communities alive and active. Would you build a real-life store and then do nothing to promote it? Real-life retailers have found that ongoing in-store events do much to strengthen their sales and consumer loyalty, and it is no different in the virtual world.

The keys to creating a vibrant virtual community include creating the right space, attracting users with ongoing activities or events, and knowing the do's and don'ts of a virtual community. We will explore each of these areas in detail.

CREATING THE RIGHT SPACE

Virtual worlds are highly visual experiences. Virtual spaces that succeed in becoming real communities have a planned design that is visually stimulating but functional. Regardless of the purpose of your space (e.g., pure fun vs. working areas for meetings and collaboration), good design is key to inviting users into your very visual space.

When it's about fun and entertainment, design ideas should include creative, out-of-the-box thinking that captures the imagination of the virtual 3D space. Design that draws virtual users back to keep exploring should include unusual features and various areas to be explored and used on a regular basis. Greenies, an island in Second Life, features a living room and kitchen designed to make the visiting avatar feels like an ant on the floor of the room. Tables, chairs, even an ironing board tower overhead and appear much larger than life. Since avatars can fly in Second Life, visitors can explore all the areas of this oversized living room and kitchen, which captures the imagination in an Alice In Wonderland sort of way. Greenies includes many hidden surprises in the space, such as tiny green Martians playing in a bag of sugar on the kitchen counter or hiding in the drawers of a living room desk. The novelty of Greenies and the opportunity to discover new things on each visit attract new and repeat visitors who come back with friends. It also offers many interesting photo opportunities around the space. This makes for more activity in the space, and, when users are regularly there, it will attract even more new users. After all, people like to be where other people are whether it's in the real or virtual world.

The physical design of a virtual community also sends strong signals about the sponsoring brand or owner of the space. When a 3D space is well built and has a strong, consistent design sense and good use of color, it feels upscale and more thoughtful, much like the design of a good retail space. Think about a design of, say, a local Dollar Store versus the lobby of a W Hotel. Both of these types of designs can be present in a virtual world as well, but they say very different things about the owner or brand who built the space. Orange Island in Second Life is one example. Orange Island is a community space of several island locations built to offer educational, cultural, and collaborative experiences to its community members. The island regularly features acoustic musicians streaming live into the space or classes on how to build 3D items or seminars on different cultures in the virtual or real world. The island is sponsored by Orange Telecom in Franc, and careful attention has been paid to the design of the island including the places where avatars meet and attend events. A rich brown floor design with a wooden texture and the subtle use of the color orange give the various spaces around the main island a warm and welcoming feel. The entry point at the island offers a map of locations to visit and features orange footsteps on the ground that follow the avatar as it walks. Avatars can take a guided tour of the various virtual gathering places that feature modern furniture surrounded by trees, hills, and natural landscaping. These added details make an island visit visually interesting and worth visiting on multiple occasions to discover more.

Some virtual locations are created expressly for in-world meetings or more formal gatherings. These types of designs tend to look more functional with less emphasis on unusual design (e.g., flying cows in the sky or furniture on the ceiling). However, good design is still important to establish the feel of the space even when it functions purely to have avatars sit and listen to live streaming speakers or chat among themselves without more active events on the schedule. In Idea City (a virtual island in Second Life owned by U.S. ad agency GSD&M Idea City), much of the island features meeting spaces and is home to a large amphitheater. While the design of these spaces is less whimsical than many areas in Second Life, the meeting areas still use lots of color, employ interesting textures (e.g., chairs covered in virtual cowhide), and feature glass walls for more visual interest.

Aside from the design itself, an active space in a virtual world must also allow for interactivity. Users of virtual spaces want to interact not just with each other but with the space itself. Three-dimensional virtual spaces can allow users to build a giant mushroom in the middle of a city street or ride a virtual train or animate their avatar to play rock-paper-scissors with another avatar. All of these examples are interactive ways that users can utilize a virtual space for more than viewing a speaker or listening to music. Interactivity adds the element of direct involvement with the space and gives it something to offer when there are no scheduled events or group gatherings. One popular interactive element for active builders in Second Life is an area called a sandbox.

Sandboxes are designated plots of virtual land where building is unrestricted and users who do not own land can use the area to build items or test out products that require land space to open or use (such as virtual cars), giving users another reason to visit a virtual location. In Idea City, sandboxes are available on both sides of the island for any builder to spend time creating products or even whole structures. The sandboxes are cleaned of any building work after a certain period of time so that space is always available for new users.

Up to this point, we have discussed the benefits of good design from a visual and interactive perspective, but if a space cannot provide good basic functionality for a visiting avatar then no amount of well-crafted visual design will help it become a location for an active community. What exactly does this mean? All virtual spaces require a certain amount of bandwidth to function properly. The developer providing the server space for the location, whether it be a virtual world such as Second Life or OpenSim, has given the builders of the virtual location a certain amount of bandwidth to work with. If the design itself uses up so much virtual space with scripts or large builds it can cause lagging which makes it difficult for avatars to move through the space or perform easy tasks like clicking on items for more information. When the design takes away from the experience, then users will also avoid those virtual locations. Designs must allow users to move easily though an area, have some way to guide users through the area with signage and arrows and illustrate how users can complete tasks or simple movements without a lot of difficulty.

ATTRACTING COMMUNITY MEMBERS

Once your space has been created, getting users to join your community is the next important step. Many accepted ways of contacting potential users in virtual worlds or spaces have sprung up as early community developers have figured out what works best in this environment. Very much like real-life store openings or the launch of a group in your community, many virtual communities start with having an event that allows them to send invitations, spread word of mouth, and set the tone for the community moving forward. For communities based in entertainment or retail, many community kickoffs can feature parties with music from virtual DJs or live musicians streaming into the space. Visitors can animate their avatars to dance, enjoy the music, and chat with other visitors. In contrast, educational communities may have kickoff events that feature a speaker series or a seminar.

Many community developers solicit visitors to join their community group, which gives them direct access to messaging those users when in-world through special notices and group IM. In Second Life, joining a group will also place a tag over the avatar's head with the name of the group. This feature can give more exposure to your group and can be a form of expression for the avatar as they let others know by wearing your group tag that they are a part of your group.

Communities will also send in-world invitations to avatars for events designed as objects that sit on the ground and can be opened or simply read. Anything from traditional cards to actual objects to books with pages to turn, these invitations can feature times, locations, and landmarks that, when opened, can teleport an avatar directly to the location. These invitations can also set the tone of your event and your community.

Being aware of other related groups in the virtual world where you are planning your community can be very useful in attracting like-minded users to your opening event and ultimately your community. Idea City in Second Life held an event with the LBJ School of Public Policy where an interview with Madeleine Albright was streamed live onto the Idea City amphitheater viewing screen. Idea City worked with virtual-worlds developer Metaversatility to contact other groups of users in Second Life who would have an interest in seeing Ms. Albright, including groups interested in social policy, politics, and education.

Reaching out to members of in-world groups is not limited to communication inside the world itself. There are blogs and Web sites dedicated to these groups on the Web where postings can be made regarding in-world events. In addition, MySpace and Facebook pages can be created where events can be posted, discussed, and promoted among virtual worlds users who maintain personal pages there as well.

THE BEST PRACTICES OF SUCCESSFUL VIRTUAL COMMUNITIES

A virtual community, much like any online social community, requires true authenticity in the way the community is set up and managed. Transparency in the intention of any events, solicitations, and communication with the members is required. Members expect to understand exactly what is being introduced into the community and what role they can expect to have because as active participants they think of themselves as "owners" as well. Input on events, openness of who is sponsoring an event, and full disclosure when events are commercial in nature are key. Full disclosure of any expected rules for the group are also required so that all members understand up front what is expected. If members suspect any less than transparent behavior, it can result in loss of members and hurt the image of the community across the virtual world in which it exists.

As mentioned previously, events are crucial to creating a new community and (as will be discussed later in this chapter) maintaining an active community. However, the quality of the events themselves is just as important. While purely entertaining events can draw members and keep some interest, over time variety and substance is what will keep a community relevant to its members. An event that offers the opportunity to learn something new or experience something unique will go a long way toward solidifying interest and connection with the current community as well as attracting more members. Orange Island in Second Life is known for its enriching culturally based events. The island held a virtual Victorian Dance in a specially designed ballroom featuring music appropriate to the era. Avatars wore authentic ball gowns and suits for the occasion and were instructed on how to move about the ballroom, fill out dance cards and understand the etiquette as was expected at such an event in its day. Both educational and fun, the event was also visually beautiful and socially compelling. It represented a truly unique experience that most of the users operating the avatars could not dream of experiencing in real life.

Successful communities also recognize that members are as much a part of running the community as are owners and managers. Virtual community members expect to have active input and in many cases may shape and form future events on their own as they become more involved in the community. Using our previous example of Orange Island, community members have taken on very active roles having conducted classes on how to build in a virtual world as well as building sections of the island themselves on land donated by Orange to its members. Creators and owners of virtual spaces must be flexible in allowing members to do much more in these types of spaces, which is a draw to social spaces in the first place. Members will want help shape a community and owners must be willing to accept the added involvement.

Much has been debated on whether brands can operate successful communities in virtual worlds. Much discussion has centered around what many feel is the resistance of the virtual world users to marketing. However, many in-world brands have been thrived with much promotion to avatars. The real issue is that any brand that can make itself relevant *inside* the virtual space has a chance for success. If a brand cannot establish a useful purpose for itself in-world, then users will indeed not see a reason to support it. Interestingly, a real-world brand does not need to create virtual clothing to make itself relevant. If it can sponsor meaningful events, bring unique opportunities to a community, or help support in-world brands, artists, or musicians, users will see a reason for its existence. In social communities, everyone must bring something to the party; real-world brands are no different. Whatever they can do to make the virtual world a better experience will buy goodwill for the brand. Orange Telecom has created a strong, positive image in Second Life for its brand through its work on Orange Island. The company does not sell phone service in-world but instead brings much appreciated events and experiences to Second Life resulting in much goodwill among users who do have an option for their services in the real world. This model for using a virtual space to further goodwill for the brand in the real world has proven quite successful.

Maintaining a Community

Communities require ongoing support in order to remain vibrant and active. Community owners and managers must find ways to keep events and activities fresh and interesting for users to stay involved. As mentioned before, one option is to draw on the community members to lead activities, but another is to come up with new things to do or update ongoing events. Successful event types include contests (e.g., trivia or in-world photography), speaker series on a topic of interest to your group, hands-on demonstrations like in-world building, entertainment (live streaming musicians or in-world DJs streaming music) and interviews with other avatars of note in the virtual space (the Metanomics show in Second Life features avatar Host Beyers Sellers interviewing business people who are active in the virtual communities from companies such as IBM, Cisco, and Linden Lab).

Another way to keep a community interesting and offer up something in exchange for the continued loyalty of the user is the "freebie." Freebies are free in-world items (virtual free clothing, furniture, animations for the avatar) that can be regularly changed out to attract and keep users. Many retailers inside virtual communities use freebies to allow avatars to experience their products before buying (much like real-world sampling or free trials). As mentioned previously in this chapter, Orange Island offered free land to users who demonstrated innovative ways to use it. Freebies foster an exchange of goodwill between community members and community owners/managers. It demonstrates that those managing communities appreciate a person's time and know that loyalty is important. Offering freebies allows communities to thank the member for continuing to participate. Freebies are also great enticements for attracting new users who may not yet be committed to frequenting your community space.

Along the same lines as the freebie are interactive activities that avatars can experience on their own when events are not available. These activities also build goodwill among current and potential members as they enjoy free experiences that can be as enriching as scheduled events. As mentioned earlier in this chapter, these types of activities can give avatars things to do and reasons to return to the space. They can also highlight the imagination and creativity of the virtual-community owners and help set the tone for the community itself. Many in-world locations feature things as simple as virtual train rides or as complex as self-guided tours of areas not easily accessed in the real world such as virtual rain forests. One virtual location allowed avatars to step inside an open chamber where users collaboratively play musical notes and create music on their own. The activity was completely self-guided, interactive and free to any user.

COMMUNITY MANAGERS

Perhaps the most overlooked function of a community in the early days of virtual worlds was the community manager. Many original locations did not have available staff to answer questions, schedule events and get to know visiting members. It was often overlooked by early brand entrants into the space, and many companies were unaware that having real-world employees regularly involved in their virtual-world community would be a necessity for keeping it alive and active. As the idea of virtual communities matured, this role of community manager became crucial to the communities that have been successful at attracting and retaining members over time.

Community managers who understand the virtual space are invaluable in ensuring development of events that will be of interest to the members, because they know who frequents the community. They also tend to be well-connected players in the virtual worlds who know other communities to draw from and have many friends in the space to network with for spreading word of mouth on their events. Much like real-world party planners or event promoters, good community managers know how to draw a crowd and keep people coming to events. These managers also make friends of frequent visitors so that they can contact certain members for help getting the word out or to take the lead on developing or participating in an event. They also have a finger on the pulse of the community itself, knowing how users are feeling about the space, the events, or other members. This is great direct input on how the community is doing and allows for a quick response to any user issues or requests of the community.

MANAGING RELATIONSHIPS

Any community with engaged users will experience both positive and negative feedback from its members and will have to deal with various personalities and incidents that result from having many users together in the same space. Any brand or company entering the space should be ready to deal with negative feedback or activity just as brands so in the social media (e.g., MySpace, Facebook) space have where community members expect to be able to express honestly how they feel about the community and its sponsor. While social media may involve simply a negative post, virtual communities can involve actual incidents inside the space (e.g., "griefing" where an avatar will harass another avatar either verbally or through scripted objects designed to disable an avatar from seeing, walking, or otherwise functioning). Most virtual communities do have ways to control the avatars that do not follow community rules and act out against others. In Second Life, community owners and managers can ban and eject unruly users with a simply right click of a mouse. However, in the interest of honest exchange, if an avatar is not hurting another but wishes to express an opinion that may be negatively disposed toward the community owners and/or managers, discretion must be used in how far an avatar can be allowed to express the opinion. Virtual communities (just like online social communities) do thrive on allowing users to feel free to express themselves but a good community manager must use good judgment in how far to let some negative situations go.

WHAT MAKES A COMMUNITY FLOURISH OVER TIME

As with real-life communities, when members of virtual communities begin to develop friendships, the community is fulfilling its purpose of bringing people together, even if it is virtually. Doing things together, chatting each week, and coming together to support the community allow users to develop connections that are more meaningful and enhance their virtual experience and ultimately their real lives. While many who are not involved in virtual worlds can struggle to see how spending time in a simulated 3D space can be real, users of virtual worlds understand that shared experience in the space does illicit emotions, strong friendships, and opportunities to meet people from around the world by simply turning on a computer. Lasting friendships and even romance have resulted from meeting other users in virtual communities and these outcomes cannot be taken lightly. They are as real as meeting someone in person or talking to someone every day over the phone.

Communities bring these like-minded people together in ways never dreamed of until the development of the virtual space. Many communities extend the identity of the user in both a virtual- and real-world way. For example, groups of DJs who stream music in-world have helped launch clubs (which become communities in their own right with "regulars" and managers) in Second Life and have joined together in their own communities. For some, the experience of being a DJ in-world has allowed them to try something not available in the real world. It also allows them to feel like they know what it could be like to be a DJ and may even see themselves as such beyond just in a virtual setting. This type of experience can extend to virtual store owners, event promoters, fashion models, photographers, and the list goes on. The virtual space gives rise to communities and roles within those communities that can extend the work experience and ultimately the identity of the user as they try new things in a space where reinvention is welcome.

SUGGESTED READING

Association of Virtual Worlds. "The Blue Book: A Consumer Guide to Virtual Worlds," 2nd Edition, May 2008.

Forrester Research. "Marketing On Social Networking Sites," July 2007.
Forrester Research. "Online Community Best Practices," by Jeremiah Owyang, February 13, 2008.
Global Kids, Inc. "Best Practices for Non-Profits in Second Life," by Rik Panganiban, Fall 2007.
interFuel. "Virtual Worlds for Kids, Tweens & Teens: 7 Must-Have Features," 2008.

14

VIRAL MARKETING: CREATING A BUZZ WITH WEB 2.0

Thomas R. Donohue

Viral marketing (VM) is currently known by several names including "buzz," "reaching the tipping point," "contagious media," and "convergence marketing," all of which refer to a specific word-of-mouth (WOM) communication generated for the Internet about a brand, product, or service that leads to self-generating demand or sometimes ruin.[1] In describing "tipping point marketing," Malcolm Gladwell argues that three factors are responsible for its occurrence.[2] The first factor is a handful of exceptional influencers (innovators) who embrace a concept and make it into a cultural phenomenon. The second factor is the "stickiness factor," which comprises specific criteria that make a contagious message memorable. The third factor is a favorable environment, one aspect being timing, that encourages a virus to be unleashed. Since the term "viral marketing" was introduced in 1997, it has evolved to mean a strategy for acquiring new customers by encouraging honest communications among consumers. Consensus appears to have emerged that VM describes any strategy that encourages individuals to pass on a marketing message to others thereby creating exponential exposure and potential influence of the message.[3]

Word-of-mouth communication is an important component of marketing communication and has proved to be an effective means of promoting products and services.[4] In fact, WOM marketing has been an important marketing tool in the movie industry for decades. Recent examples include the phenomenal success of *My Big Fat Greek Wedding*, which was released in 2002 as a throw-away movie on fewer than 800 screens. It received positive reviews and began to attract larger audiences each week as the "buzz" and WOM worked. As the momentum increased, more screens were added and it became the sleeper film of the year as it grossed ten times its cost. On the negative side, the film *Gigli* in 2003 generated such negative reviews and buzz that it was pulled after two weeks of devastating WOM and movie-audience shunning.

The difference between traditional word of mouth and viral marketing is that VM uses the Internet and its networks and links to deliver brand and product messages. The challenge in viral marketing is managing the advocacy or referral rather than allowing a virus to spread in a random, uncontrolled fashion. Viral marketing can be defined as using e-mail to distribute advocacy and referral endorsements from one consumer to a host of potential consumers. The idea is to get people to forward a favorable message or advertisement to people in their e-mail address books, thereby creating an inverse pyramid effect.

There are two kinds of VM—passive and active. Passive refers to non–marketing-controlled pass-along where the form and content of the message causes people to forward it to their cohort groups. It can be humor or information oriented, but the pass-on is driven by the fact that the person is spontaneously intrigued and wishes to share the message. Active viral marketing is strategically crafted to be passed along because of some inherent benefit, disclosure, or inducement. Passive VM is unpredictable and often surprising in its spread. Active VM is designed to follow a specific path to targeted potential customers. Its predecessor is guerrilla marketing, where unorthodox strategies, tactics, and media were used to appeal to difficult-to-reach potential customers in offbeat contexts.

Origins of Viral Marketing

The WOM/VM phenomenon was originally described by Rogers and his associates as The Diffusion of Innovations,[5] in which the diffusion of innovations—new ideas, products, behaviors, and trends—could be described as approximating a bell curve. Adoption is based on attitudes of people as they evaluate new ideas or products. People differ dramatically in value constructs that make them anxious, willing, slow, or resistant to trying new things. The best example of the diffusion life cycle is found in the adoption of new technology. There are those anxious to try any new computer game, visit new Web sites, and acquire new electronic gadgets and those who will never have a personal computer, play a computer game, or figure out how to get the DVD/VCR player to quit blinking 12 o'clock.

Adopters come in five types: (1) Innovators; (2) Early adopters; (3) Early majority; (4) Late majority, and (5) Laggards. The key group from a VM perspective is the innovators. Innovators are adventuresome. They take chances, are attuned to emerging trends, and are called the "cool" people in adolescent groups. Innovators "discover" new bands, new clothing, and about-to-become-hip forms of expression. To their non-innovative friends, they also possess two major traits that make them "cool."

The first trait is credibility. Innovators know a lot about the category in which they have acquired expertise. Music innovators, for example, spend vast amounts of time scoping out new forms of music, new bands, and potential stars and can speak knowledgeably about most aspects of contemporary music. Consequently, people further back on the diffusion curve look to innovators for emerging trends.

The second trait of innovators is trust. People trust innovators' recommendations because of their credibility and are willing to accept their recommendations. There is also a third, minor characteristic termed "dynamism." Dynamism is based in action and commitment. Innovators tend to be passionate about their interests and willing to share enthusiastic opinions with friends and followers. In a PBS documentary, "The Merchants of Cool," marketing researchers are shown frantically attempting to discover and define teen coolness—that is, to find the innovators—so their cachet can be attached to teen products. Innovators constitute the smallest segment of adopters. However, their numbers belie their importance in viral marketing.

In the original diffusion model, mass media were the primary sources for awareness and information in the discovery of new cultural phenomena. Innovators would comb traditional and underground media for undiscovered and future icons. Their recommendations were then passed to early adopters who are credited with mainstreaming innovative trends. By the time the early majority were finished embracing a trend, nearly half the life cycle had been completed and the trend may have lost its "coolness."

In the VM model, innovators discover new trends at new and obscure Web sites, drill down for more information and, after they have digested it, pass it along (via e-mail) to early adopters who are eager to be in on the "next big thing." Traditional mass media are too slow and "late majority" audience oriented to be of much use to innovators. The problem with innovations and their diffusion over the Internet is that time is being compressed and there is a constant decrease of time between discovery and popularity of a trend. That means that viral marketers must identify trends instantly and act quickly as the window for spreading the word becomes smaller each month.

THE CASE FOR USING VIRAL MARKETING

Viral marketing is an important marketing tool for four reasons:

- It is not expensive for marketers—the individual passing on the referral carries the cost and invests the time of forwarding the brand or product message.

- Because the act of forwarding a message is voluntary, rather than a paid endorsement, the message has more inherent credibility and is likely to be viewed with less skepticism by recipients.
- Those forwarding messages are most likely to know which among their cohort groups have an interest in the topic thereby performing a nifty targeting function and ensuring a higher probability that the message will be read.
- The strategic aspects of the message—humor, irony, or pathos—may contribute to the enjoyment of the message and enhance a brand's image.

According to Douglas Holt, in his book *How Brands Become Iconic: The Principles of Cultural Branding*, one needs the assistance of stories, identity myths, and urban legends to move a brand from a mere mortal status of "identity brand" to an immortal status of icon.[6] It appears that the Internet is well poised as a tool to help brands achieve the rarified air of icon. The Internet possesses homogeneous cohort groups for targeting potential customers and creating devotees; it has democratized the review process (blogs and Zagat-like review Web sites) and fosters the connection of like-minded individuals. Personalized video sites, such as YouTube.com, augment the text component of communication with videos that can enhance legends and myth creation.

On the other hand, viral marketing has its detractors who argue that because of cheap gimmicks, sophomoric attempts at humor, and witless videos, viral marketers have inoculated customers by being boring, derivative, and/or tasteless. The rash of supposedly humorous video clips has become tiresome and viewers are increasingly more difficult to engage, setting the bar for a successful VM campaign yet higher.

How Effectively Does Viral Marketing Work?

N. Hermann and C. Fiteni have devised a five-step sequence that describes how viral marketing works. They argue that VM should be treated like a real virus whose survival advertisers want to ensure while encouraging exponential growth.[7]

Step One—Fast and Effective Transfer

The more easily a virus transmits, the more it will spread, so the medium used to carry the message must be easy to transfer and replicate. The Internet boom in viral marketing is due to the fact that communicating has become fast, efficient, and relatively inexpensive. Moreover, messages should be short and to the point—through both visuals and text—so to be understood quickly and require less time and effort to digest.

Step Two—Exploit the Carrier

The best viruses are those that exploit common high-interest topics including sex, humor, irony, and gender differences. Some would argue that incorporating basic human needs in a viral message increases its chances to be passed along. The need to stay connected with one's cohort group also plays a role in viruses. Most Internet users like to communicate with their frequent e-mail partners. Forwarding a message one knows to possess interest for the recipient is an easy way to stay connected.

Step Three—Prepare for an Epidemic

If one seeks to create a virus, preparations need to be made to ensure its success does not overwhelm. If a viral campaign is successful, the product's Web site has to be able to handle the hits and follow-up communication. That means e-mails and queries have to be answered in a timely manner. If there is a telephone component, sufficient capacity has to exist for an increased call volume. The best commercial Web sites are those where queries, orders, and customer complaints are handled quickly, efficiently, courteously, and professionally.

Step Four—Proliferate from Within

It has been said that humans are separated by no more than six degrees—that our social networks are overlapping and that generally fewer than six people separate one person from another unknown person. If that is true, if one communicates regularly with a dozen people who communicate with a dozen people each, the exponential spread of a virus is assured—if the message is compelling and fits the reference criteria of the recipients.

Step Five—Affiliate and Breed

Convergence marketing argues that there is a plethora of communication tools that can help spread one's message. Hermann and Fiteni suggest that viral marketers should use affiliate programs—billboards on other sites—to generate high traffic volume. In addition, the authors recommend using Internet news releases that can be picked up by periodicals, which would be captured by portals such as Yahoo and Google News, thereby spreading a message with rapidity and economy to millions of Web surfers daily.

BOTTOM LINE

The litmus test for creating a message intended for viral distribution is embedded in the answer to the question, "What would cause me to forward it to people whose time I respect and for whom I think the message is appropriate and interesting?" Hermann and Fiteni offer a checklist for determining the efficacy of any viral strategic effort:

- Is it Easy? Make it easy to use and abuse—forward—and the chances for success are greater.
- Is it Entertaining? People spend a great amount of time on the Internet entertaining themselves and like to forward content to others who will be similarly entertained.
- Does the Message Have Pass-along Legs? Will people like the message enough to pass it along? Does the message resonate with themes that will be appreciated by thousands of people?
- Can you fulfill Expectations? Does the company have the capacity to deliver what it claims it can when it says it can and meet customers' service expectations?

MOTIVATIONS FOR FORWARDING MESSAGES

As one creates messages designed for viral distribution, the question of what motivates people to forward these messages emerges. What types of messages get passed most often and what are the circumstances that encourage pass-along? J. E. Phelps and his associates queried people about their motivations for forwarding pass-along e-mails and found that many experience positive emotions when sending such e-mails. The emotions reported the most were excitement, being helpful, happy, or satisfied. However, they also reported that certain conditions must be met before they forward e-mails.[8]

For frequent e-mailers, the forwarded message had to be important or relevant or contain something that the sender was positive the recipient would like. Also, having sufficient time (not in a rush) and being in a good mood were said to be important motivating factors for people to forward e-mails. Frequent e-mailers also reported that they like to be the first with information their cohort groups would find useful, much in the same way people like to break important news stories to one another.

People reported that fun, entertainment, enjoyment, having a good time, a distraction from what they are doing, and rejuvenation from boring tasks are among the personal gratifications from forwarding eye-catching e-mails. Senders also reported that their messages affect recipients by helping them, letting them know that they care, thanking or encouraging them, and helping them "be in the know." Clearly, the overriding motivation for people to forward e-mails to others in their networks is that it makes them feel good to do so.

IMPLICATIONS FOR MESSAGE CREATION

Content analysis of forwarded e-mail would demonstrate what most e-mailers know intuitively: messages that evoke strong emotional responses—through humor, empathy, indignation, inspiration—and offer new insight are the most likely to be forwarded. Messages about free stuff, consumer tips, new applications for existing products, and warnings are likely to be passed along, as well. The key to creating messages that get passed along is that they should be consistent with the product they wish to promote.

Common-denominator or low-brow humor is inappropriate for icon brands, status brands, emerging brands, and new products. Mature brands' messages can be crafted with more leeway than new products and brands. Because consumers commonly know the mature brand, more message options are available to its viral marketer. For example, Coke has been an icon brand for more than 75 years, so now the company's strategy is to entertain customers in order to protect market share, nibble at market share held by close competitors, and maintain a formidable presence in the market place. To the contrary, for emerging brands and new products, a key consideration is a brand's benefits, unique selling propositions, and competitive positioning. Thus a new brand or product's viral campaign needs to be reasons-why oriented and should offer a free sample, trial, and/or coupon as a way to provide a money-saving offer for e-mailers to encourage forwarding the message.

PLANNING THE VIRAL MARKETING CAMPAIGN

Strategic planning for viral marketing plans is remarkably similar to that for traditional media. A full assessment of the product, target market, goals, strategies, and tactics are requisites before a campaign is initiated.

- **Product**. One has to assess if the product can be virally marketed. Typically, low-involvement commodity products such as tissue, gasoline, and household products do not lend themselves to the kind of engagement and self-involvement necessary to create a viable viral campaign. At best, e-mail receivers may be entertained by a marketer-generated message, but the nature of the product is unlikely to attach to an increased appreciation for the product. Generally, as ego-involvement increases for a brand, so does the possibility that it is an appropriate viral-marketing candidate.

  A downside assessment of the product's negatives is also necessary. In instances where products have potentially controversial components (cigarettes, alcohol, gas-guzzling cars, shoes produced in countries without child labor laws, and the like), the way in which the negatives could be used to tamper with the message must be assessed. Otherwise, the buzz could become negative as the intended viral message is ridiculed or becomes the recipient of editorial content as it is forwarded.
- **Target Audience**. Knowing the target audience is necessary but not sufficient. Marketers have to know the targeted consumers' lifestyle and entertainment habits and preferences. For example, a viral message fashioned after a droll New Yorker magazine cartoon would be inappropriate in some geographic areas, irrespective of peoples' education and income,

not because they wouldn't understand it, but because they would not find the message engaging enough to forward. Engagement is crucial in forwarding, so viral marketers have to know and understand the cultural icons favored and appreciated by potential customers.

- **Innovators**. As was pointed out previously, innovators are product and content specific. Innovators in music and fashion may not be innovators for electronics and automobiles. It is crucial to understand who the innovators for the product/brand are and where they live on the Web. YouTube is researching its users and is able to identify specific target markets based on content preferences and the number of viewers. YouTube is a great site for viral market campaign initiation.
- **Message Verity**. Consumer messages need to be honest and truthful with "puffery" left at the door. Consumers will not participate in the exaggeration of product claim by passing it on to their cohorts. After all, their credibility is at stake, as well. It is especially important not to dupe bloggers or forum users as they will savage the company once they discover they've been duped.
- **Irretrievability**. Once released, the viral message cannot be retrieved. There are short-term and long-term implications to the existence of a viral message. For the short term, it may or may not be successful and have the desired effect. However, as cultural and societal norms change, one must consider how consumer history will judge the effort. One only has to think of 1930s and 1940s cigarette ads that touted tobacco's health benefits. Web ads can come back to haunt.

USING SOCIAL NETWORKS FOR VIRAL MARKETING

Social networks have become particularly attractive to marketers. Three networks are of particular note as this is written. MySpace went online at the end of 2003. It was designed as a place for friends to meet and encourages the creation of private communities in which people exchange photos, journals, and specific interests with members of the network. Facebook, which launched in 2004, began as a network for university and college students and faculty. It began unprecedented growth when it removed the .edu e-mail suffix requirement for membership.

YouTube was launched in 2005 and positioned itself as the premier designation for sharing and viewing original videos from electronic devices that allow access to the Web. Data from 2006 indicate that Facebook dominates the 18–24 demographic, while over half of users of MySpace and YouTube are over 35. Collectively, the three social networks are a "must" in viral marketing plans.

Most who use the three networks mentioned above consider themselves to in the upper 25 percent of the innovation curve. They are socially astute, trend conscious, and not easily persuaded to forward mundane or end-of-trend messages and videos. For those constituencies, messages have to have three additional components. The content should be new, provocative, and/or shocking. According to Jonah Peretti, the guru of social marketing, well-used ideas, formats, hooks, and executions are unlikely to be forwarded because once a phenomenon has been diffused into the general population, it loses "its cool."

Messages with shocking content work because they push the envelope of social norms and accepted behaviors. An additional attraction to forwarding shocking material is that the sender gets "street cred" for uncovering and sending "wow" messages. Provocative content also works because it may cause the recipient to be sufficiently interested in the content to "drill down" or seek other links of similar material.

The impact of blogs is not quite certain in the social networking mix as they tend to be more specific and topic oriented. However, when news reporters surf blogs for stories, they may uncover a nugget, that once revealed, sends hoards to the blog site. One need only consider the blog in the 2004 Presidential election campaign that uncovered the fact that the documents used by Dan Rather on CBS News to question President Bush's war record were fake. The buzz and viral activity that resulted was picked up by other media and led to the resignation of Rather and two of his producers.

If the history of media content is any barometer, social networks will become more narrowly focused, which will result in more targeted audiences. This phenomenon will lead to greater opportunities for advertisers to reach homogeneous audiences with tailored, targeted messages.

- **Viral Marketing is Evolving**. Since its inception in 1997, viral marketing has been undergoing more permutations and developing more tentacles. One must understand that today's viral is likely to be tomorrow's cliché.
- **Idea Generation**. Most advertising is derivative and the ideas are not unique. A marketer doesn't necessarily need to come up with the "big" idea; often a new twist on classic or culturally embedded ideas would work, as well.
- **Timing is crucial**. Understanding the cultural times, in which a viral marketer is creating a message is the difference between an explosive success and barely being noticed. In television advertising, the "Mean Joe Green" and the "Hilltop" Coke commercials were recognized for being perfect in using America's racial tension and civil unrest to tremendous advantage.
- **Viral Messages and the Traditional Campaign**. Current wisdom supports the idea that viral and traditional media campaigns should be well coordinated, synergistic, and perhaps the viral campaign could jump start the traditional media campaign.
- **Quality**. Viral campaigns need as much thought, execution, and production support as traditional marketing communication campaigns. Thus personnel and budget allotment should reflect viral message's integral importance to the overall effort.

- **Timidity**. Viral marketing is not for the timid. Timid, conservative, demure, and pulled punch viral attempts are not going to win the pass-along message derby. Viral marketing messages are going to get the same critical analysis television commercials receive. Edgy, hip, clever, and resonant messages will receive good reviews and be forwarded.

QUESTIONS FOR THE VIRAL CREATIVE TEAM

- What are the objectives for the viral campaign?
- Who are the influential consumers (innovators) in your product category?
- Can you rise to the creative challenge of resonating with the "cool" people?
- How and where do you plan to "seed" or "salt the mine?" Find Web sites that are known for seeding (Kontraband and BoreMe.com, for example).
- Are you comfortable with the approach(es) you select? Will it make the brand message stand out?
- Are you being honest with the consumer?
- Is there a sufficient budget to achieve articulated goals?
- Will you be proud of the campaign in five years?

In the final analysis, viral campaigns have to be of the moment and have "talkability"—meaning a word-of-mouth aspect as well as a Web life. The best campaigns are not derivative and cloned from other media. Rather, they are created from scratch for the Internet and are consistent with the overall advertising strategy.

One must remember that a hard sell does not work on viral and for most people, it is the equivalent of fingernails scratching a blackboard.

It is also important to track the results to determine whether the campaign has been successful. For example, Kontraband has software that tracks how many views a viral receives when played through QuickTime. Often the tracker can provide anecdotal evaluations of the viral campaign.

NOTES

1. A. Dobele, D. Toleman, and M. Beverland, "Controlled Infection! Spreading the Brand Message through Viral Marketing," *Business Horizons*, no. 48 (2005): 143–149.

2. Malcolm Gladwell, *The Tipping Point: How Little Things Can Make a Big Difference* (Little Brown & Company, 2000).

3. Clay Shirky, "The Toughest Virus of All," *Business 2.0* (2000).

4. T. Meyer, K. Gettelman, and T. Donohue, "Word-of-Mouth Advertising: A Comparison of Internet/Technology Channels versus Face-to-Face Communication," *Journal of Contemporary Business Issues* 13, no. 2 (2005): 11–17.

5. Everett Rogers, *Diffusion of Innovations* (Free Press, 1995).

6. D. Holt, *How Brands Become Icons* (Harvard Business School Press, 2004).

7. N. Herrmann and C. Fiteni, "Let It Breed; Traditionally You Might Refer to This as 'Referral Marketing', but on the Web, It's Viral," *Metro Magazine*, no. 137 (2003): 168–170.

8. J. E. Phelps, R. Lewis, L. Mobilio, D. Perry, and R. Niranjan, "Viral Marketing or Electronic Word-of-Mouth Advertising: Wxamining Consumer Responses and Motivations to Pass along Email," *Journal of Advertising Research* (December): 333–348.

15

DIGITAL GIFTS: EVOLVING PATTERNS IN GIFT EXCHANGE

Erika Pearson

Web 2.0 is often referred to as the social Web, and interactions between people and groups have become a core part of users' experience of the Internet. The importance of these social interactions cannot be understated, as users turn to their online social networks for ideas, help, support, and information as well as friendship.

As such, the ongoing maintenance of this social network is one of the more important tasks users undertake in their online daily lives. Alongside the obvious social primers, such as conversational intimacy and the development of trust, the exchange of gifts plays a key role in the upkeep of social life online just as it does in offline spaces.

Gifts online can take on a more diverse range of forms and modes than their offline equivalents, and this has implications for how the gift operates in Web 2.0–supported social relations. Different types of gifts are given to represent different types of relations, and different modes of gift-giving behavior act as online public displays to signify different interpersonal relations to the group as a whole. The gift as a concept operates on multiple levels of meaning to those involved in its exchange, and by teasing out those layers, it may be possible to reveal more intimate details about hard-to-observe online social ties, social dynamics, and trust relations.

This chapter explores the role of the gift in online social interactions, specifically how users give and receive gifts to define not only their online social network but also their perception of their place in that network and the contribution they make to the networks' accumulated social capital. Just as in offline groups, gifts online help members develop a sense of belonging and obligation to the online social network, and they help sustain the group over time. The difference with online groups is the nature of the gift, the type of exchange, and the subsequent social ties that can be sustained through gifting behaviors.

To understand this, it will first be necessary to define what is understood by the concept of the gift and the gift exchange as a social act. The gift must be considered as a form of display that is both generous and calculated. This chapter will then trace how the movement of gifts online can be used as a way of understanding the dynamic, complex, and fluid network of social ties that constitutes Web 2.0–enabled social relations. By doing this, it will be possible to demonstrate the importance of gifts to the ongoing health and vibrancy of online social networks. Taken together, these various aspects of gifting behavior at first reveal a social function familiar from offline gift exchanges. What is novel to online gifts is the ease of gifting, in part due to the low barriers to entry for online gifts. This in turn means that, through such gift exchanges, online social networks can be shared among a larger social network than could be sustained in an offline physical space. This has implications for how we understand both Internet users as social agents and the repercussions for users who participate and can access the resources of such large and often physically dispersed social networks.

What Is a Gift?

In the general usage, gifts are thought of as one-off tokens of affection or regard, boxes tied with a bow and given to mark special occasions. But at a deeper, more critical level, gifts can be seen as part of a system of exchanges that help foster and maintain social relations.

The gift as a sociological construct traces its theoretical origins to anthropology, but the concept of gifting has subsequently spread to be used in a diverse number of fields. The gift was first used to help describe the exchange of valued objects—including crafts, objects de art, and tools—between individuals or groups who maintain social relations without any expectation of immediate recompense.[1] However, gift exchanges cannot be understood as momentary events—rather, they are better comprehended when seen as part of a series of interactions occurring over time that reflect the evolution and long-term maintenance of a social relation.

It is perhaps due to this genesis in anthropology that for a long time gift giving was perceived as something primitive or premodern, something that was irrelevant to modern societies and capitalist systems of exchange brokered on a culturally agreed currency. This perception has been slowly shifting, fueled in large part by the observed exchanges occurring among social groups in cyberspace. Internet users, who in the main reflect the most wealthy, educated, and technologically literate segments of the global community, often participate in online gift exchanges. Indeed, it has been noted that the Internet itself developed out of an ongoing series of gift exchanges between the developers of the architecture and tools that define the Internet a user now experiences.[2]

Theorists on the gift, including Marcel Mauss[3] and Alexander Gofman,[4] have argued that the gift acts as a "total social fact"—that is, something that signifies or represents the entirety of a social phenomenon. A gift is not *just* a present. It carries with it ties to the social, legal, economic, political, and cultural mores and expectations of the social context in which it is exchanged.[5] A gift represents the whole of the social system, where the system is dynamic, irreducible, and complex. The gift exists within a historical frame, linking to past events and exchanges and anticipating future interactions.

As already mentioned, the gift can take a number of different forms and be exchanged in a wide variety of social contexts. So in order to develop a working definition of the gift as it occurs today, it is necessary to move away from thinking of the gift as momentary object in order to fully understand and define the function of the gift.

It is useful to think of the gift as a representation of a social phenomenon. It has been noted that gifts "encapsulate the concern with what it means to be human,"[6] and as a total social fact a gift can be understood as an enactment of the abstract social obligations gift givers and receivers feel toward their social network. Comprehending the gift in this way opens up a number of interesting ramifications. For a start, it means that gift exchanges can be used to trace social ties and the movement of social capital, the nebulous bonds of obligation and affection we feel for those to whom we socially belong. Reciprocation of gifts (either through a sense of obligation or off a social impulse) means that the participants in the network are constantly reenacting these abstract social ties over time, further deepening the strength and the history of those ties and improving network cohesion. Failure to participate, or incorrect participation, indicates that the non-gifter either feels no such abstract bonds or has failed to comprehend the totality of the social frame in which those bonds occur. Either way, that nonparticipant may be ostracized or excluded and eventually entirely cut out of the social network.

It has been noted elsewhere[7] that it is difficult to develop a definition of gift that encompasses all the forms a gift can adopt. However, by taking a symbolic approach to the concept of the gift, it is possible to outline a few interlinked characteristics that act to define a gift.

First, gifts are unique. Unlike purchased commodities, which are divorced from any kind of identity or real history, gifts have identity and history that is enmeshed in the act of giving and the social fact of the gift. For example, a gift of a toy given by a little girl to her best friend differs from all the other toys that child owns (which have been bought as commodities). That toy is unique because it becomes "the toy that my friend gave me," and stands in for that relationship, a tangible reminder of a social bond and interpersonal history. The weight these unique gifts carry to the people who receive them can be seen in the social taboo of "re-gifting" or on-selling of physical gifts they have accepted from their social network. They cannot usually be passed on or sold because, beyond the capital worth of the base object, they are also imbued with the symbolic worth of being a gift. As will be discussed in a later section, this taboo is extended to online gifts and is one way to measure their symbolic worth to the participants in the online gift exchange.

Second, a gift carries with it an expectation of some kind of reciprocity. Given that the gift is a social construct representing the totality of the social network, it must be emphasized that this reciprocity does not mean direct and immediate reciprocity between the two individuals involved in the original gift exchange. Rather, reciprocity in this sense refers to the overall balance of gifts given and received within the social network as a whole.[8] Reciprocation may involve someone receiving a gift from one individual in her social network then going on to give a gift to another member. This collective indebtedness (in a social or moral, rather than capitalist sense) reinforces the qualitative nature of the gift (as opposed to a quantitative or commodity value). Failure to reciprocate or acknowledge this shared communal indebtedness may ultimately lead to ostracizing from the social network.[9] Reciprocity also carries with in an assumption of long-term relations and ongoing public displays of gifting. These two assumptions are necessary in order to ensure that the overall amount of gifts given and received balances, even with the absence of direct reciprocation. Inversely, it also implies that true gift exchanges can only occur where there is an expectation that social relations will endure beyond the moment of the gift exchange itself.

Finally, and tied to the other two characteristics, gifts are marked by a sense of social acceptance. In other words, the gift is welcome and generates a kind of gratitude (in the broadest sense) for the offer of the gift. A gift that fails to generate this social acceptance may imply that the gift offered deviates from the total social fact as shared and understood by the rest of the social network—it was inappropriate or unwelcome. An example of this from everyday life might be an extravagant or excessively expensive first date gift. The offer of such a gift and the discomfort the intended recipient feels reflects the differing expectations and social mores surrounding the social structures of a first date.

So far, the gift has been dealt with in very general terms, where the gift has been considered as a concept, marked by the broad social pressures and contexts that imbue the gift exchange. This chapter will now turn to look specifically at the gift in cyberspace, and explore how online gifts match up with and deviate from current understandings of the gift. It will consider issues unique to online gifting behavior, particularly questions of social symbolic value in online social groups.

THE GIFT IN CYBERSPACE

In much of the theoretical and critical studies of gifting, the gift has taken the form of a physical object that can be traced as it moves from individual to individual, both within and between social and kinship groups. The common example of this is the North American potlatch,[10] where invited guests of a tribal social group would be lavished with gifts as part of the display of the wealth and power of their hosts in a moving cycle of invitations and presentations. The gift itself, the method of exchange, and the quality and value of the gift were all carefully calculated in regards to prestige, social status, and past and anticipated future relationships, and thus helped balance long-term symmetrical reciprocity of the social relationship among interlinked groups.[11]

Such historical examples of gifting were often highly ritualized and structured, with the act of gifting an overt gesture of exchange of objects in the context of the gathering. Online, gifting behaviors are often far more subtle and difficult for nonparticipants to identity. There are a number of reasons, but one key reasons is the different forms the gift can take online.

The Internet fosters an entirely mediated social experience—while individuals and groups who develop high levels of trust may exchange physical objects through the postal service, for the most part social interaction online is done virtually, with users socializing with others online through digitized words, symbols, and multimedia transmitted electronically over the Internet. Any sense of "closeness" is entirely experiential, and has little to do with physical proximity as would have been experienced by those exchanging gifts at a potlatch.

Online, gift exchanges can take on a number of different forms, but generally fall into two general categories: object gifts and effort gifts. Object gifts include gifts of physical or monetary items, and often require sufficient trust between giver and receiver for personal physical information such as a postal address to be exchanged. Effort gifts are gifts that are created in the virtual environment through the time and skill of the gift giver. Such gifts include virtual art objects, services, or online items such as Web pages and layout designs. Effort gifts may also have a monetary value if sought as a commodity, but are created by the gift giver themselves and thus possess a qualitative rather than quantitative aspect.

Though the gift itself varies widely in form and method of delivery, when considered as a gift concept as previous defined, both object and effort gifts retain the key definitional qualities required—gifts are unique (i.e., "this layout was made for me by my friend"), carry an expectation of reciprocity (Social networking sites [SNS] often have a function for tracking birthdays, a very common and socially emphasized occasion for reciprocating gifts), and come with an expectation of social acceptance (i.e., publicly thanking a giver for their gift, even if the gift was delivered in a very low-key or non-public way). There is continuity between offline and online gifts, and this familiarity ensures that gifting behavior and expectations of gifts are governed by implicit understandings developed offline and subsequently brought into the online environment, rather than by any formal rules.

However, online gifting is not a direct analog of offline gifting behavior. Some issues pertaining to online gift exchanges need to be explored before the role of the gift in online social networks can be understood. These include negotiating the dispersed online social network, issues of anonymity, questions of scarcity and reproduction, and assessing the "value" of digital gifts within the fluid social dynamics of the online network.

Unlike physically based networks, where individual members share a physical environment and are more likely to also share certain cultural values or expectations, an online social network is bound instead by common interest. These communities of interest, to borrow Benedict Anderson's phrase from his book, *Imagined Communities*, may draw their members from a wide variety of backgrounds. As such, they may bring with them different cultural expectations, social mores, even language. When an online group forms, the members bring with them this cultural "baggage," and part of the formation of the group is to renegotiate, often implicitly through give and take and developing trust, a common social expectation. Gifts, symbolic representations of a social totality, can only be exchanged under the above definition once there is social stability in this nascent online network.

Of course, the development of these social formations is unique to every group, and different problems arise based upon the unique constellation of expectation, identity, and personal understanding of the group and the individual's place in it. But misinterpretation is common, particularly in groups or between individuals who do not have extensive social histories. However, developing such histories is one of the symbolic functions of the gift, and misgifting and even freeloading (taking gifts without giving back commensurate gifts to the network as a whole) can arguably be tolerated to a degree as part of the stresses of community formation.

Anonymity in gift giving is something that is fostered and made perhaps more easier by the mediated and technologically supported nature of the exchanges. As the famous cartoon notes, "on the Internet, no one knows you're a dog." Anonymity, aliases, or constructed identities allow individual users to present any virtual face, or no face at all, to the social group as a whole, as well as their intended recipient. That said, for true gifting behaviors (with their expectations of reciprocity) to occur, some kind of traceable identity, or identity that has history within the group, is required.

An interesting example is the 4Chan community and their spin-off network, Anonymous. As suggested by the group name, no traceable identity markers such as a name or an alias can be used within the network. Anonymity is a social requirement for participation. All users post messages and participate in online exchanges under the user name "anonymous." But by being stripped of individual identity in this way, the participants instead adopt a group identity—We Are Anonymous, as one of their group-produced videos begins. Gifts are given and received by the anonymous members of Anonymous. These are still gifts because the overall capital exchange is constant—there is reciprocity, both directly through the creation of new gifts to the Anonymous group, such as videos, interesting diatribes, or even pranks that are part of the social mores of the group, and indirectly through the praise and public merit award to the gifts as they circle among the unknown number of members. The shared history and identity of Anonymous is represented through the gifts that are anonymously given.

The flip side of anonymity and gift exchange is the practice of free-loading. As mentioned already, freeloading is the practice of being in a social group and accepting gifts and other benefits of social group membership without giving gifts back to the community in turn. Because gifts occur in historical time, a certain amount of freeloading is tolerated with the implicit expectation that a gift or other suitable contribution to the group may be forthcoming. However, unlike gift giving, which can occur without individual identity in the appropriate social context, freeloading requires that the freeloader can be individually identified and marked out as the freeloader.

These different identification requirements for gift giving and free-loading behaviors may have implications for how the group as a whole operates. Given that gifts are total social facts, the method for accounting for gifts and the ability to account for freeloaders may either shape or be shaped by the implicit social expectations of the network as a whole and of individuals' perceptions of their place in it. This may have flow-on effects as to the strength of ties and the level of trust different social networks can achieve, but to date there has been little research in this area, and the full implications are still unclear.

The third issue that needs to be assessed in terms of online gift-giving behavior is the question of scarcity. While high-trust online relationships may include the exchange of object gifts, it is arguable that the majority of gifts exchanged online are effort gifts, which often take the form of digital artifacts. Digital artifacts are infinitely reproducible due to the nature of digital copying, and as such, once the original investment of time and effort is made, the gift can be given without the gift giver losing the "original." While there are some arguments that this potential to circum-navigate traditional capitalist notions of scarcity diminishes the value of the gift, it needs to be remembered that the gift value inherent in the gift lies not with the object of the gift (whether that be a tangible object or an intangible service or virtual piece), but in the social implications tangled up in the act of gifting itself.

Another argument against the issue of scarcity and online gifting is that of time. While the creation of an online gift, particularly an effort gift, may not represent a large investment of physical or financial capital, it does involve an investment of time of behalf of the gift giver.[12]

While the finished gift may be replicable without loss of the original item (such as, for example, a digital music recording), the gift still represents a non-reclaimable investment of resources. Along with the social implications tied up in the gift, this gives online gifts contextual value.

Alongside scarcity remains the question of reproduction. Earlier in this chapter, it was noted that re-gifting is a taboo in most offline social networks. Does this taboo hold when the digital artifact of the gift can be *copied* and returned to the social network as a gift? Again, there is little empirical research in this area, but there are anecdotal examples of online social network participants sharing gifts—for example, making available a sound recording with the message "My friend made this for me; I want you all to hear it." These messages sometime carry a rider to the effect of asking those who share the gift to praise the original giver or creator of the gift. These riders suggest that such sharing behaviors are not re-gifting in the offline sense but rather a way to reward the giver of the gift by turning the gift into a display that channels praise, social merit, and even social elevation back toward the original giver.

Many of the questions around gift behavior, and especially whether a gift is appropriate, revolve around a negotiation of symbolic and tangible gift value. Unlike a commodity, in which the value can be reduced to a dollar amount, the value of a gift must refer to a calculus of economic, personal, social, and historical factors that are symbolized by that gift. Questions such as uniqueness (a pro-forma gift generated by a Facebook widget versus an effort gift crafted expressly for the recipient would carry different weight), appropriateness (especially in terms of commodity value—the first date example applies just as much online as off), the levels of trust between participants, and even remembered past and anticipated future interactions all help determine the appropriateness and acceptability of a gift from both an individual and a communal perspective. To return to the concept of the gift as a total social fact, the gift must be exquisitely crafted so as to convey the exactly correct proportion of symbolic value within the dynamic social context and social historical moment in which it is exchanged.

Online, all exchanges are made through symbols, and the gift is one of the strongest and most complex symbols that can be exchanged. Just as the gift in the North American potlatch served as a display of wealth as well as a maintainer of a social tie, so the online gift must serve as a display of the self in a virtual community, a marker of participation and merit. Therefore, this chapter will now turn to consider the gift as altruistic offering, as a lure for public reciprocity, and as a display to the virtual community.

ALTRUISM, RECIPROCITY, AND DISPLAY

It has been established that the gift is a symbol that represents a wealth of information about the social network in which it circulates. But the gift operates on other levels simultaneously with this symbolic function. Gifts are often given publicly, or at least it becomes common knowledge that a gift has been exchanged. Therefore, gifts have a display, almost performative, function. The importance of this function is highlighted when tied back to the common social capital and reciprocal expectations inherent in a gift.

The gift itself encapsulates the social experience and helps to maintain long-term social bonds through the reciprocal exchange of unique gifts among members of a social group or network. But what of the gift givers and gift receivers? What motivates them to create or obtain, offer, and receive such gifts? Gifts can act as prestige markers, a way of displaying wealth, merit, or power to the community, or they can be thought of in terms of the "warm glow" of giving. Gifts can also function as part of an online identity construct and a way for an online participant to signify to others who they think they are and how they fit in the network. Finally, there is also the problematic concept of the altruistic or "free" gift.

Gifts as prestige markers presume that the gift exchange is a public act, a display in which the act of giving yields immediate benefits for the giver in terms of public merit and perceived generosity. This prestige earned through giving gifts may help the individual move through the social hierarchy of their social network. Therefore, the gift takes on an added dimension, one in which the act of giving away gives back to the originator the gift of social standing.

Even in social groups where achieving a good position in the hierarchy is not an explicit or dominant aim of group members, the act of giving for prestige may help individuals build a reputation for generosity, willingness to participant, or even for more nebulous qualities such as engagement or friendship. This reputational prestige is reliant on the giver's maintaining a stable identity within the social network—other network members have to know who is offering these gifts, and have a way of remembering and tracking past gift activities.

When two or more group members are vying for social status or position through prestige gifting tactics, prestige gifting may take on a competitive element. Prestige in this sense carries problematic implications of uniqueness. If all members of the group displayed extreme generosity, then gift giving becomes part of the character of the group, and no individual can attain status through such giving. As such, giving to obtain prestige involves giving beyond the standards of regular social maintenance exchanges. In fighting for prestige through giving, there is a challenge among the givers to give the most gifts, unique gifts, or special gifts. At its most extreme, givers can exhaust their resources, or even potentially be ostracized as the intended recipients are overwhelmed with an inability to maintain their reciprocal obligations. As with freeloading, extreme deviation from social norms affects the balance of the social relations as a whole.

Similarly, there is prestige to be had in being offered and accepting gifts from others in the network. By being offered a gift, especially when the offer is made public, a recipient also receives the prestige of being singled out of the social network and deemed worthy of receiving the gift. As with bestowing gifts, uniqueness is a kind of social currency, and being offered a gift marks the potential recipient as being worthy within the community as a whole. Recipients can develop this honor as they simultaneously make a gesture of reciprocal social capital by openly and publicly thanking the gift givers for their generosity. As noted at the beginning of this chapter, such exchanges are part of the core definition of gifts as social concepts.

Another, more abstract reason for gifting behavior may be found in the act of identity construction. While it can be argued that all identity is, to a greater or lesser extent, constructed, online this identity construction is explicit, symbolic, and total. Everything an online social network knows about its members, it knows through the symbols, ideas, and contributions an individual participant makes to that network. Given that gifts themselves are powerful symbols, the act of gift exchange may be thought of as part of this wider symbolic construction of personal identity. By participating in gift exchanges, an individual is making a statement about belonging to a group and the identity facets that it provides.

Of course, not all gift exchanges have such overtly mercenary motives. The phenomenon of the warm glow cannot be completely excluded from the calculus of gifting motivation. Warm glow refers to the private good feelings and internal satisfaction experienced by a giver upon giving a suitable and well-received gift (which links back to one of the key characteristics of the gift, social acceptance). Warm glow is separate but related to the concept of altruism and the free gift, but when considering motivations for gifting, the warm glow can neither be completely discounted nor made to serve as the sole motivation for gifting.

Pure altruistic, or the so-called free gifts, are problematic concepts. Anthropological research demonstrates that the line between altruistic and free gifts is a hazy one,[13] tangled up with notions of common humanity, recognizing relations, and free redistribution of wealth in times of crisis. This is an interesting area of gift economies in its own right, but for the purposes of this discussion, it is sufficient to note that, even if the gift givers' intentions were purely altruistic, gifts within a social context always carry some expectation of reciprocation, even if is for a warm glow and the public noting the act of generosity, which in turn may lead to future tangible or intangible benefits for the gift giver.

One final potential motivation for gift giving, which is tied into and underlies many of the previously discussed rationales, is the element of display. It may prove useful to consider the display elements of gift exchanges separately for a moment, to further unravel the complex interplay of the varying rationales for exchanging gifts.

Display and performance of gift exchange are interesting ways of conceptualizing the gift, because it considers the exchange from the perspective of the wider social network. In other words, how does it look to the network when two individuals exchange a gift? Displays of gift giving may demonstrate an individual's wealth (particularly capital wealth when considering object gifts), power, established and developing prestige, and position, both in terms of social hierarchy (bestowing a gift that demonstrates superior skill within a meritocratic network, for example), and in terms of social network (i.e., demonstrating the wealth of friends and social contacts who will accept such gifts).

Display is also a motivation for receiving gifts, and the rational is nearly identical to those used to help justify offering gifts. Apart from demonstrations of wealth, choosing to receive a gift allows the recipient to display his power, network position, and social prestige by declaring both his self-worthiness and socially perceived worthiness to be offered a gift.

For both participants, such displays form part of the social ritual required to negotiate the presentation of a public face or recognized identity to others.[14] Giving and receiving, and being seen giving and receiving, not only maintain general social bonds but also help maintain individual presentations of identities. This display aspect of gifting is arguably vital in online communities, where all interactions are mediated within the shared virtual space of the social network; all identities are deliberately constructed and reshaped within the social network.

As this chapter has demonstrated so far, gifts are complex social concepts that act to help gift givers, receivers, and their social networks maintain a number of personal and group benefits, including social cohesion, social elevation, identity formation and maintenance, as well as demonstrations of social and personal wealth and status. This chapter will now turn to explore how gifts act online as symbolic assets, and how the gift operates to achieve these functions within the special conditions of virtual environments.

Symbolic Assets and the Cumulation of Social Capital

So far, this chapter has explored the total social fact of the gift, and the function it fulfils as part of acts of social maintenance, prestige display, and long-term engagement. As has already been noted, the gift online brings with it many of the expectations and understandings inherent in offline gifts. Yet the gift online has some situationally specific characteristics which affect how the gift functions in *online* social environments.

Online social networks are constructed symbolic environments. Everything a user knows about their online social network comes to them through mediated and constructed signs, including avatars or identity representations, word choice and conversational tone, even the virtual location of the engagement (such as a specific SNS, a bulletin board, or a topical Usenet group). The constructed nature of the spaces means that every engagement, every communication or identity facet, is part of a deliberate performance using the symbolic structures shared within that group. That these symbolic spaces are also deliberately entered into as extensions of an individual identity also implies that online social engagements can take on multiple forms, and different depths of engagement, trust, and social investment.

Where does the gift, as described above, fit in this mediated, symbolic virtual social environment? It can be argued that the gift plays an important role in maintaining the health of a virtual social network. Gifts are symbols of worth in a symbolic space and convey notions of value and merit. They are reciprocal and unique, and effort gift exchanges in particular have low barriers to entry. This chapter will consider each of these roles of the gift in online networks in turn, drawing on examples from various SNS gift behaviors, in order to demonstrate the multifaceted and complex role of online gift exchanges.

First, as has already been noted, gifts can be thought of as symbols that stand in for or represent the entire complex, irreducible system of a social network. They are symbolic representations of participation, belonging, and social investment. As such, the exchange of gifts in the symbolic environment of online social networks is even more important to the articulation of the ephemeral ties of a virtual social bond. Both effort and object gifts, to different degrees, make the symbolic statement of the existence of a relationship between two or more members of an online network. Such declarations are vital given the stripped-back nature of online communication, where exchange is often reduced to a single channel of communication, and where all information has to be deliberately coded and transmitted. Even the most simple of gifts is entangled with very complex symbolic representations of belonging, social capital, and social history, and thus acts as a potent symbol that can be reciprocally exchanged to represent and thus maintain the social bond.

The reciprocal aspect of such exchanges cannot be understated. Online, identity is a deliberate construct, and as such can be see as fluid, even ephemeral. Internet users take advantage of the mediated symbol nature of the space to play with identity, how they represent themselves, and how they read and relate to the identity representations of others. The gift in this aspect of online social life acts to create longevity of social relations as individual online identities move, shift, and develop. By agreeing to be involved in a gift exchange (often implicitly through the act of accepting a gift), it is arguable that online identities find a kind of situational permanence. Even though individual identities are seen to be shifting and developing, there is a stability of relational identity when taken in relation to other identities in their network. In other words, people in the network know and remember who the others are, even if the symbols, expression, and orientation of that identity have developed over time. In this way, the exchange of gifts, and the expectation of reciprocity, helps construct and maintain longitudinal cohesion and trust within the network. By becoming indebted to a network, there is an impetus for maintaining stable social bonds over time regardless of other changes.

Finally, it is worth considering the specific place of the effort gift in an online social network. Whereas object gifts have clear capital value that is enhanced by its conversion into a gift, effort gifts have a more situational value. Though effort gifts could, in the free market, be assigned a dollar value, within the context of a gift exchange it is rare to find effort gifts evaluated in this way. Effort gifts are seen as having low capital value, but high social-capital value. As such, they are given more freely and are exchanged between individuals or groups whose social ties or network relations might not have justified an object gift. Given that gifts represent total social facts, and that gift exchange is a finely tuned calculus of expectation, reciprocation, status, and merit, this lower entry point for effort gift exchange online has interesting ramifications for social network cohesion. What effort gifts enable is for users to establish reciprocal social relations with others who are further away, socially, in the social network, and with whom they may share weaker ties as compared to their more traditional gift exchange partners. This, combined with the symbolic nature of the exchange and the delocalization of social interaction online, means that individuals can maintain social relations with a far larger and more dispersed social network than might otherwise have been possible. This has implications not only for how users negotiate and understand their own social networks but also for how scholars and researchers negotiate the nebulous and tangled web of social relations that make up online friendship. However, it might help explain the shifting meaning of the word "friend" online and how it can now be applied to both the closest of intimates and the most distant of online acquaintances.

Even though these aspects have been drawn out and examined separately here, in practice they are intertwined, each aspect of gift behavior online reinforcing others. A good example can be found in the social expectations and taboos surrounding effort gifts of graphic designs made on SNS such as Livejournal. Livejournal, like many networked blogging platforms, allows users to customize their blogs in terms of their appearance, and many users customize their spaces as part of their expression of their online identity on the site. However, even the simplest customization, such as a unique avatar, requires skills such as graphics design—and more advanced customizations may require CSS coding ability. As such, users who have such skills often give customizations of varying types away as gifts to other users on their networks, despite the significant effort and time investment some of these customizations represent.

The exchanges themselves carry the hallmarks of gift exchanges as noted earlier: offer and acceptance within social context, gratitude, uniqueness, and some notion of reciprocity. Giving such gifts is in itself a gesture in prestige, for both gift giver (who has such skills) and receiver (who merits such a gift). What is interesting in terms of gift exchanges online is what happens when there is a breakdown or disruption to the gift exchange process, such as with the "theft" of an effort gift. "Theft is a politically loaded term, but is used here to refer to someone who takes or benefits from a gift not intended for them, often without credit or gratitude back to the original gift giver. For example, on Livejournal, users are represented by 100x100-pixel user pictures, referred to as icons. Gift givers may give to their network (either strong and/or weak ties relations) as a group a range of such icons that they feel will appeal to the group as a whole—such as icons that represent some aspect of the collective identity. When a theft of such a general effort gift occurs, it is usually in the form of a user taking such a gift without credit (gratitude). In many cases, it is arguable that the network and the gift giver in particular see this as a declaration of freeloading: taking without giving back. It also diminishes the symbolic worth of the gift by attempting to circumvent the unique value of the gift by removing it from the exchange context. Such theft behaviors often result in severe censorship and even exclusion from the social network itself. This critical backlash betrays the social importance of gifts in online contexts.

GIFTING IN PRACTICE

This chapter will now turn to look at some actual examples of different types of gifts given online. Even though there is a enduring and widespread practice of interpersonal gifting going on online, this chapter will focus specifically at gift exchanges made between companies or corporations and their users, client base, or target market. But before looking at some examples of online gifting practices, it is first necessary to recap three critical points about digital gifts.

First, as was discussed at the beginning of this chapter, a gift is a total social fact. It carries with it, and therefore must reflect, everything about the giver and the recipient, their relationship to each other, and their relative places in the wider social context. A gift remembers past exchanges and anticipates futures actions. Therefore, the quality and nature of the gift must be appropriate to, and reflect, these factors. This means a gift that is of inferior quality may be taken as implying the low regard the giver has for the recipient. Conversely, an extremely extravagant gift may place too great a burden of reciprocity on any future relations.

In practice, this can be seen in a number of common examples of gifting. Take, for example, a situation where a long-term loyal client, who has brought significant business over the shared history of the interaction, is "rewarded" with a low-quality gift—say, a cheap hat or a pen with the company logo inscribed on it. By giving such a low-quality gift to a client who has such an extensive and important history with the company, the company is sending a message along with the gift that they consider their total social fact—their past history and any future relations, their interactions, and their positions in regards to each other—to be inferior or insignificant, and thus unworthy of a more substantial gift. By receiving such a gift, the client may reconsider their relationship to the company, and downgrade it accordingly.

On the other hand, extravagant gifts are also problematic. Continuing this hypothetical situation, if a company lavished expensive gifts on a client, this might also upset the social relation between the two (leaving aside for one moment the actual cost of such gifts). Extravagant gifting, considered as part of a total social fact, unbalances the dynamics of the social relation and puts the recipient in a position where they may feel indebted to the giver or even threatened by the extravagance displayed. This was seen in the earliest potlatches right through to modern gifting behaviors. At its most extreme, extravagant gifting behavior may ultimately force the recipient to cut off social relations rather than endure such an unequal relationship.

The second critical point that needs to be revisited is that gifts imply belonging. To give a gift is a public act of claiming a relationship. In terms of a commercially based social relationship (such as those with a client), the act of gifting can in some cases be linked with branding. By accepting a (publicly given) gift with brand connotations, the recipient can, in a sense, become "branded" as well—that is, part of the overall image that the brand invokes. However, given that the gift also functions as a status symbol, the brand must be suitably elite, high status, or desirable for the recipient to *want* such a relationship to be invoked. If the brand invoked by the gift carries connotations of a low-status relationship, the gift may fall foul of the inferior gift problem noted above.

Third, by giving socially appropriate and relevant gifts, the gift giver will receive gratitude from the recipient for the gifts. If the gifts are socially inappropriate, inferior or extravagant, or irrelevant, gratitude will not be forthcoming. This lack of gratitude is a good test of whether a gift was well judged. It must be noted that gratitude is not the same as the platitudes of good manners required for a gift, but true appreciation that will facilitate further interactions.

In regards to the gift itself, as was noted above, there are two forms the gift can take online: object gifts and effort gifts. These online gifts must conform to several key characteristics, such as being unique, carrying with them an expectation of reciprocity, and having a public or social acceptance by the recipient. Online gifts must also negotiate issues specific to the online environment, such as being distributed across dispersed networks to potentially anonymous or pseudonymous recipients. Online, gifts also face challenges in terms of scarcity and reproduction, especially in regards to effort gifts. Because of this, there are also questions about the "value" of digital gifts. To explore how gifts operate in this digital context, this chapter will now turn to briefly sketch out two examples of online gift exchange.

A recent example of online object gifting comes from the Web site provider Moonfruit. Moonfruit was capitalizing on the growing popularity of the microblogging site Twitter to run a promotion where Twitter users were encouraged to mention Moonfruit in their posts, known as tweets, to go into the running to win one of ten high-end laptop computers. During this competition, a number of Twitter users did more then mention Moonfruit, but composed haikus and songs, created animations, and other forms of creative endeavors to promote the brand, completely unprompted by the company.

In recognition of this fledgling community of Moonfruit fans, the company decided to randomly give out a number of branded mp3 players to some of these creative posters. Though an mp3 player might be seen as an extravagant gift when taken in isolation, it came across to the users as appropriate when seen in comparison to the laptops on offer as part of the competition. The gifting of mp3 players, which among the high-end technology users that represent Moonfruit's client base are seen as disposable items, fit the gift criteria as being neither too cheap nor too extravagant and reinforced the perception that Moonfruit was valuing the creative efforts of these users (which, ultimately, were helping to elevate Moonfruit's public profile in a way no advertising campaign ever could).

By giving out multiple mp3 players, the gifts also helped reinforce the sense of belonging among these Twitter users, and helped strengthen the growing ties of community that were forming between them, and between the user group and the company itself. The mp3 players and the creative works also worked together in an interesting cycle of reciprocal gratitude—both the creative works and the mp3 players operated as gifts to the company and the user base, respectively, and as such took on an aspect of gratitude for the efforts of the other. Therefore, even though the mp3 giveaway was occurring alongside a more traditional "lucky draw" competition, the mp3 giveaway is better understood as an object gift exchange that ultimately fostered enduring social ties between these users and the company.

In regards to effort gift, a good example comes from the music industry. The large independent label Fueled By Ramen manages and produces approximately a dozen bands from hip-hop to pop-punk. Many of these bands have overlapping audiences, developed and cultivated particularly through co-touring and guest appearances on one anothers' albums. The label also has a strong history of exploiting Web 2.0 tools such as blogs, MySpace, and other media sharing tools, to promote these bands. The label's most famous alumni, the band Fall Out Boy, or FOB as they were referred to online, were strong bloggers and supporters of the site, and still maintained management ties with the label and its vanity spinoff label Decadance.

In August 2008, a viral campaign that came to be known as Citizens For Our Betterment, or CFOB, was launched. Through a clever series of links, cryptic media files, and references to the Web presence of different parts of Fueled By Ramen and its signed bands, CFOB lured the fans of the bands into a kind of constructed conspiracy theory. In doing so, the label created a sense of belonging—the Fueled By Ramen blog and message board, plus literally thousands of fansites, were abuzz with discussion as to what these links and cryptic clues meant. As the clues were decoded and assembled, they began to construct a postmodern narrative of alienation and political apathy, themes common to and resonating with the punk ethos of the core of the fan base, or what in gift theory terms could be part of the total social fact of the relationship among bands, management, and fans.

CFOB culminated in the free online release in the *CFOB Mixtape*, made up partly of samples and remixes from Fueled By Ramen bands, and partly of snippets and sound bites from the band Fall Out Boy's forthcoming album, *Folie à Deux*. To access the mixtape download, fans had to be able to follow the clues (or know where to find the blogs where other fans explained the clues) to get the download code that would enable them to access this gift.

The mixtape is clearly a gift from the band/label to the fanbase. It recognizes the total social fact of their relationship, both in terms of their relationship to each other as music producer and consumer, and in terms of their shared position in both the pop-punk subculture and the wider cultural moment. The mixtape (as suggested by the label Citizens For Our Betterment) made strong reference to the politics of the (then) current U.S. presidential elections, in which the fan demographic had a strong current interest. The gift was seen as appropriate, in that it targeted the recipients' interests, but was neither excessive nor cheap (the download was free of both up-front cost and paid advertising, and the remixing and sampling were done by noted DJ Clinton Sparks). As noted, the form of both the gift (a mixtape) and its method of delivery implied belonging by tapping the historical cues of the subculture. And, finally, the gift invoked gratitude, both in word-of-mouth publicity (a public gratitude) and in ongoing loyalty to the label and the bands involved.

CONCLUSION AND DISCUSSION

This chapter has argued the importance of the gift in the representation and maintenance of social relations. In particular, it has focused on how online networks both reinforce and renegotiate the meaning of the gift. The gift plays a multifaceted role in online social relations. In many ways, it operates online in ways very similar and familiar to offline gifts, and this may be due to the behaviors and expectations users bring with them from their offline cultures and experiences. However, the Internet allows new modes of gifting and new ways to extend and expand a gift network.

Online, gifts can take a number of different forms. Both object and effort gifts play a role in online social networks. Object gifts online closely map the giving of objects in offline social networks and require trust, social history, and a reasonable expectation of an enduring relationship. Effort gifts are more flexible in terms of how they can be exchanged and with whom. Effort gifts can be folded into the symbolic exchanges of online environments, and can be separated out (if not divorced entirely) from other forms of capital. As such, the exchange of effort gifts can be made between individuals who might otherwise not have sufficient history or trust for a gift exchange to occur. This means that social networks can be expanded outward in ways that are just not feasible in offline social networks. It may also have implications for the speed or scope of trust and social-capital development between new contacts online.

In terms of the two examples briefly outlined above, it can be seen that both forms of gifts, object and effort, managed to be appealing to the target group without being excessive or insulting. The gifts were appropriate in that they were selected to reflect both the nature of the recipient and the shared history and wider social context of both gift giver and recipient, as reinforced by the public gratitude and appreciation for the gifts. And in the long term, both forms of gifts reinforced a social relation—whether it be brand loyalty, the future purchase of music, or the word-of-mouth publicity of the company.

In conclusion, gifts are an important part of the ongoing maintenance of online social relationships and can also help foster new social ties. Appropriate gifts, whether they be physical objects such as an mp3 player or virtual artifacts such as a bundle of mp3 tracks, can reinforce a sense of belonging and identity among a group and make them feel special and appreciated—and therefore more inclined to continue to put in the effort to maintain an online social relationship. Online, where social ties might be spread over vast geographical distances, or conducted anonymously or through pseudonyms, gifts (particularly effort gifts) can help foster a sense of trust. Gifts can be used to link online and offline interactions—there a many small-scale examples of this on geo-local social networking sites such as Facebook. Done with appropriate sensitivity to the complex social markers and taboos surrounding gift exchanges, the giving and receiving of gifts can be an important part of ongoing social relations and even become a status symbol for those who receive such gifts.

NOTES

1. Peter Kollock, "The Economies of Online Cooperation: Gifts and Public Goods in Cyberspace," in *Communities in Cyberspace*, ed. Marc A. Smith and Peter

Kollock (London: Routledge, 1999); Mark Osteen, "Introduction: Questions of the Gift," in *The Question of the Gift: Essays across Disciplines*, ed. Mark Osteen (London: Routledge, 2002).

2. Magnus Berquist, "Open Source Software Development as Gift Culture: Work and Identity Formation in an Internet Community," in *New Technologies at Work: People, Screens and Social Virtuality*, ed. Christina Garsten and Helena Wulff (Oxford: Berg, 2003).

3. Marcel Mauss, *The Gift: Forms and Functions of Exchange in Archaic Societies*, trans. Ian Cunnison (London: Cohen and West Ltd., 1954).

4. Alexander Gofman, "The Total Social Fact: A Vague but Suggestive Concept," in *Marcel Mauss: A Centenary*, ed. Wendy James and N. J. Allen (Oxford: Berghahn, 1998).

5. See Note 3.

6. Karen Sykes, *Arguing With Anthropology: An Introduction to Critical Theories of the Gift* (London: Routledge, 2005), 4.

7. Aafke E Kompter, "Introduction," in *The Gift: An Interdisciplinary Perspective*, ed. Aafke E. Kompter (Amsterdam: Amsterdam University Press, 1996); Aafke E Kompter, "The Social and Psychological Significance of Gift Giving in the Netherlands," in *The Gift: An Interdisciplinary Perspective*, ed. Aafke E. Kompter (Amsterdam: Amsterdam University Press, 1996); Maurice Godelier, *The Enigma of the Gift* (Cambridge: Polity Press, 1999).

8. See Note 3, 18.

9. See Note 6.

10. See Note 3 and Note 6.

11. David Cheal, *The Gift Economy* (London: Routledge, 1988).

12. Berquist, "Open Source Software Development as Gift Culture," see Note 1.

13. See Note 6.

14. Erika Pearson, "All the World Wide Web's a Stage: The Performance of Identity in Online Social Networks," *First Monday* (2009).

SUGGESTED READING

Marcel Mauss. *The Gift: Forms and Functions of Exchange in Archaic Societies*. Trans. Ian Cunnison. London: Cohen and West Ltd., 1954.

Aafke E. Kompter (Ed). *The Gift: An Interdisciplinary Perspective*. Amsterdam: Amsterdam University Press, 1996.

Wendy James and N. J. Allen (Eds). *Marcel Mauss: A centenary*. Oxford: Berghahn, 1998.

16

SOCIAL COMMERCE: E-RETAILERS AND TODAY'S SOCIAL CONSUMERS

Tracy L. Tuten

Social commerce and social shopping shouldn't come as a surprise to anyone. Shopping has perhaps forever been a social experience; one that is shared with friends, family, and sometimes even strangers nearby. Purchase decisions at large may be individual or group-oriented, but the act of shopping is inherently a social behavior. At its core, social shopping refers to our propensity as consumers to interact with others during a shopping event, which introduces an enhanced potential for the influence of others on the purchase decision. Social shopping primarily refers to online shopping, though, simply because of our ability to share information electronically, easily share opinions and access the opinions of others, and communicate with friends, family, and associates about the shopping decision from a geographic or time distance. Whenever consumers navigate product information online using social commerce tools, such as bookmarking their favorite products, e-mailing product summaries, and subscribing to RSS feeds of other users' favorite product lists, they are social shopping.

Consider this example: During the 2009 inaugural festivities, I watched many of the events on television while microblogging on Twitter and Facebook. When Mary J. Blige performed in the pre-Inaugural Celebration, I was spellbound by her boots, rumored to be Christian Louboutins. I posted a status update about my boot envy. A girlfriend responded within moments with a link sent via Facebook to the Victoria's Secret Web site and a very similar pair of boots. A few conversational exchanges later (with input from several friends by that point), I had made my purchase and promised to post pics when the boots arrived. Without my friend's response to my post, I wouldn't have known about Victoria's Secret's product offering. Even if I did, I wouldn't have had that little nudge one sometimes needs to validate a somewhat frivolous purchase. This is what social shopping offers the Web 2.0 consumer.

Social commerce is the retailer response to the behavior of social shopping. Though offline shopping may certainly have a social aspect to it, social commerce and social shopping are online phenomena related to the Web 2.0–enabled accessibility of our social networks. You may be thinking that social commerce then is not so different from traditional retail commerce. Prima facie, you'd be right. The power of social commerce as a platform for social shopping resides in the functionality Web 2.0 technology brings to the shopping experience. E-retailers, social shopping networks, and social networks can provide many tools for the online shopper including offering product reviews, wish lists and shopping lists, e-mail-a-friend notifiers, recommendations based on other shopping behaviors, and chat functions. These tools enable online shoppers to access influential others at critical points in the purchase process and to organize the shopping process in a manner that is not easily accomplished in offline shopping situations. Such functionality is increasingly offered by commercial online sites. Even without tools designed for social commerce, social networks can play a role—just as Facebook did in my acquisition from Victoria's Secret.

THE BEHAVIOR OF SOCIAL SHOPPING

The consumer decision-making process includes five basic stages: (1) problem recognition, (2) information acquisition, (3) alternative evaluation, (4) decision, and (5) post-purchase evaluation. Whether shopping offline or online, socially or not, these are the five stages of product choice. However, the tools of social commerce have expanded the manner in which we gather information and the quantity and quality of information itself. One of the first insights marketers acknowledged about the Internet was its transfer of power from the marketer to the consumer because of the product information it made freely available and easily accessible. Web 2.0 continues this trend by adding social influence to the information available online. While Web 1.0 enhanced information acquisition, Web 2.0 means that consumers can access information on the experiences of others and use those experiences and opinions to aid in their evaluation of alternatives. It is from this systematic use of online information that the role of social shopper evolved. But, it isn't all about making better more informed decisions. Social shopping means that social pressure now exists for the online shopper just as it has for the more visible offline shopping experience. We'll explore these consumer shifts in online shopping behavior and the responses from e-retailers, social commerce sites, and networks.

Social shoppers, as a distinct consumer segment, are consumers who actively seek out and place great importance on the reviews and feedback offered online about products and services. Social shoppers do more than consider online opinions while shopping—studying product reviews and consumer feedback is something that they do consistently and systematically when shopping online. What's more, this is not a niche group. In a study of 1200 online shoppers conducted by the e-Tailing Group (Social Shopping Study 2007), 70 percent reported using online consumer reviews and 65 percent were classified as social shoppers.[1,2] They are 20 percent more likely than the average online shopper, according to the report, to seek out customer reviews and top-rated product lists online, and they participate in these activities for at least 50 percent of all their shopping choices, whether shopping off or online.

Social shoppers, more frequently than other online shoppers, reported that online reviews were preferable to speaking with a knowledgeable sales associate about a product at a store. They also were more likely to shop at a competitor site rather than their brand favorite if the competition offered social shopping tools and the favorite brand did not. All in all, social shoppers use the feedback contributed by others to narrow their product selections. Further, online shopping has long emphasized sales of specific types of products including electronics, toys, books, music, and travel, but social shoppers use reviews and social commerce tools for a wide variety of product categories.

This narrowing of product choices (part of the third stage of the purchase process) using social commerce content is known as social navigation. Social shoppers "navigate" the Internet's shopping choices, narrowing their product selections based on the reviews and comments of their online peers. The term "peers" is used loosely in that the primary credibility component is the assessment of whether the comments are posted by like-minded people. One may or may not know whether comments come from "people like me" depending upon whether the others involved in the purchase are really a part of the shopper's social network or represent comments from unknown others.

Five key factors explain why reviews and feedback from "people like me" are such powerful sources of influence in online consumer shopping: (1) accessibility, (2) trust, (3) perceptions of authority, (4) similarity, and (5) the impact of social proof.[3] First, the information is easily accessible for online shoppers who already use the Internet to find product-related information prior to purchase. As shoppers enter search terms for product information, reviews, blog posts, and other content is easily indexed and retrieved. Trust is enhanced by the lack of motive present in the posting of reviews. Consumers tend to discount opinions or recommendations offered by paid endorsers, whether celebrities or sales people. Other online shoppers, though—"people like me"—are not motivated by an endorsement fee. There is no clear benefit to those contributing product information, other than the knowledge that they have served as a benevolent purchase pal.

These online purchase pals do still maintain an image of authority in the minds of other consumers. When people who rely on heuristics, or mental shortcuts, in making decisions have access to the recommendation of another, who is perceived to be an expert, they will tend to follow said recommendations. In the case of social shopping, the authority or expertise is based upon the product experience of the person providing the opinion. This tendency to follow the recommendation from someone with experience is heightened by the perception that the person offering the feedback is also similar to us. When people are perceived as similar, they gain credibility. Finally, people tend to be influenced by the belief that others are behaving similarly. When we have evidence that others are making a specific decision, we are more likely to make that same decision. Social proof is at the heart of social commerce tools like Amazon's "What Do Customers Ultimately Buy After Viewing this Page?" listing and its "Customers Who Bought This Item Also Bought . . . " In seeing these recommendations, the social shopper is able to make a sort of collective decision rather than an individual one.

Even among those who did not meet the characteristics to be classified as a social shopper, social influence still may play a role in their online shopping behaviors. Key findings in the e-Tailing Group's Social Shopping Study report revealed the following insights about those surveyed:[4]

- 86 percent reported that customer reviews were very important as they made purchase decisions.
- 82 percent found reading reviews better than researching a product in-store with a knowledgeable sales associate.
- 81 percent rely on customer reviews to decide between two or three products or to confirm that their final selection is the right one.

These high percentages of respondents indicating social influence in their online consumer behavior suggest that consumer-generated reviews and social shopping are more than just a trend, but represent a new paradigm in shopping behavior. What we see here is that while social shoppers are a powerful breed of online shopper, representing masters of social navigation in the online space, the vast majority of online shoppers are still navigating somewhat socially in order to make better purchasing decisions. For instance, results from a survey conducted by Yahoo and OMD found that 75 percent of study respondents used trusted, well-known Web sites when making purchases online, and 54 percent said the Internet was their most trusted shopping source.[5] Another study conducted by the American Marketing Association[6] concluded that:

- 47 percent of consumers used social networks to discuss and find holiday gift ideas.
- 29 percent would buy products through those social networking sites.
- 51 percent would look for discounts on social networking sites.
- 18 percent would read or write product reviews for social networking sites.

Still, despite what may appear to be a seemingly endless amount of product information available online, a study by the Pew Internet and American Life Project found that out of 2,400 online shoppers interviewed, 43 percent have been frustrated by the lack of information available.[7] Social shopping enables consumers to get the information they need from people they perceive to be credible and trustworthy. Further, social shopping enables consumers not only to research specific product choices, but also to ask for the aid of others to even identify possible solutions to a problem. Gordon writes that consumers who submit reviews to social commerce sites and read reviews on these sites have a sense of knowing that they are making better product decisions.[8] This enhanced confidence in the choice process leads to an increased likelihood that these consumers will return to the social commerce sites and encourage other online shoppers to do so as well. Before we delve more deeply into the social commerce side of social shopping, let's take a closer look at the behavior of social navigation.

SOCIAL NAVIGATION

To review, social navigation refers to a consumer's ability to both explore and narrow certain product selections based on recommendations and reviews from other consumers with similar interests. Today, consumers are more likely to rely on product reviews from other consumers when making purchasing decisions online than they are just to trust their own judgment or to be persuaded by advertising and other branded promotional materials.

Software providers, such as Bazaarvoice and PowerReviews, have given online retailers the ability to turn consumers into reviewers without the need for a custom-developed information system.[9] User-controlled content sites are assisting in the shift of power from the retailer to the consumer; therefore, more and more consumers are taking part by voicing their opinions and feelings.

Bazaarvoice, the leading provider of social commerce tools for e-retailers, conducted a study on the use of consumer reviews. Jesse Goldman, reporting on that study, highlighted the following findings:

- 55 percent of study participants said they were more likely to buy from a Web site with customer reviews than one that did not offer reviews.

- 63 percent of participants reported that reading consumer ratings were helpful when making a purchase.

Not only do online shoppers prefer sites with social commerce tools, but these consumers are also more likely to start their shopping on a site that offers the tools enabling them to navigate product information.

Social Commerce

Thus far, we've focused heavily on consumer-generated product reviews as a featured tool for social commerce sites and resource for social shoppers. In truth, there are several methods of making e-commerce more social and several types of social commerce offerings. Jordan Kasteler, of Search & Social, coaches that e-marketers must consider the following factors if they wish to excel at social commerce: (1) credibility, (2) utility, and (3) realistic sales expectations.[10] As noted above, consumers will value a recommendation only if they feel that it originates from a credible source. It may be tempting for sites to introduce product reviews that are scripted rather than organic from real product users. Social shoppers will recognize these reviews as phonies if they spot "pitch diction" in the copy. Pitch diction is a phrase used to denote copy that too perfectly capture product features and benefits and may be fraught with persuasive calls to action (e.g., buy now before it's too late!). For sites that truly wish to grow as a social commerce choice, providing tools for posting and accessing consumer-generated product reviews is critical.

Kasteler advises that social commerce sites also focus on utility. Social shoppers want tools that will make it easy for them to shop collaboratively online. While product reviews are an important resource for social shoppers, it alone cannot meet the needs of the social shopper. Social commerce sites should also consider offering bookmarklets, shopping-oriented widgets (like sale announcements), wish lists, shopping profiles (like the virtual model at Land's End), recommendation agents, and share tools. For instance, the JCPenney Web site offers share tools such that social shoppers can easily share product pictures and information on Facebook, MySpace, StyleHive, and Kaboodle networks. With the click of an icon, an online JCPenney shopper can easily share an outfit and message with his or her social network and request guidance before adding the product to the shopping bag. Some sites allow consumers to bookmark, tag, share, and even post blogs about specific products that they like and dislike. E-retailers can embed tools that enable two or more customers in different geographic locations to shop together online, viewing the same products and chatting.[11] Charlotte Russe, for instance, has adopted a tool from DecisionStep called ShopTogether, which enables dispersed co-shopping. The store made the decision to offer the tool in order to leverage the peer pressure its target market of teenagers typically feel when making clothing choices. Since the launch of ShopTogether, new customers have come to the online store, average time spent at the site has increased, and average order values and conversation rates are up.

These kinds of utility, as they become more readily available to social shoppers, are certain to enhance the shopping experience online. Utility is the premier benefit of social shopping tools that are not in and of themselves social commerce sites. For instance, Snipi is a browser plug-in application that allows utility such as sharing across social networks. Such utility applications will be discussed shortly.

The third factor important to social commerce sites is sales. And this factor is perhaps counterintuitive. Rather than anticipating sales, or requiring evidence of sales brought about by social commerce efforts, sites must acknowledge that the purchase may follow several online episodes. Social shopping may not lead directly to sales, or the trail to the point of conversion may not be traceable. Social commerce has been criticized by some as an effort that cannot monetize because of its inability to properly scale. Denise Zimmerman, in an article for iMedia Connection on social shopping, pointed out that social shopping is not yet mainstream.[12] Social commerce sites have just 1.43 percent of the traffic of a major social network like MySpace.

Instead, social shopping affects more indirect marketing objectives including brand awareness, purchase consideration, and purchase intent. Social commerce sites must see social shopping and the tools required to enhance the social shopping experience as beneficial to meeting the retailer objectives of building overall sales, market share, customer satisfaction and loyalty, and positive word-of-mouth communication.

SOCIAL COMMERCE SITES AND FUNCTIONALITY

There is no lack of social commerce sites despite the issues with return on investment plaguing social commerce. Indeed, at this writing, there are no less than 50 such sites not including e-commerce power houses with social commerce features, like Amazon. Some of the more well-known social commerce sites include Kaboodle, StyleHive, ThisNext, Wists, StyleFeeder, FiveLimes, Woot, Fluid, Shopflick, DesignSociety, Etsy, ShopFiber, GoToDaily, Glimpse, StyleHop, Fruugo, and Snipi. Kaboodle, ThisNext, StyleHive and StyleFeeder are the leaders in the social shopping market. Kaboodle has the most traffic to date with about 1 million unique visitors per month.[13] Kaboodle has also best monetized social shopping by partnering with Shopping.com. Shopping.com posts prices and merchants for products noted by Kaboodle users. Kaboodle then earns a fee for clickthroughs to merchant Web sites.

All incorporate the social aspects of sharing and collaboration in their service offerings, along with at least one point of differentiation. Kaboodle enables its members to save things it finds online, share the page, request comments from friends, and publish recommendations from friends.

It also summarizes the information from saved Web pages, making it easy to review key product information. A customizable style area lets members coordinate outfits and room décor before deciding if a product fits the desired look.

StyleHop lets users define a fashion peer group and adjust who the peers are for each search. This enables users to filter results based upon the rankings of their peers when they are shopping online. The feature enhances the social proof, credibility, and similarity influencers for social shopping by ensuring that the people offering opinions are in the user's reference group. StyleHive partners with brands to create brand community pages called "Nectar Hives." StyleHive members create bookmarks around the brand, and these bookmarks are available on the Nectar Hive landing page.

Shopflick stands out as a video-shopping site, which also incorporates StyleHive and Kaboodle. The sellers enhance the social shopping experience by telling a story about the product. ShopSeen incorporates location-based search, mobile uploads, and social network integration to enhance social shopping. Operating in real time, ShopSeen puts an emphasis on sales and events as they happen and events in one's geographic region. Retailers can interact with ShopSeen and create event announcements and product listings.

Fruugo aggregates multiple social commerce tools including a search utility, price comparison tool, and a sales site for European retailers. Fruugo acts as the e-retailer for merchants, reaching customers, promoting products, and managing the exchange process. Select2gether stands out as a primarily mobile service allowing users to get real advice no matter when or where they are shopping. Its Web site also includes a database and collaborative tools. Of course, there are many others, but this overview provides a picture of the range of services offered by social commerce sites.

In addition to these social commerce sites, there are also social communities that revolve around specific products and product categories. Though not developed exclusively for social shoppers, these communities can certainly influence the shopping choices of their users. For example, StyleZone exists for discussions on the latest fashion trends; All Lacquered Up is a blog devoted to nail polish.

Possibly the most advanced social shopping service available is Snipi. Snipi is a new service that lets people literally drag and drop content (products, photos, and videos) from virtually any Web site on the Internet to save into collections for themselves or to share and collaborate on with others. All of this snipped content is saved on Snipi.com; can be shared via Facebook, Twitter, and WordPress; and is immediately accessible through Snipi's free iPhone application—all from the point of capture—not requiring users to leave the page where they find their interests. These data are aggregated into the Snipi network and cataloged in detail by domain, category, title, description, price (where applicable), tags, and user (along with demographic information). Snipi's "Interest Network" creates links between people's product, photo, and video interests and correlates them to other users and their interests. Snipi also provides collaborative capabilities that allow multiple users to participate in the collection of content around general interests or specific topics. The relationships between people and their interests (from any online destination in almost all categories) gives Snipi a unique opportunity to analyze a broad scope of consumer behavior and produce the most innovative and effective semantic tools for its users, partners, and advertisers. Snipi's technology is unparalleled and is developed to provide end users with the simplest and most innovative collecting, organizing, sharing, and collaborative tools; retailers with the tools to access and analyze de-identified consumer data (for marketing optimization and site personalization); and to give advertisers the tools to target.

SOCIAL COMMERCE AND ENTERPRISE 2.0

Social commerce is still at an early stage of evolution and adoption. In fact, social-media marketer Jeremiah Owyang described social commerce as the fifth and final stage in a blog post on the future of the social Web.[14] The five eras Owyang describes are the Era of Social Relationships, the Era of Social Functionality, the Era of Social Colonization, the Era of Social Context, and the Era of Social Commerce. The Era of Social Commerce is not expected to really begin to influence the Social Web until 2011. As of this writing, we are solidly into the Era of Social Functionality and beginning to see just the early indicators of the Era of Social Colonization. What is recommended for social commerce as we seek to realize a time when community drives product development and choice? Owyang recommends that organizations ensure their Enterprise systems are fully evolved. It is not enough that Enterprise technologies connect within the organization; the enterprise systems must also connect to the social Web. As organizations seek to meet the needs of customers in the social marketspace, we will see an increased emphasis on Social CRM—social customer relationship management.

CONCLUSION

Already a substantial portion of online shoppers can be characterized as social shoppers. They want social commerce tools to aid their online shopping efforts, and they will seek out those retailers, networks, and services that provide the tools they need. We also know that online shoppers in general also use some social tools, even if their affinity for these tools does not warrant their classification as social shoppers. Innovative e-retailers like Amazon, JCPenney, and Overstock are meeting these needs with collaborative tools, recommendation agents, and customer-generated product ratings and reviews. Social commerce network sites like Kaboodle are building communities around the shopping activity.

Though social-media experts believe we are still early in the life cycle for social commerce, the collaborative nature of the social Web is no doubt influencing online shopping patterns. Ultimately those organizations that link their Enterprise systems to both internal and external stakeholders, employees and customers, will be able to leverage the social Web for sustained competitive advantage.

Notes

1. The e-Tailing Group, "Merchant and Customer Perspectives on Customer Reviews and User-Generated Content," White Paper, February 2008, http://www.e-tailing.com/content/?p=37.

2. The e-Tailing Group report termed these shoppers "social researchers." However, this term is not utilized here as the author does not agree that there is sufficient distinction to be made between online shoppers, social shoppers, and social researchers at this stage of development in social shopping behaviors. Consequently, those who use social commerce tools considerably more frequently and for more product decisions compared to the average online shopper are deemed social shoppers.

3. Tracy Tuten, *Advertising 2.0: Social Media Marketing in a Web 2.0 World* (Westport, CT: Praeger Publishers, 2008).

4. Marketing Charts, "Social-Shopping Study' Defines New Breed of Shopper—the 'Social Researcher'," November 12, 2007, http://www.marketingcharts.com/direct/social-shopping-study-defines-new-breed-of-shopper-the-social-researcher-2347/.

5. Kim Gordon, "The Power of Social Shopping Networks," Entreprenuer.com, March 2007, http://www.entrepreneur.com/marketing/onlinemarketing/article174746.html.

6. Jessica Guynn, "Next Big Trend: Social Shopping?" *The Technology Chronicles*, November 2006, http://www.sfgate.com/cgi-bin/blogs/techchron/detail?blogid=19&entry_id=11274.

7. Amanda Kooser, "Net Profits Social Shopping," *Entrepreneur*, July 2008, 112.

8. See Note 5.

9. Jesse Goldman, "A Rave Review for Social Navigation," *E-Commerce Times*, April 23, 2008, http://www.ecommercetimes.com/story/A-Rave-Review-for-Social-Navigation-62695.html?wlc=1221332584.

10. Jordan Kasteler, "Why You Should Get Involved with Social Shopping: E-Commerce 2.0," Search Engine Land, July 28, 2009, http://searchengineland.com/why-you-should-get-involved-with-social-shopping-e-commerce-20-22995.

11. Chantal Tode, "Social Shopping Is Poised for Growth," DM News, August 24, 2009, http://www.dmnews.com/Social-shopping-is-poised-for-growth/article/147162/.

12. Denise Zimmerman, "Get In On the Social Shopping Craze," iMedia Connection, March 19, 2008, http://www.imediaconnection.com/content/18641.asp.

13. Ibid.

14. Jeremiah Owyang, "The Future of the Social Web: In Five Eras," Web Strategy, April 27, 2009, http://www.web-strategist.com/blog/2009/04/27/future-of-the-social-web/.

About the Editor and Contributors

TRACY L. TUTEN, Ph.D., author of *Advertising 2.0: Social Media Marketing in a Web 2.0 World*, is an associate professor of marketing at East Carolina University. Frequently quoted in the press, including the *New York Times, Brandweek*, the *International Herald Tribune*, and the *Washington Post*, she is a leading contributor to industry views on leveraging the Internet. Her research has appeared in such journals as *Psychology & Marketing*, the *Journal of Business Research*, and the *Journal of Marketing Communication*, among others. Dr. Tuten has served consultant and guest professor roles internationally (in Korea, Germany, France, and Argentina) and in the United States with organizations that include Samsung Electronics, Royall & Company, The Martin Agency, and the NFL Coaches Association. Dr. Tuten has twice served as a Fulbright Scholar and won the 2006 Excellence in Scholarship Award during her tenure at VCU. She also won two national awards for teaching excellence (Association of Business Administration and Society for Marketing Advances), a teaching innovations award from the Society for Marketing Advances, and a university-wide teaching award at Longwood University.

CHERYL L. ADKINS, Ph.D., is Professor of Management and Chair of the Department of Management, Marketing, and Information Systems at Longwood University. She earned her Ph.D. in organizational behavior/human resource management from the University of South Carolina in 1990, her MBA from Salisbury University in 1985, and her B.S. from Longwood College in 1981. Cheryl's research interests include work-family conflict, person-organization fit, and work values. She has published research in journals such as the *Academy of Management Journal*, the *Journal of Organizational Behavior*, the *Journal of Management*, and *Personnel Psychology*. She serves on the editorial review board of *Human Resource*

Management Review and has served as an ad hoc reviewer for several other scholarly journals and conferences.

JOSH BERNOFF, a Vice President and Principal Analyst at Forrester Research, Inc., is the coauthor of *Groundswell: Winning in a World Transformed by Social Technologies* (Harvard Business Press, May 2008), a comprehensive analysis of corporate strategy for dealing with social technologies such as blogs, social networks, and wikis. Josh joined Forrester in 1995. In 1996, he created the Technographics® segmentation, a classification of consumers according to how they approach technology. Forrester has used this segmentation as the basis of its consumer research offering, also called Technographics, since 1997. Josh's research, analysis, and opinions appear frequently in publications like the *Wall Street Journal*, the *New York Times*, *Broadcasting & Cable*, and on national television news programs. He writes a column for *Marketing News*, a publication of the American Marketing Association. Josh's blog is located at blogs.forrester.com/groundswell.

BARRY BREWTON received his bachelor's degree in Business Administration from Longwood University and won Entrepreneur of the Year from the College of Business & Economics at Longwood University in 2009. Mr. Brewton has worked as the Director of Human Resources for New Horizon Security company. He is a Certified Compliance Agent through the Department of Criminal Justice Services for Virginia and is a Member of the Society of Human Resource Management since 2007.

THOMAS R. DONOHUE, Ph.D., is a Professor of Mass Communications and Psychology at Virginia Commonwealth University in Richmond, Virginia. He received his Ph.D. from the University of Massachusetts Amherst. His research during the past 30 years has focused on the social impact of media, including television and the Internet. He has published over 75 articles, papers, book chapters, and monographs. Most recently, he has been researching social networks, including their use as an advertising tool.

DEEPAK KHAZANCHI, Ph.D., is a Professor of Information Systems and Quantitative Analysis, as well as Associate Dean of Academic Affairs, in the College of Information Science and Technology at the University of Nebraska at Omaha. His research interests include virtual-project management, virtual worlds, and B2B assurance services in extended enterprise environments. Khazanchi has a Ph.D. in business administration (with a specialization in management information systems) from Texas Tech University. Contact him at khazanchi@mail.unomaha.edu.

ELLEN KOLSTÖ, Planning Director at GSD&M Idea City, has over 18 years of advertising and marketing experience. In her 4 years at GSD&M Idea City, Ellen has served as a senior planning generalist, having worked directly on the AT&T Search business, L. L. Bean, American Red Cross, and AARP accounts uncovering insights on those businesses. On the other hand, she has also carved out a role as the one of the agency's resident experts on online community-building and digital consumer insights having conducted qualitative research inside the virtual world space and currently working on some online community research projects. Prior to joining GSD&M Idea City, Ellen crisscrossed the country, working at agencies such as The Richards Group (Dallas), J. Walter Thompson (Chicago), Young & Rubicam (San Francisco), and Mullen (Boston). During that time she worked on such iconic brands as Motel 6, Kraft, Neiman Marcus, and TripAdvisor. Ellen received her M.A. in Advertising at the University of Texas. The author acknowledges the contributions from Metaversatility in writing her chapter.

ROBERT V. KOZINETS, Ph.D., is a globally recognized expert on online communities, online market research, and online marketing strategy, whose opinions and work have been featured in global media from the *New York Times*, the *Chicago Tribune*, and *Newsweek* to the Discovery Channel, the CBS National News, Brazil's *Bites* Magazine, and Australia's *Boss* Magazine. His interests look at the interface of technology, culture, and entertainment. He has extensive speaking and consulting experience, working on research projects with a range of companies, including Campbell Soup Company, PepsiCo, American Express, eBay, and Merck. An anthropologist by training, he is Associate Professor of Marketing at York University's Schulich School of Business (Toronto), with research published in over 50 chapters, proceedings, and articles in some of the world's top marketing journals. Brandthroposophy, his popular blog about branding, marketing, and technology, is available at www.kozinets.net. His book about online communities and ethnographic methods published by Sage in 2009 is entitled *Netnography: Research Cultures and Communities*.

CHARLENE LI is the Founder of Altimeter Group and coauthor of the business bestseller *Groundswell: Winning in a World Transformed by Social Technologies*, published by Harvard Business Press in May 2008. She is currently working on her next book, *Open: How Leaders Win By Letting Go*, to be published in May 2010 by Jossey-Bass. She frequently consults and speaks on social and emerging technologies and publishes a blog, The Altimeter. Charlene is one of the most frequently quoted industry analysts and has appeared on *60 Minutes*, *The MacNeil/Lehrer NewsHour*, ABC News, CNN, and CNBC. She is also frequently quoted by the *Wall Street Journal*, the *New York Times*, *USAToday*, Reuters, and the Associated Press. She is a much-sought-after public speaker and has presented frequently at top technology conferences such as Web 2.0 Expo, SXSW, Search Engine Strategies, and the American Society of Association Executives. Previously, Charlene was a Vice President and Principal Analyst at Forrester Research, Inc.

ALANAH MITCHELL (NÉE DAVIS) completed her Ph.D. in Information Technology (IT) in the College of Information Science and Technology at the University of Nebraska at Omaha. Dr. Mitchell is an Assistant Professor of Communication at Appalachian State University. Her research interests include virtual and face-to-face collaboration, and e-commerce. Davis has an MS in e-commerce from Creighton University. She can be reached at davisa1@appstate.edu.

JOHN D. MURPHY is pursuing a Ph.D. in Information Technology (IT) in the College of Information Science and Technology at the University of Nebraska at Omaha. His research interests include collaboration, design science, and interdisciplinary research. Murphy has an MS in computer science from Troy State University. Contact him at jmurphy@mail.unomaha.edu.

RUDY NYDEGGER, Ph.D.. is Professor of Management and Psychology at Union Graduate College and Union College in Schenectady, New York. He also has a private practice and is Chief of the Division of Psychology at Ellis Hospital in Schenectady. He has served on the New York State Board of Psychology and has also been President of the Psychological Association of Northeastern New York, and also of the New York State Psychological Association. He has over 35 years of experience in teaching, research, practice, consulting, and writing.

JASON D. OLIVER, Ph.D., is Assistant Professor of Marketing in the Department of Marketing and Supply Chain Management at East Carolina University. He previously worked with Fidelity Investments, most recently as a Product Manager. His research interests include green marketing/sustainability, behavioral decision-making, and consumer loyalty. He has an article forthcoming in the *Journal of Advertising*.

PETER OTTO, Ph.D., is Associate Professor for Management Information Systems at Union Graduate College, School of Management. He also holds a visiting teaching position at the Graduate School of Business Administration (GSBA) Zurich, Switzerland, and IESEG School of Management, Lille Catholic University, Paris, France. Dr. Otto has extensive consultancy experience and holds an MBA and a Ph.D. in Information Science and Technology, with primary specialization in Decision Support Systems, from the University at Albany, New York. His present research focuses on group decision-making, IT systems implementation, and online communities.

DAWN OWENS is pursuing a Ph.D. in Information Technology (IT) in the College of Information Science and Technology at the University of Nebraska at Omaha. Her research interests include project management, virtual teams, and software quality assurance. Owens has an MS in management information systems from the University of Nebraska at Omaha. Contact her at dmowens@mail.unomaha.edu.

ERIKA PEARSON, Ph.D., is a lecturer in media, film, and communication at the University of Otago, Dunedin, New Zealand. Research interests focus around social life on the Internet and include issues such as identity, performance, social network construction, and social-capital exchange. She is also the founding convener of the Internet Research Group of Otago, an interdisciplinary research network studying all aspects of the Internet in everyday life.

SONYA F. PREMEAUX, Ph.D., is Associate Professor of Management and Associate Dean of the College of Business Administration at Nicholls State University where she also holds the Gerald Gaston Endowed Professorship of Business Administration. She obtained her Ph.D. in organizational behavior/human resource management from Louisiana State University in 2001 and her B.S. and MBA from McNeese State University in 1986 and 1988, respectively. Sonya's research interests include work-family conflict, speaking up in the workplace, and multicultural issues. She has published research in journals such as the *Journal of Management Studies, Journal of Organizational Behavior, Human Resource Planning,* and the *International Journal of Selection and Assessment.* She serves on the editorial review board of the *Journal of Business and Psychology* and has served as an ad hoc reviewer for several other scholarly journals and conferences.

ELIZABETH C. RAVLIN, Ph.D., is Associate Professor of Organizational Behavior and Management on the faculty of the Moore School of Business, University of South Carolina. She received her Ph.D. degree in Organizational Behavior from the Graduate School of Industrial Administration, Carnegie Mellon University.

Dr. Ravlin currently serves on the editorial boards of the *Journal of Management* and *Human Resource Management Review* and has also served on the boards of the *Academy of Management Journal* and the *Academy of Management Review.* Her research examines interpersonal processes and team effectiveness, work values and ethics, and status influences in organizations and has been funded by grants from such organizations as CIBER and the Riegel and Emory Human Resource Research Center. Her publications have appeared in such journals and annuals as *Journal of Applied Psychology, Organizational Behavior and Human Decision Processes, Personnel Psychology, Journal of Management, Journal of Organizational Behavior,* and *Research in Organizational Behavior.*

Her teaching and consulting are in the areas of team and organizational processes. Dr. Ravlin has served as Research Director of the Riegel and Emory Human Resource Research Center, Director of the Management Organizational Behavior Ph.D. Program, and as Chair of the University Graduate Council.

RUN REN, Ph.D., is an Assistant Professor in the Department of Organization Management, Guanghua School of Management, Peking University, China. She received her doctorate in Management from Texas A&M University. Her research focuses on organizational justice, employee creativity, cross-cultural studies, and various human resource management. Dr. Ren's work has appeared in such journals as *Human Resource Management Review, Journal of Business Ethics,* and *Basic and Applied Social Psychology.* She has also written a book chapter for the *Sage Handbook of Organizational Behavior.*

SCOTT SHERMAN has lived in many places, having grown up in a Navy family, but he has called Virginia home since he was in middle school. Sherman holds an associate's degree in business administration, a bachelor's degree from James Madison University, and a master's degree in advertising design from Syracuse University. He also studied advertising at Virginia Commonwealth University. Sherman has worked as a freelance advertising consultant, but most of his 20-year ad career was in the creative departments of two Richmond advertising agencies—where he applied his knowledge in guiding strategic creative and design. He is an Assistant Professor at Virginia Commonwealth University where he focuses on the strategic side of the ad business. He states, "I am passionate about the ad business and passionate about teaching. How I teach is to focus on the learning; it's paramount. What I teach is simple, too. Superior communication design is always collaborative, always creative, and always based on a thorough understanding of the business objectives and the strategy." Sherman uses sunscreen regularly, likes surprises, and enjoys funny jokes. He, his wife, and their three children live in Richmond.

NATALIE T. WOOD, Ph.D., is Assistant Professor of Marketing and Assistant Director of the Center for Consumer Research in the Haub School of Business at Saint Joseph's University in Philadelphia. Her research on avatars and virtual worlds has been published in journals such as *Marketing Education Review, International Journal of Internet Marketing and Advertising, Journal of Website Promotion,* and *Journal of Advertising Education.* She is also an advisory editor for the *Journal of Virtual Worlds Research.*

ILZE ZIGURS, Ph.D., is a Professor and Department Chair of Information Systems and Quantitative Analysis in the College of Information Science and Technology at the University of Nebraska at Omaha.

Her research interests include design, implementation, and use of collaboration technologies, particularly in virtual teams and projects. Zigurs has a Ph.D. in Business Administration (with a specialization in Management Information Systems) from the University of Minnesota, Twin Cities. Contact her at izigurs@mail.unomaha.edu.

INDEX